A History of T
Presence in

A History of the British Presence in Chile

From Bloody Mary to Charles Darwin and the Decline of British Influence

William Edmundson

A HISTORY OF THE BRITISH PRESENCE IN CHILE
Copyright © William Edmundson, 2009.
Softcover reprint of the hardcover 1st edition 2009 978-0-230-61849-7

All rights reserved.

First published in 2009 by PALGRAVE MACMILLAN® in the United States—a division of St. Martin's Press LLC, 175 Fifth Avenue, New York, NY 10010.

Where this book is distributed in the UK, Europe, and the rest of the world, this is by Palgrave Macmillan, a division of Macmillan Publishers Limited, registered in England, company number 785998, of Houndmills, Basingstoke, Hampshire RG21 6XS.

Palgrave Macmillan is the global academic imprint of the above companies and has companies and representatives throughout the world.

Palgrave® and Macmillan® are registered trademarks in the United States, the United Kingdom, Europe and other countries.

ISBN 978-1-349-38109-8   ISBN 978-0-230-10121-0 (eBook)
DOI 10.1057/9780230101210

Library of Congress Cataloging-in-Publication Data is available from the Library of Congress.

A catalogue record of the book is available from the British Library.

Design by Scribe Inc.

First edition: November 2009

To Daniel, David, and Olivia, whose formative childhoods were spent in Chile; to their descendants, who will wonder why they have British genes; and to my wife Verônica, whose unfailing support and encouragement helped make this book possible.

Contents

List of Illustrations		ix
Acknowledgments		xi
Introduction: A Mysterious Sympathy		1
1	Pirates, Buccaneers, Privateers, Corsairs, and Circumnavigators	7
2	Explorers by Sea	27
3	British Naturalists in Chile	41
4	Chile's Wars	55
5	Visitors and Explorers on Land	83
6	British Artists in Chile	95
7	British Communities in Chile	103
8	Commerce and Industry	131
9	Mining	147
10	Banking	169
11	Railways	175
12	Education	191
13	Religion	197
14	Sports	215
15	The Battle of Coronel	221
16	The Decline of British Influence	229
17	The Imprint That Remains: Family Names and Geography	233

Appendix A: English Newspapers in Chile	243
Appendix B: British Diplomatic Representation in Chile	247
Select Bibliography	251
Index	267

Illustrations

4.1	Arco Británico (British Arch) in Valparaíso © William Edmundson	56
7.1	Memorial in Punta Arenas to those who died on HMS Doterel © William Edmundson	119
7.2	Commemorative plaque on the Clock Tower, Antofagasta © William Edmundson	129
8.1	Steam engine in southern Chile, imported by Williamson Balfour © William Edmundson	141
9.1	Swimming pool at the Oficina Humberstone © William Edmundson	168

Acknowledgments

There is probably no other country in the world, that never was a part of the British Empire or Commonwealth, where British associations and sympathies are so strong.

—L. C. Derrick-Jehu, "The Anglo-Chilean Community"

My first words of thanks go to members of the Anglo-Chilean community of descendants of British immigrants in Concepción, who warmly welcomed me and my family when I lived in Chile for six years, recruited by the British Council as Director of the Chilean-British Cultural Institute, in the years 1984 to 1990. They told me stories of pirates, of the English Club, of Scottish coal miners, of the British-built railway bridge over the River Bío-Bío, and of Admiral Cochrane, and an Irishman named O'Higgins. I was immediately fascinated and started to research the history of the British presence around Concepción, and I made a promise to myself that one day I would sit down and write a history relating to all of Chile.

This is the book, and I am grateful to the many individuals who have helped me with this research: my friend Armando Baltra, for encouraging me to go to his country when I had doubts; Anthony Adams, then Director of the Chilean-British Cultural Institute in Santiago, for loaning me valuable old books; historian friends in the Sociedad de Historia de Concepción; Alejandro Pizarro in Concepción, who gave me newspaper and magazine cuttings relating to the Battle of Coronel; the late John Carlyle, with whom I corresponded in 1994, when he was researching the history of the Scottish presence in Chile; Donald Binns, for publishing my articles on railways in Latin America; Mary Stathers, for correspondence on the *Colinda* story and kindly allowing me to quote from her article published in *The Scottish Genealogist*; Judith Hudson Beattie Valenzuela, for sharing with me her research into *The Colinda* (forthcoming) and kindly allowing me to quote from our correspondence; Paulina Ruiz, of the Chilean-British Cultural Institute in Santiago, for her encouragement and comments on an early draft of the chapter on British naturalists; Andrew Robshaw, Managing Director of the Chilean-British Chamber of Commerce in Chile; Leslie Hemery OBE, President of the Prince of Wales Country Club, for comments on the chapter "Commerce and Industry"; and Dick Wilkinson, President of the Anglo-Chilean Society in London, for helpful advice.

The epigraph from "The Anglo-Chilean Community" in *Family History* is used by kind permission of the Trustees and Principal of the Institute of Heraldic and Genealogical Studies, Northgate, Canterbury. I am grateful to Lloyds TSB Group Archives for permission to quote from David Joslin's *A Century of Banking in Latin America* (London: Bank of London and South America Ltd., 1963). I am also grateful to *The Scottish Genealogist* for permission to quote from Mary Stather's article "The Colinda Voyage—An Emigration that Didn't Make It—Or Did It?" (vol. 34, no. 2, 1987).

Every effort has been made to trace all copyright holders, but if any have been inadvertently overlooked, the publisher will be pleased to make the necessary arrangements at the first opportunity.

I am also grateful to acknowledged experts on parts of the story. The Chilean historian Juan Ricardo Couyoumdjian generously guided me with comments and suggestions relating to the introduction and the chapter "Commerce and Industry." Duncan Campbell, site administrator for the excellent "British Presence in Patagonia" site (http://patbrit.org/eng/index.htm), gave me comments and corrections. Ian Thomson Newman suggested revisions to the "Railways" chapter. Cecilia Polo and Doralisa Duarte, library researchers at the Museo Nacional de Bellas Artes Santiago, gave comments and suggestions on "British Artists." I also owe a tremendous debt to my friends David Shepherd, for reading the manuscript so meticulously, and especially Roddy Kay, who not only commented on my first drafts but also engaged in a rich dialogue that immeasurably improved the text.

All errors are, of course, my entire responsibility.

William (Eddie) Edmundson
Recife. December 2008

Introduction

A Mysterious Sympathy

The Byrons of England have had a mysterious sympathy for this land of Chile, whose gate of entrance was called since its conquest "The Valley of Paradise."

—Benjamín Vicuña Mackenna,
The First Britons in Valparaíso 1817–1827

The British have been involved at nearly every turn of events in Chilean history since the Spanish Conquest, and not as bystanders but as key players. This is no exaggeration. Even that quintessential hallmark of Britain, the monarchy, has left its stamp on Chile. The history of the British in Chile starts with an English Queen who also held the title of Queen of Chile.

The Captaincy-General of Chile was an administrative territory of Spain from 1541 until full independence in 1818. Although Chile had several governors during its long colonial history, including the Irish-born Ambrose O'Higgins, it also technically had a king and a queen, from which was derived its other designation as the Kingdom of Chile, a status enjoyed by no other Spanish possession in the New World. This kingdom was a possession of the King of Castile, and later the Spanish kings, and was ruled as a captaincy-general from the viceroyalty in Peru.

Mary Tudor (Mary I, also known as Bloody Mary), the eldest child of Henry VIII, and the only surviving child of his first marriage to Katherine of Aragon, succeeded to the throne of England in July 1553. She married Philip, her cousin and eleven years her junior, when he was still heir to the Spanish throne. Philip was the only legitimate son of the Holy Roman Emperor Charles V and is remembered as Philip II. He was given the title of King of Chile by his father to make him more regal—he was at the time a mere prince, and Mary was already a reigning monarch. They married in July 1554, and Mary became Queen of Chile until 1556, when the Kingdom of Chile was absorbed back into the Spanish monarchy. As consort to Mary, Philip was styled King of England, a title he relinquished on Mary's death in November 1558, when the English throne passed to Elizabeth I.

The marriage treaty summed up both Mary's and Philip's joint dominions: "Philip and Mary, by the grace of God, King and Queen of England, France, Naples, Jerusalem, Chile and Ireland, Defenders of the Faith, Princes of Spain and Sicily, Archdukes of Austria, Dukes of Milan, Burgundy and Brabant, Counts of Habsburg, Flanders and Tyrol." (http://www.nationmaster.com/encyclopedia/Mary-I-of-England).

Following his father's abdication, Philip II reigned as King of Spain from 1556 to 1598. In 1556, Chile merged back into the Spanish crown, continuing with its practical identity as a captaincy, but also keeping its honorific title of kingdom. Although the marriage of Mary and Philip was consummated, they failed to produce an heir, and Philip left England in August 1555 to take up his duties as ruler of the Netherlands and only returned to England once, for three months in 1557. Mary Tudor, then, was Queen of Chile from 1554 to 1556.

Henry Lyon Young (1963, 12) reports the existence of a painting with the inscription *Maria Tudor: Regina Chiliae*, hanging in the Museo de Bellas Artes in Santiago, "perhaps the only one in existence, of Bloody Mary in her robes as Queen of Chile." Regrettably, it has proved impossible to trace this painting to the present day.

Mary Tudor is not the only foreign monarch whose name can be linked with Chile. For students of the "what if?" current of history, there is the tantalizing story of Admiral Cochrane's intrigues to bring a deposed emperor to Chile. Thomas Cochrane was born in Scotland and is better known in Britain as Lord Cochrane, Tenth Earl of Dundonald. His exploits as "Commander in Chief of the Naval Forces of the Republic of Chile" in the War of Independence are told in Chapter 4. When the representative of Chilean independence in England offered Cochrane command of the patriot naval force, one decision Cochrane made on accepting this post was to rescue Napoleon Bonaparte (then in exile on the island of St. Helena) on his journey out to Chile and to place him on the throne of South America once independence was achieved.

Still on the theme of monarchy, there was the self-styled "Nitrate King," Colonel John Thomas North, born near Leeds, who controlled companies that had a near-global monopoly on Chilean nitrates following the War of the Pacific between Chile and the forces of Peru and Bolivia. Colonel North's story is told in Chapter 9. Another British-born "king" in Chile was Leslie Greer, the General Manager of the Tierra del Fuego Exploitation Company, known by some as the King of Patagonia (while others simply called him God). The lands he ruled over were on a royal scale; in 1898, the Company owned 1,109,000 hectares of sheep-grazing land. The story of British, mainly Scottish, involvement in farming in Patagonia is told in Chapter 7. There was also the "Wheat King," José Bunster, a Chilean born of Welsh (or possibly Cornish) descent, who opened the Banco José Bunster in the south of Chile in 1882, following the "pacification" of Araucanía—the southern mainland region of Chile inhabited by Mapuche Indians, whom the Spanish never conquered.

A real prince—the Prince of Wales—visited Santiago and Valparaíso in 1925, and Queen Elizabeth II came to Chile in 1968. However, not all British visitors had such pleasant intentions. There were plans made to colonize parts of Chile for Britain.

The sixteenth century was an age when the European powers were competing to establish overseas colonies, including the Americas, and it was inevitable that England should consider settling parts of the New World and come into conflict with Spain. As early as 1570, a group of Englishmen thought of establishing a colony near the Magellan Strait as a base for incursions into the Pacific, but it was not until 1574 that the venture was given shape. Queen Elizabeth's Privy Council was led by Francis Walsingham, principal Secretary of State for Foreign Affairs. Together with the queen's confidant, Robert Dudley Earl of Leicester, Walsingham led the faction arguing for more aggressive action against King Philip II of Spain, the widower of Mary Tudor.

In March 1574, the Council received a petition from Richard Grenville, representing William Hawkins and a group of West Country investors, for a voyage to the South Sea. The alleged purpose was to form a peaceful expedition aimed at founding settlements near the Rio de la Plata and, once through Magellan Strait, along the Pacific coast of America south of the lands occupied by Spain; that is, south of the River Bío-Bío in Chile. Since Richard Glenville had the reputation of having acted as a pirate, there is considerable doubt over the peaceful intentions of this enterprise. Seven ships and 1,500 men were brought together at Plymouth, but then Queen Elizabeth listened to wiser counsel and ordered the preparations to stop. She feared the voyage was bound to rouse Spain to hostilities with England at a sensitive moment when political relations between the two countries were actually improving.

Francis Drake knew of this proposal, and when he set out in 1577 on his great voyage of circumnavigation, he followed a plan drafted by Walsingham that had been presented to, and sanctioned by, Queen Elizabeth. This document survives, although badly damaged by fire, and it instructs Drake to proceed toward "the pole . . . the South Sea then . . . far to the northwards as . . . along the said coast," and "he should spend 5 months in tarrying upon the coast to get knowle[dge] of the princes and countries there" (see Sudgen 1990, 97). In 1578, Drake named the Elizabeth Islands in Tierra del Fuego in homage to the Queen and claimed them for England.

John Narborough's expedition in the *Sweepstakes* and the *Batchelor* was commissioned by the British Crown, and one aim was to explore the possibilities for British occupation in the region of Valdivia, in the south of Chile. It is claimed that in 1670 Narborough took possession of territory comprising the southern coast of Patagonia from Rio de la Plata to the Magellan Strait. He did this in the name of Charles II, thinking of making it a British dominion. Francis Drake and John Narborough, and other British pirates and privateers, are described in Chapter 1.

Manchester-born Father Thomas Falkner was the last to seriously suggest that the British establish a settlement in Chile, in 1774, leading the Spanish court to take fright, realizing that they were weak on detail and vulnerable to a British grab at territory in the south. This story is told in Chapter 5. Perhaps this nervousness helps account for the unfounded allegations that Ireland would set up a colony in southern Chile. These suspicions were leveled in 1796 against the Irish-born Ambrose O'Higgins by the Captain General of Chile, Gabriel de Avilés. Ambrose O'Higgins was then Viceroy of Peru, with tutelage over Chile, and his story is told in Chapter 4.

Not to be outdone, it would seem, there was very nearly a Welsh settlement established in Chile. A group of mainly Welsh colonists arrived in 1888 to settle on the banks of the River Percey and the upper reaches of the Chilean River Futaleufú, in valleys high in the Andes. The history of British frontier arbitration and the Welsh colonists is told in Chapter 4.

Of course, no autonomous colony (other than Spanish) was established in Chile, whether English, Irish, Welsh—or Scottish, for that matter. Talk of this kind was abandoned from the time of Chile's conflict with her colonial masters, which was a turning point in the history of the relationship between Chile and Britain. Instead, there was a radical redirection of policy. The geopolitical strategies of British foreign ministers Castlereagh and Canning—during and following the wars of independence in Latin America—favored trade and investment with the newly independent republics to any further thought of colonization or continuing with the centuries-old belligerence against Spain. And they were in a position to enforce this creed, with British naval might, and defuse any pretensions other powers might have to snatch land in colonial South America as it broke up. British involvement in commerce, mining, banking, and railways is described in chapters 8, 9, 10, and 11.

While all thought of establishing an independent British colony in Chile was abandoned following independence, there were attempts made in the nineteenth century to bring British settlers to colonize parts of the country. An outstanding example was a scheme of assisted immigration in the late 1880s under the Presidency of José Manuel Balmaceda, specifically designed to bring British settlers to Araucanía, in Mapuche Indian country, in the south of Chile. The story of immigration and the growth of British communities is dealt with in Chapter 7.

This book tells the history of the British presence in Chile, straddling the pivotal War of Independence, from Francis Drake to the start of the Second World War. While some stories are traced beyond 1939 to briefly round off what happened in relevant cases, and the concluding chapter examines the imprint that remains on the geography of modern Chile, this timeline has been chosen because it is a watershed, signaling the sharp decline of British influence in Chile, and the region in general, from that time on.

This is the story of several of the countless British pirates, privateers, explorers by sea and on land, naturalists, soldiers, sailors, artists, merchants, engineers, farmers, teachers, and missionaries who have left their stamp on the history of Chile. The structure is topical, but also generally chronological, so that, for example, the chapter "Pirates" (sixteenth to eighteenth centuries) precedes "Naturalists" (focused on Darwin in the early nineteenth century), which precedes "Railways" (late nineteenth century) and "The Battle of Coronel" (early twentieth century). The protagonists come from the four corners of Britain, from Scotland (for example, Lord Cochrane), from Ireland when under English domination (Ambrose O'Higgins), from Wales (Chilean President Aylwin's Welsh ancestor), and from England (John Thomas North, the Nitrate King).

In his lecture to the YMCA in Valparaíso in 1884, Chilean historian Benjamín Vicuña Mackenna spoke of Chile as "The England of the Pacific." Some will say that it is no mere coincidence that Chileans are sometimes known as "the English of South America." I am not convinced that the Chilean traits of reserve, of gentlemanliness, and proud national identity can be traced to the influence of the British.

I believe it is more a matter of what the two countries have in common—especially the same insularity. For centuries, Chile shared with Britain the sense of being an island. It is hemmed in on two sides by the Andean mountains and the Pacific Ocean. In the north, there is the driest desert in the world, the Atacama. Mainland Chile in the south ended for the Spanish at the River Bío-Bío for nearly three centuries, from the 1599 Mapuche Indian uprising in Araucanía until the founding of Temuco in 1881 and Colonel Urrutia's arrival at the ruins of Villarrica in December 1882. And beyond Araucanía lay the forbidding Magellan Strait.

Nevertheless, these two insular nations became linked in *a mysterious sympathy*, and, as we shall see, there is no doubt that the British presence was critical and influential at many of the twists and turns of the history of Chile since the Spanish Conquest.

Chapter 1

Pirates, Buccaneers, Privateers, Corsairs, and Circumnavigators

> *I heard Mr Caldcleugh say that sitting by an old lady at a dinner in Coquimbo, she remarked how wonderfully strange it was that she should live to dine in the same room with an Englishman. Twice as a girl, at the cry of "Los Ingleses," every soul carrying what valuables they could had taken to the mount.*
>
> —*Charles Darwin's Beagle* Diary, May 12, 1835

After the conquest of territory on the western coast of South America, from Panama down to the Magellan Strait, Spain came to regard the Pacific Ocean—better known then as the South Sea—as its own monopoly, a kind of privately owned lake. With this in mind, two Spanish viceroys were established—the one in Lima covered Chile. Britain strove to break this monopoly, both officially and unofficially, motivated by the prospects of plunder against the Spanish, often backed by the legitimacy of a state of war existing between the two countries. A secondary motive was that, from the British perspective, the land mass of Latin America acted as a barrier to the important spice trade in the east. There was no Panama Canal, no passage in the northern hemisphere, and for many years it was believed that the only sea route from the Atlantic to the Pacific was through the Magellan Strait. Britain's efforts to harass Spain in her imperial backyard and to get around this barrier brought her into continual conflict with Spain.

Naturally, Spain resisted these incursions into her territory and accused Britain (and other European nations) of acts of piracy, but to label all who came to fight the Spanish as pirates is to oversimplify what happened. Some definitions are needed.

The word *pirate* comes from the Old French *pirate*, which derives from the Latin word *pirata*, meaning "sailor, sea robber," and in turn from the Greek *peirates*, meaning "one who attacks," and *peiran* meaning "to attack, assault." Pirates acted beyond the protection of the law. Strictly speaking, "privateers" existed in times of war only, and this is the key difference. The usage dates from 1646 and originates from the phrase *private man of war* and may also be modeled on the words *volunteer* and *buccaneer*.

Unlike pirates, the privateer vessels and their commanders were authorized by *letters of marque* (from the French *lettre de marque*) issued by governments or monarchs to harass or capture the enemy's merchant ships. This cover of legitimacy to otherwise piratical acts originated with the French but had been adopted by Henry VIII in his war against France to encourage private investment by shipowners in order to increase the strength of the Royal Navy. Although the distinction between privateers and pirates was often blurred, privateering was an accepted norm of naval warfare from the sixteenth to the nineteenth centuries and practiced by all the major sea powers. The cost of fitting out a privateer was borne by investors who hoped to profit from the prize money awarded when the captured ships and their contents were sold.

Corsairs were originally French privateers from the Brittany port of St-Malo, and the name derives from the French *corsaire*, as well as Medieval Latin *cursarius* meaning "pirate," and Latin *currere*, "to run." Some also argue that it comes from the French King's *lettre de course* (racing letter) with 'race' as a euphemism for the pursuit of foreign merchant ships.

The word *buccaneer* was first used to describe the pirates who attacked Spanish shipping in the Caribbean and comes from the French word *boucanier*. This was the name for French settlers in Hispaniola who smoked and cured their meat on wooden frames called *boucans*, following the practice of the indigenous Arawak Indians, who called the grill a *buccan* or *barbacoa*, a word (and custom) handed down to our times as *barbeque*. Over time, *buccaneer* came to mean any pirate who raided Spanish possessions and ships along the American coast in the second half of the seventeenth century.

By these definitions, Sir Francis Drake was a privateer or corsair. He was an instrument of government policy, since in his famous voyage to the Pacific he was almost certainly acting with the consent and support of Queen Elizabeth, although it is very doubtful that she signed her name to a privateering commission for the venture. Nevertheless, Drake would show a document to his prisoners alleging that he had the Queen's commission—but only to Spaniards who could not read English! For the Spanish he remained a pirate and the scourge of Spain and her colonies. Drake reported that the Queen had contributed a thousand crowns to the enterprise that culminated in going round the world, although there is no documentary proof of this investment. What is certain is that Drake was the *first* ship's captain to circumnavigate the globe; Magellan (known in the Spanish-speaking world as Magallanes) had died en route on his voyage.

Francis Drake's career against Spanish interests started in the 1560s, when, as captain of the *Judith* in a fleet of five ships commanded by John Hawkins, he saw action at San Juan de Ulúa near Vera Cruz in Mexico in 1568. This was an experience that inspired in him a life-long pursuit of vengeance against the Spanish for the perceived treachery of Philip II's Viceroy of New Spain, Don Martín Enriquez, who broke a truce agreement.

Drake returned to the New World, and his two independent voyages to the Caribbean in the 1570s soon brought his name to the attention of the Spanish crown, especially after his audacious attack on the town of *Nombre de Dios* and the seizing of bullion from the Panama mule-trains in 1572 to 1573. The fame of his exploits spread to the extent that by the mid 1570s, Philip began to refer to him as *Draque, Francisco Draque, El Draque,* and even more intimately as *El Capitán Francisco*. Educated Spaniards called him *Francisco Draguez,* and Spanish mothers warned their children that if they did not behave, *El Draco* would come and take them away—a play on words, since *el draque* in old Spanish means "the dragon," derived from the Latin *draco,* meaning "serpent." Many years later, in 1829, a British visitor to Chile named Samuel Haigh wrote, "The Chilean and Peruvian mothers on the coast, when trying to hush their babes, cry '*aqui viene Draake*' (here comes Drake!)" (1829, 175).

By his skills as a navigator and his ability to out-maneuver and out-think his pursuers, Drake acquired the status of a legend in his own time. Regarded as a heretic by the Spanish (since he was Protestant) and a pirate, both revered and reviled, he was also thought to have supernatural powers and that his successes were aided by the devil.

It is very likely that after seeing the Pacific Ocean from the Panama Isthmus, Drake decided on the bold strategy of attacking Spanish interests in the South Sea from below and behind, where they were least prepared, by entering through the dreaded Magellan Strait. This led to the famous voyage and unintended circumnavigation that started in Plymouth in November 1577, and ended with his return to Plymouth in September 1580. Queen Elizabeth met with Drake in private before he sailed, presented him with a sword, and according to legend spoke the famous words "We do account that he which striketh at thee, Drake, striketh at us."

There is no documentary evidence that survives of what the Queen's real opinions were, but it is probable that she understood the geopolitical potential of Drake's ambitious plan to strike at Spain and the riches of Chile and Peru through the open basement door of the southern sea and that she swore everyone to secrecy. The account of the subsequent voyage, *The World Encompassed by Francis Drake*, compiled by the fleet's pastor, Francis Fletcher, was deemed so sensitive that its publication was delayed until 1628, fifty years after the expedition. When the famous contemporary historian Richard Hakluyt published his *Principal Navigations, Voyages, Traffickes & Discoveries of the English Nation* in 1589, there was an account of Drake's voyage, but no mention of the open water passage to the south of Cape Horn—Drake's Passage.

Of the five ships assembled for the voyage, the *Pelican*, the *Elizabeth*, the *Marigold*, the *Swan*, and the *Christopher*, only the *Pelican*—renamed the *Golden Hind* (or *Hinde*) completed the circumnavigation. By the standards of today, the *Pelican* was extremely small, just 150 tons, with a length of around eighty feet. The crew of about 160 men and boys were told that they were going to the Mediterranean; the fact that the fearsome Magellan Strait was in prospect was only communicated to them when at sea.

On entering the Strait, Drake named three islands—Elizabeth (after the Queen), St. George, and St. Bartholomew—shown in a map of Levinus Hulsius of 1606 as the "Francisci Draco Ins[ulae]." No one on board had been through the Strait before, and Magellan had left few details of his route, which must have tested Drake's navigational skills to the full. He crossed the 363-mile strait in only sixteen days. This was probably the fastest journey through the strait in that century—Magellan had taken thirty-seven days.

On their way through the strait they saw penguins, "strange birds, which could not fly at all, nor yet run so fast ... In the space of 1 day, we killed no les [*sic*] than 3000" (*The World Encompassed* 1628, 35), and the usage possibly dates from this expedition. The pastor, Francis Fletcher, noted the "fowle," which the Welsh sailors named "penguin," a term borrowed from the Celtic word for the great auk (from the Welsh *pen* "head" + *gwyn* "white"). This was a flightless sea bird that became extinct in the late nineteenth century. They also met a group of Alacaluf Indians in a canoe near Cape Froward, "The people are of a meane stature, but well set and compact in all their parts and lims [*sic*]; they have great pleasure in painting their faces" (*The World Encompassed*, 37).

When they emerged from the strait on September 6, 1578, the ships turned northwest and therefore into the open ocean, but later discovered their error in "shaping our course right Northwest to coast along the parts of Peru (for so the generall maps set out the land to lie)" and concluded that "the generall maps did erre from the truth" (*The World Encompassed*, 45–46). That the coast in fact tends northward was one of the two notable geographical discoveries of the voyage. But this lay ahead, for the flotilla's luck ran out and they were now hit by a succession of terrible storms that battered them southward. The *Marigold* was lost in the high seas, overwhelmed by a great wave. Under Captain John Winter, the *Elizabeth* turned back to the strait, making the first west-east navigation by a British sailor, and then made for England. The *Golden Hind* remained the only ship of the group in the Pacific, remorselessly pushed southward by the raging storms that lasted for fifty-two days.

This led to a second and even more momentous discovery; that the Magellan Strait was not just a passage between two continent masses arranged north to south, the Americas and Terra Australis, as shown in Mercator's map of 1541. Another widely held version had the same geography—Diego Gutiérrez's map of 1562. This was the most detailed map of the sixteenth century showing the New World; it showed that the strait divided Tierra de Patagones from Tierra de Magallanes. What Drake's voyage discovered was that the Atlantic and the Pacific actually joined in a confluence and that open sea lay south of Tierra del Fuego. *The World Encompassed* (1628, 44) recorded this discovery: "The uttermost cape or headland of all these islands stands near in 56 degrees, without which there is no main nor island to be seen to the southwards, but that the Atlantick Ocean and South Sea meet in a most large and free scope." This new fact has been commemorated ever afterwards in the naming of Drake's Passage—the sea between Cape Horn and the Antarctic.

Having been driven south, Drake discovered some islands, but it is uncertain exactly which islands he reached south of the Magellan Strait. Francis Fletcher recorded that the ship was pushed down to the "utmost island of Terra Incognita." No one can be sure, but this "utmost island" may have been Cape Horn. Drake formally claimed the islands in the south for England and called them the Elizabeth Islands.

There is an intriguing detail. Drake sheltered from the incessant storms for three days and four nights in the lee of an island he also called Elizabeth Island, where he recorded a depth of twenty fathoms. This island was shown for more than 170 years on maps as Port Sir Francis Drake. The curiosity is that this island, given the coordinates recorded by Drake, lies well to the west of Cape Horn and away from the Tierra del Fuego archipelago, where no modern map shows land and where it is known that the ocean is enormously deep. For example, Emanuel Bowen, engraver to George II, shows in his map of 1747, *A New and Accurate Map of Chili, Terra Magellanica, Terra del Fuego &c*, that at longitude 78 just north of latitude 57 south there is a "Port discovered by Sr F. Drake." Felix Riesenberg (1950) hypothesizes in his chapter on "The vanished island of Sir Francis Drake" that this might have been the crater of a volcano, since reclaimed by the sea.

The storm now abated, and Drake's instructions from England were to carry out a reconnaissance of the coast as far north as 30 degrees south, along what is now Chile. This territory was free of Spanish occupation at the time, and England recognized neither the strait nor this southern coastline of Chile as belonging to Spain. Drake's first contact with the natives, when he anchored off Mocha Island near the Chilean coast, nearly ended in disaster. The Indians were members of Araucanian (Mapuche) groups living south of the River Bío-Bío who, with their fierce spirit of independence and fighting ability, had so far repulsed all European incursions into their lands. Drake knew of this hostility toward the Spanish and hoped to turn it to his advantage.

The first day ended well, with the Indians showing signs of friendship, but on the second day, when Drake went looking for fresh water with only ten men, they were set upon by large numbers of natives. Two men were immediately killed and the rest, including Drake, wounded in this skirmish. When he returned to the *Golden Hind*, there was a general shout to exact revenge by firing on the natives, but Drake, showing the compassion and humanity that he was capable of on several occasions, and believing that the natives had mistaken them for Spaniards, ordered that no shot be fired.

Sailing north, Drake turned his attention to Valparaíso and, in December 1578, he brazenly entered the bay and pulled alongside a solitary Spanish ship, the *Los Reyes*. Since the Spaniards "knew" there was no foreign presence in the Pacific, there was no reason to suspect the *Golden Hind*, and the Spanish crew even drummed a welcome as a boat from the *Hind* came alongside. The Spanish ship was quickly overcome, the crew taken down to the hold, and the small settlement of Valparaíso ransacked. Drake left the following day, towing the Spanish ship as a prize behind him. This action put the Governor of Chile, Rodrigo de Quiroga, on alert, and he prepared a ship with a hundred men to go after Drake and sent another boat to Callao to warn the Viceroy in Lima of the raid on Valparaíso.

Drake spent several days looking fruitlessly for the *Marigold* and the *Elizabeth*, and then, while at anchor in the Bay of La Herradura, south of Coquimbo, he suffered his first reverse to the Spanish. When a shore party of around a dozen men was looking for fresh water, they were set upon by a group of Spaniards on horseback and on foot coming from nearby La Serena, aided by Indian auxiliaries. One of the English sailors was shot and then executed by the natives. Drake sailed to the Bay of Salada, one hundred miles further north, to complete the final preparations for his main action against Spanish interests, an attack on Arica.

Drake arrived at Arica on February 6, 1579. Arica at that time was a small settlement of fewer than one hundred houses. Drake had hoped to profit from sacking the town, since it was the port from which the silver of Potosí was shipped to Panama, but the residents prepared to defend themselves and the pickings from the boats in the harbor were disappointing. However, Drake learned that a treasure ship had just left for Chule, the port of Arequipa in present-day Peru, and set off in pursuit. Unfortunately for Drake, it was now clear that after the events in Valparaíso and Coquimbo, the Spanish were running ahead of him, northwards along the coast, with dire warnings about the English pirate. As a result, the treasure was taken out of the ship and hidden.

Nevertheless, Drake sailed on and got into the harbor at Callao at night unobserved, causing considerable damage and havoc. He learned that another treasure ship, the *Nuestra Señora de la Concepción*, had recently left Callao for Panama, and he set off and finally overtook it. Having decided that the return to England by Cape Horn was too risky, Drake continued to Mexico, then to what is now northern California, searching for a possible northwest passage, and then crossed the Pacific to the Philippines, the Moluccas, the Indian Ocean, the Cape of Good Hope, Sierra Leone, and back to Plymouth.

In his study *Sir Francis Drake*, John Sugden (1990, 122) writes that "Drake's raid on the Pacific coast of South America was remarkably bloodless. None of his prisoners was killed. . . . This was sixteenth century warfare, and by its standards Drake was far from cruel or brutal. Even when Spaniards resisted capture, and might have expected their lives to be forfeit, Drake generally received them with some respect and consideration."

But the Spanish in South America were definitely not amused. The Viceroy in Lima sent Don Pedro de Sarmiento y Gamboa to find

Drake in the Magellan Strait (which of course he did not), and then on to Spain with the news of these exploits. It is said that in Spain Philip II asked Sarmiento if it was possible to close the Magellan passage with a chain and padlock! Clearly not, but Sarmiento responded that it was possible to fortify the strait. Philip II's reaction to the menace represented by Drake was to send, in 1581, a fleet of twenty-three ships with around 3,500 men to guard the River Plate region on the eastern coast and the Magellan Strait and to reinforce Chile. This force was under the command of Diego Flores de Valdez, with Sarmiento second in command.

The aim was to land five hundred men and leave some ships, all under Sarmiento, to colonize and defend the region. Two other groups of ships were intended, respectively, to garrison the ports and patrol the coasts of Chile and Peru and to sail across the Pacific to consolidate Magellan's discoveries in the Philippines. But the journey south was beset with problems, and only four ships under Sarmiento actually entered the strait in 1583. Once there, three ships deserted, and Sarmiento struggled to establish the settlements they called Nombre de Jesus and Rey Felipe. This enterprise in Tierra del Fuego was an unmitigated disaster, with more desertions, mutinies, executions, and murders. Very few of these men and women ever saw Spain again, and the settlements were decimated within a few years by abject starvation. This was the pitiful situation that Thomas Cavendish encountered on his 1586 voyage.

Although there was no formal declaration of war, England and Spain were in conflict continuously between 1585 and 1604, spanning the invasion attempts of the Spanish Armada in 1588 and the English Armada in 1589. It was in this period of hostility that Sir Thomas Cavendish, or "Candish" in older accounts, led the third expedition to successfully circumnavigate the world, and he was the *first* to deliberately set out to do this. Known as The Navigator, Cavendish was stimulated by Drake's success, and he commanded a voyage that started and ended in Plymouth: July 1586 to September 1588. It seems he successfully sought a commission from Queen Elizabeth, but there is some doubt about whether Queen Elizabeth knighted him on his return.

The flotilla comprised three ships, the *Desire*, the *Content*, and the *Hugh Gallant*, with a total of 123 sailors. The *Hugh Gallant* was scuttled off the west coast of South America, and only the *Desire* made it back eventually to England. Port Desire was discovered by Cavendish and was named after this ship. In January 1587, Cavendish came across the small Spanish settlements set up at Philip's command. While numbers vary according to sources, most agree that at Nombre de Jesus, Cavendish came across eighteen starving survivors and that he embarked one (perhaps three) of them, leaving the rest behind. Worse off was Rey Felipe, where he found only corpses. This was then renamed Port Famine by Cavendish. The crossing of the strait took Cavendish forty-nine days, due to contrary winds. He fixed the most southerly point of the continent, calling it Cape Froward. These names of Port Desire, Port Famine, and Cape Froward remain in use today.

On his way up the coast of Chile, Cavendish captured and plundered several Spanish ships. He summed up his first incursions into the Spanish New World in a letter (quoted in Hakluyt 1589, vol. 12, 70) with this blunt narrative: "I navigated alongst the coast of Chili, Peru, and Nueva Espanna where I made great spoils: I burnt and sunke 19 sailes of ships small and great. All the villages and townes that ever I landed at, I burnt and spoiled: and had I not bene discovered upon the coast, I had taken great quantitie of treasure."

Andrew Merrick was the next British adventurer to arrive. He organized with John Chidley an expedition of five ships that departed from Plymouth in 1589. A storm dispersed the group off Africa, and only Merrick's *Delight* got to Port Desire. After waiting for two weeks, the ship left to cross the strait, but a mutiny obliged Merrick to return to Europe, where the *Delight* was wrecked on rocks near Cherbourg, with only six survivors, including Merrick and yet another Spanish survivor of the ill-fated Spanish settlements in Patagonia.

Thomas Cavendish departed from Plymouth in 1591 on his second voyage to the southern latitudes, this time accompanied by John Davis (or Davys). Cavendish captained the *Leicester* (or *Lester*), with John Davis on the *Desire*. They were accompanied by the *Roebuck*, the *Dainty*, and a pinnace called the *Black*. In March 1592, Cavendish reached Port Desire and reunited with the rest of the fleet. However, the crew was in a terrible state, and after failing to get much further than Cape Froward, Cavendish decided to return to England and died on this return journey while off Ascension Island. On this voyage, his companion John Davis discovered the Falklands/Malvinas Islands, in August 1592.

Since the ships were separated, and searching for Cavendish proved unsuccessful, the *Desire*, with Davis on board, and the *Black* set off to get through the strait. On their third attempt, they managed to sail into the Pacific, where the *Black* sank with all its crew. With his men dying from scurvy and his sails in tatters, Davis decided to cut his losses and return to England. He attempted to provision his men at Port Desire, where Indians killed nine of his sailors, and finally arrived in Ireland in June 1593 with just sixteen survivors from the original seventy-six sailors, of whom only Davis and four others were in any kind of fit condition.

Sir Richard Hawkins left Plymouth in the same year. Richard was the last member of the remarkable Hawkins dynasty, and the only son of John Hawkins, who had suffered with Drake the treachery at San Juan de Ulúa. Richard Hawkins' ship was the *Dainty*, 350 tons, originally named the *Repentance* and built specially for the Pacific voyage. He was joined by the *Fancy* and the *Hawk*, as well as a store ship and two pinnaces. While the equipping of the expedition was certainly undertaken by Hawkins, Queen Elizabeth gave it ample support and the Privy Council its consent. Richard's plan was to follow the route taken by Francis Drake, for fame and fortune, and in fact he received guidance and advice from Drake.

Captain Tharlton of the *Fancy* deserted in a storm off the River Plate, and the *Dainty* sailed with difficulty through the Magellan Strait in February 1594, spending more than a month in a battle against the gales, but eventually emerged to sail on to Mocha Island, Valparaíso Bay, Coquimbo, and Arica in present-day Chile, attacking Spanish shipping. The Spanish reacted by assembling a small armada of six heavily armed ships to pursue him. Three of these ships eventually cornered Hawkins in a bay off present-day Ecuador, and, despite the odds, the English sailors fought on for three days but were finally subdued. In 1597, Hawkins was sent back to Spain, and then, in late 1602, he was freed following the payment of three thousand pounds, a ransom set aside in his father's will, and he returned to England. His book, *The Observations of Sir Richard Hawkins* (published posthumously) became the inspiration for Charles Kingsley's *Westward Ho!*

Benjamin Vicuña Mackenna (1884, 5) tells the story of Richard Hawkins throwing a crucifix into the Bay of Valparaíso, adding that this may not really have happened. Nevertheless, it provoked an angry reprisal in Santiago. This was "a famous procession called *Del Desagravio*, intended to appease the anger of the Almighty, celebrating every year in commemoration of the offence, and in a solemn and pompous manner, the recovery of the sacred relic by the net of a Valparaíso fisherman."

The Anglo-Spanish War ended in 1604 with the Treaty of London, negotiated between Philip III (Philip II's son) and James I. The terms committed England to renounce its buccaneering ways against Spain. There was yet another Anglo-Spanish War in the middle of the century (1654–1660), which closed with the Treaty of Madrid signed in

July 1670. The terms of this agreement stipulated that England could keep Jamaica and the Cayman Islands in exchange for guarantees that Spain's commercial monopoly in America would not be challenged.

It was during this period of peace between England and Spain that Sir John Narborough came to Chile. His expedition in the *Sweepstakes* and the *Batchelor* lasted from 1669 to 1671 and was commissioned and paid for by the British Crown. The objectives were to explore the Magellan Strait, appraise the power of the Spanish in southern Chile, and assess the possibilities for British commerce, possibly by occupation, in the region of Valdivia.

The voyage provided accurate soundings and descriptions of the strait that were the source over many years for future charts. Narborough's *Journal* reports his taking possession of the bay and river, on both banks, at Port Desire in the name of Charles II (the recently restored monarch) and his descendants. There may in fact have been more territory claimed for the King. Barros (1988, 43) quotes from the diary of Richard Williams, who traveled on the *Sweepstakes*, that Narborough took possession in April 1670 at Port Desire of the southern coast of Patagonia, from Rio de la Plata to the Magellan Strait, thinking of making it British colony. There is a map of the strait made by Narborough, found today in the British Library, where the British flag appears both north and south of the strait. Other maps omit this claim but carry the flag of St. George on Elizabeth Island.

Suggested tactics included taking Valdivia and making an alliance with the Mapuche natives to throw the Spanish out. Barros tells the story of a mysterious adventurer who traveled with Narborough and passed as Spanish with the name Don Carlos Henríquez. Narborough calls him "Don Carolus" in his journal. He was possibly one of a number of foreign residents in London who lobbied the Court for England to promote trade with the colonies in the New World, and it seems that he served as a translator on the voyage and mediator in negotiations. There is a document in the Public Records Office in London, dated July 14, 1669, that outlines a project by which Don Carlos petitioned the King to consider establishing an English colony near the strait (see Barros 1988, 51–57). He claimed to know the coasts of southern South America, but on arrival there he showed that he was ignorant of the region. At his request, he was put ashore in the Bay of Valdivia near a Spanish fort, and he never returned to the ship. Don Carlos was captured with four English companions and interrogated in Valparaíso. They were then sent on to Lima, where they were executed.

The *Batchelor* separated from the *Sweepstakes* during a storm and returned to England with the news that Narborough's ship was lost.

Narborough spent a month at Port Desire then wintered from April to September 1670 at San Julián—the agreed rendezvous point—before returning to Port Desire and exploring the Magellan Strait in October and November. He stopped at what is today Isla Isabel (Elizabeth Island), near Punta Arenas, where they met with Fuegians and attempted to explain that they were looking for gold, all to no avail. Narborough left a description of their physical characteristics in his *Journal* (published 1694), where he described meeting Indians "of a middle stature, both Men and Women, and well limbed, and roundish Faced, and well shaped, and low Foreheaded . . . their Faces dawbed in spots down their Cheeks with white Clay, and some black streaks" (1694, 65).

The *Sweepstakes* passed by the island of Chiloé and arrived at the mouth of the River Valdivia in December 1670. Narborough made contact with the Spanish garrison, and when he requested water, they were directed to Fort San Pedro, where an officer (Lieutenant Thomas Armiger), a "gentleman" (John Fortescue), and two sailors went ashore. They were initially treated cordially, but then the Governor had them arrested and demanded that Narborough's ship enter the bay and position itself under the fort's cannons. The sailors were released to take this demand to Narborough, who decided the risk to his ship was too great, and so he left the prisoners with the Spanish and returned to the south of Chile. He was unable to make contact with the natives near Valdivia, nor in the strait to which he returned, and he turned home, arriving back in England in June 1671.

Nine years later, there started a period of intense British piracy against Spanish interests in Latin America, including Chile. The story is complicated, and not all sources agree on the details. Nevertheless, it all began in April 1680 when a contingent of 331 buccaneers, led by Captain Peter Harris, landed on the Isthmus of Panama. This group included Bartholomew Sharpe and William Dampier—names that became well known in Chile.

They divided into five companies, led by Sharpe, Richard Sawkins, Peter Harris, John Coxon, and John Cook. After several skirmishes with the Spanish, and desertions, two ships remained in the Pacific, the *Trinity*, commanded by Sharpe, and John Coxon in charge of the *Mayflower*. The *Mayflower* was sailing badly and was abandoned. Notwithstanding these several reverses, Sharpe drove on south in the *Trinity*, and on October 23, 1680, he attempted the first of many landings on the Chilean coast in search of wood and water. In the same month, Sharpe attempted to extort cattle from inhabitants of Port Hillo, near Arica, but he scurried back to his ship when Spanish horsemen challenged his party. In December, they attacked Coquimbo and La Serena, capturing the settlements in fierce fighting, but were again sent packing by the Spaniards.

Having had his fill of action, Sharpe sailed to the Juan Fernández Islands for rest and recuperation, with the intention of returning to England via the Magellan Strait. The crew opposed this decision, mutinied, and put Sharpe in irons, electing John Watling as the new leader. Leaving quickly from the islands on sighting Spanish warships, they left behind an Indian called William—the first of the "Robinson Crusoes" on these Chilean islands. The *Trinity* turned north and engaged Arica in a second attack in January 1681, which was also beaten off by the Spanish. Watling was killed in the attempt on this strongly defended town, and Sharpe was reinstated as commander. This time he agreed to the general view that they should continue to prowl the Pacific coast for shipping to plunder. However, a few weeks later, a group of forty-seven men under John Cook (including William Dampier) journeyed in canoes to the Isthmus of Panama and from there returned to the Caribbean.

Sharpe remained with about seventy-five men on the *Trinity* and stayed in the Pacific for several months longer. Among the prizes taken was the *Rosario* off what is now Ecuador, with valuable and detailed charts of the west coast of the Americas. In November 1681, Sharpe headed for the Magellan Strait, but his ship was pushed down past the entrance to the strait by a fierce storm. He was forced to try Cape Horn instead, becoming the first English captain to round the Cape from west to east and thus to prove that there was no great southern continent nearby—the legendary Terra Australis Incognita. On his arrival in England, Sharpe was tried for piracy in London. He was saved from execution because he had taken from the *Rosario* a manuscript describing all the ports held by the Spanish from California to Cape Horn, complete with instructions on how to get into the harbors. This implied challenge to Spanish hegemony in the Americas was in contravention to the Treaty of Madrid but of great value to the English.

To this day, Bartholomew Sharpe's pirating exploits in Chile are remembered in the expression *llegó charqui a Coquimbo* ("*charqui* has arrived in Coquimbo"; *charqui* is an indigenous name for dried meat, jerked beef, but in this case it is also a corruption of the name Sharpe). The expression conveys the sense of someone having arrived who is not welcome. Agustín Edwards (1937) tells the story that at La Serena, Sharpe stole a silver statuette of the Virgin Mary from one of the altars in the Iglesia de los Agustinos. He returned a short time later and, under the astonished eyes of the faithful, took the image of Saint Joseph, saying by way of excuse that the Virgin Mary could not continue living without her husband and missed him terribly. Charles Darwin heard the same story from Joaquín Edwards, which he retold in his *Beagle* journal:

> [Joaquín] told me he recollected being at school in Coquimbo, when a holiday was given to all the boys to see the Captain of an English Ship, who came on some business from the Port to the city. He believes that nothing would have induced any body in the school, including himself, to have gone close to the Englishman; so fully had they been impressed with all the heresy, contamination & evil to be derived from contact with such a person. To this day they hand down the atrocious actions of the Buccaniers [sic]; one of them took the Virgin Mary out [of] the Church & returned the ensuing year for St. Joseph, saying it was a pity the Lady should not have a husband. (Beagle *Diary*, May 12, 1835)

Picking up the story of William Dampier's connections with Chile: After arriving in Panama by canoe, he suffered greatly crossing the Isthmus as part of John Cook's group. William Dampier is no longer a household name, but he was very well known to and had a great influence on his generation and beyond. He was a pirate for part of his life, but he preferred to see himself as a keen observer and at worst a privateer, which, strictly speaking, he only became when the War of the Spanish Succession started in May 1702.

The survivors of the overland trek found a fleet of eight pirate ships on the Caribbean coast, four of which were commanded by Englishmen, one of whom was John Coxon. John Cook went as second-in-command on a Dutch ship, and William Dampier as navigator on a French ship. Later, Cook and Dampier traveled (separately) to Virginia, where they joined a buccaneer named Edward Davis and a navigator named William Ambrosia Cowley on a ship called the *Revenge*. They sailed to the west coast of Africa, where they captured a Danish ship and called her *The Batchelor's Delight*, and set off for Cape Horn, which was rounded in February 1684. Off the coast of Chile they met up with another buccaneer, Captain John Eaton on the *Nicholas*. The two ships sailed to Juan Fernández Island, where they found the Indian, William, left behind by Sharpe. John Cook became ill and died soon afterward at sea, being succeeded in command by Edward Davis. Davis and Eaton separated, unable to agree on their shares of eventual plunder, and Cowley joined Eaton on the *Nicholas*, which set off across the Pacific. Although Davis, Cook, Cowley, and Dampier started in Virginia, this voyage can be called a circumnavigation, since it is probable that the ships and crews originated in Britain.

Edward Davis may well have been the first European to sight Easter Island, in 1687, on board *The Bachelor's Delight*, and this was the opinion of William Dampier, who joined him on this voyage. An account by Lionel Wafer, a member of the crew, refers to coming across a "small flat island" where "to the westward about 12 leagues, by judgement, we saw a range of high land, which we took to be islands," some five hundred leagues from Copiapó, which was "almost due east," and six hundred leagues from the Galápagos (see Thompson 1891, 447). Errors in these distances may be explained by drift due to strong currents. Unfortunately, Captain Davis did not permit anyone to land upon this island, and there is no mention of the famous Easter Island statues. There is today a *Bahía Inglesa* (English Bay) five kilometers south of Caldera in northern Chile that dates from when Edward Davis called there, and the bay became known as *Puerto del inglés*—the Englishman's port.

Dampier published his first book in 1697—*A New Voyage Round the World*—which was an immediate bestseller, with three printings within nine months followed by translations into Dutch, German, and French. The Royal Society described the book as a "factual, talented, and richly detailed account of people, places, things, plants, fishes, reptiles, birds and mammals." This book, and his later publications, influenced other writers, including Jonathan Swift and Daniel Defoe. William Dampier's talent for observation and analysis of natural history helped Darwin and Humboldt in the development of their theories, and he made innovations in navigational technology that were studied later by James Cook and Horatio Nelson.

William Dampier undertook a second circumnavigation, the first person ever to do this *twice*, leaving England soon after the start of the War of the Spanish Succession (1702–1713) on a voyage that lasted from September 1703 to 1707. The small flotilla comprised two government ships, the *St George* and the *Cinque Ports*, the latter captained by Charles Pickering. Several members of the crew of the *Cinque Ports* died of fever, including the captain. Thomas Stradling assumed command, with the sailing master—a Scotsman named Alexander Selkirk—as his second-in-command. Unfortunately, they did not get along, and Selkirk was left marooned in September 1704 on the uninhabited islands of Juan Fernández and became the model for Defoe's *Robinson Crusoe*. Most versions of the story say that Selkirk asked to be put ashore because of his disagreement with Stradling and because he feared the *Cinque Ports* was not seaworthy; and indeed this ship did later sink off the coast of Peru with the loss of most of the crew.

In 1966, Chilean President Eduardo Frei Montalva renamed the two main islands of the Juan Fernández archipelago in an effort to increase tourism. The closest to the Chilean mainland, Isla Más a Tierra, was renamed Robinson Crusoe Island, and Isla Más Afuera was given the name of Isla Alejandro Selkirk, even though Selkirk never actually set foot on this island. There is a bronze plaque in memory of Selkirk on a hill, called Selkirk's Lookout, near the village of San Juan Bautista on Robinson Crusoe Island. This plaque was erected by Commodore Powell of the frigate *Topaze* in 1868. Modern maps of Robinson Crusoe Island still show the bay of *Puerto Inglés* (English Port), the anchorage favored by the English pirates, and Cumberland Bay (named by Lord Anson), and in both these places cannon pieces remain as testimony to the Spanish colonial efforts to keep these unwelcome visitors from landing.

Not content with two circumnavigations already under his belt, Dampier agreed to serve Woodes Rogers as his pilot and sailing master on a voyage in the *Duke*. This expedition left from Bristol in August 1708, and arrived back in The Downs in October 1711. This made Dampier the first person to go round the world *three* times. This expedition rescued the marooned Alexander Selkirk in February 1709. Dampier recognized him as the sailing master from the ill-fated *Cinque Ports*, even after his four years and four months' solitude on the Juan Fernández archipelago. Selkirk had forgotten how to speak but was otherwise in good health. Woodes Rogers published his account of *A Cruising Voyage Round the World* in 1712, which is likely to have been the main inspiration for Daniel Defoe's novel.

The War of the Spanish Succession ended with the Treaty of Utrecht in 1713, but soon another conflict broke out involving Spain and England as adversaries, this one called the War of the Quadruple Alliance (1718–1720). In what was probably the last English privateering expedition to the southern seas, John Clipperton and George Shelvocke set out from England in February 1719. Clipperton was the master of the *Success*, and he seems to have focused on following his military orders. Shelvocke in the *Speedwell*, on the other hand, was more interested in piracy. They returned separately to Galway in Ireland in June 1721 (Clipperton), and to London in August 1721 (Shelvocke). An incident on Shelvocke's ship where a crewman shot an albatross which had followed the ship for several days, thinking it a bad omen, was used by Coleridge in his *Rime of the Ancient Mariner*.

Two decades later, there was another conflict with Spain, the War of Jenkins' Ear (1739–1742), and it was in this period that George Anson commanded the last British Navy expedition against the Spanish in the southern seas. Anson left from St. Helen's Road (near Portsmouth) in September 1740, intent on attacking Spanish settlements on the west coast of South America, and returned to Spithead in June 1744, after the war had finished. Six ships left England in a debacle of a voyage that from the first showed the signs of widespread corruption in the Royal Navy, with the ships leaking and the provisions almost inedible. Commodore Anson led in HMS *Centurion*, but two ships in his fleet failed to round Cape Horn. After clearing the Le Maire Strait, Anson wrote, "We had a continual succession of such tempestuous weather as surprised the oldest and most experienced mariners on board, and obliged them to confess that what they had hitherto called storms were inconsiderable gales compared with the violence of these winds" (1748, chapter 6).

Another ship in the fleet, HMS *Wager*, with a midshipman called Byron on board, was wrecked off Chile in the Guayanecos Islands. After the ship struck rocks off the island that now bears the name of Isla Wager, many of the crew reached the shore in safety. Since the ship was a store vessel for the fleet, the survivors were able to salvage sufficient supplies to spend several months on the island. Nevertheless, a dispute broke out regarding the powers of command of the captain over the soldiers on board, and over the sailors too, since on land away from a ship they would no longer be paid by the navy. These grievances climaxed in the captain shooting dead a midshipman and the party splitting into two groups.

Captain Anson and around twenty officers and men, including Byron, sailed northward in open boats in search of civilization. After tremendous suffering, they were helped by Chonos Indians, who took the remaining four survivors to Chiloé Island. The Spanish treated them surprisingly well, both at Chiloé and later in Valparaíso and Santiago too, considering that the two countries were at war. All four eventually made it back to England. The other group, of about eighty crew and soldiers, decided on the opposite direction and went south and east in an extended longboat journey through the Magellan Strait to Brazil, and eventually twelve survived the nightmare voyage to Britain. On his return to England, Byron wrote his *Narrative of the Loss of the Wager till their Arrival in England: With an Account of the Great Distresses Suffered by Himself and his Companions on the Coast of Patagonia from the year 1740*. He was grandfather of the poet Lord Byron, who used details of the shipwreck in Canto II of *Don Juan*.

The three surviving ships, the *Centurion*, the *Gloucester*, and the *Trial* (and the provisions boat *Anna*, later abandoned at the Juan Fernández Islands) got into the Pacific and visited the Juan Fernández Islands and Valparaíso, but only the *Centurion* managed to return to England, since the other two were scuttled as unseaworthy in the Pacific. Of the 961 crew on the three boats, only 335 were alive when the group reached Juan Fernández Island; the rest had died, mainly through scurvy. Of these survivors, around two hundred returned to England, in June 1744, with just one ship—the *Centurion*, laden with so much treasure that thirty-two ox-carts were needed to take it to the Tower of London. George Anson published in 1748 his account, *A Voyage round the World in the Years 1740–1744*, one of the most popular books of maritime adventure in the eighteenth century. Moreover, Anson, now an Admiral following his return to England, introduced an Act of Parliament in 1748 extending naval discipline to crews wrecked, lost, or captured.

An intriguing sequel to this story followed in 1761, when Admiral Anson dispatched an English sailor, Cornelius Webb, on board the *Unicorn* to recover Spanish treasure buried on Más a Tierra (Robinson Crusoe) Island. It seems that Webb found the treasure and took it on board, only to return to the island after a storm split his mast. The treasure was then reburied so that Webb could sail to Valparaíso for repairs before continuing with his venture. Hearing that the crew planned to mutiny on their return to Más a Tierra Island and seize the treasure for themselves, Webb started a fire on the ship which killed everyone except himself, and as the only survivor he rowed himself to Valparaíso. According to some versions, Webb then sent coded messages back to Lord Anson explaining where the treasure had been reburied, but Anson had died suddenly in June 1762 before Webb's envoy arrived in England.

The last piratical acts involving the British occurred during Chile's War of Independence. Strictly speaking, these were privateers who acted with at least the informal understanding of the Chilean patriot forces that any attack on Spanish interests was to be welcomed. In 1817, Captain Mackay led a party of six unemployed English sailors on a sortie against Spanish shipping in a launch called *La Fortuna*. Their motives were probably more piratical than altruistic. They left Valparaíso and captured two Spanish ships, the *Minerva* off Arica, and then the Spanish brig *Santa María*, which had dispatches from the Spanish authorities in Peru to the royalists in Chile. Mackay passed these documents to the patriot forces in Valparaíso, and for this act his activities as a privateer were given a degree of official approval.

A little later, in 1819, John Illingsworth with a crew of Chileans in the frigate *Rosa de Los Andes* was also operating off Panama. They had skirmishes with the Spanish frigates *Piedad* and *Prueba*, captured the Spanish brig *Canton* in the Galápagos, and sacked the Spanish settlement on Taboga Island.

Since the new republican government did not always pay wages on time, it is hardly surprising that some sailors became pirates and attracted deserters from the navy to their side. These men contributed a great deal to the patriot cause in the War of Independence against Spain, harassing and attacking, to the point that a fleet of Spanish merchant ships was tied up in Callao harbor. However, the Commander of the Chilean patriot navy, Admiral Cochrane, was eventually compelled to contain such excesses, and he did so by adopting the British naval code. Maria Graham (May 30, 1822) comments on the complaints she heard among British naval officers, "the disappointment of . . . hopes too highly raised," and hoped they would not turn to pirating, "unless indeed, what I should shudder to think true, any English officers expected that their service in Chile would be only a kind of licensed buccaneering, where each should be master of his own ship and his own actions, without rule or subordination."

Chapter 2

Explorers by Sea

> *The inhabitants of Tierra del Fuego have . . . been spoken of as if they were beings possessed of little more than animal instinct, and incapable of being instructed. This may, perhaps, be the case; arising however, out of the peculiar situation in which they are placed. Give them intercourse with foreigners and they will improve in understanding; for I have found them to be not only tractable and inoffensive, but also, in many of their employments, active and ingenious.*
>
> —*James Weddell*, A Voyage towards the South Pole, *1825*

At the close of the Seven Years' War (1756–1762), there was at last a period of peace between England and Spain, during the reign of George III. At that time, the British Admiralty was worried that the Spanish, Dutch, and French might overtake England in overseas trade and decided to send Commodore John Byron, who had sailed as a midshipman on Anson's expedition, to explore the southern Pacific, with the additional task of finding whether a southern continent really existed. This led to another circumnavigation of the globe, and, since the Royal Society gave its support, the expedition is regarded as the first world voyage of scientific investigation. There are suspicions too that the expedition was also expected to keep an eye open for unknown lands which could perhaps be claimed for Britain.

John Byron has gone down in history as "Foul Weather Jack." The voyage started from The Downs in June 1764, and Byron returned in May 1766, a voyage of only twenty-two months, and the fastest circumnavigation to date. The Admiralty ordered that Byron sail through the Magellan Strait after Anson's difficulties rounding Cape Horn, which resulted in important surveying. Byron had overall command of the expedition, but of the two ships, the *Dolphin* and the

Tamar, only the *Dolphin*, captained by Philip Carteret, returned to England. The *Tamar* developed rudder problems and ended its voyage in Antigua. Byron searched for survivors of the wreck of the *Wager* in the Guayanecos Islands, allegedly finding children with blue eyes and fair hair. He also made contact with several Indian groups—the Tehuelches, Selk'nam, and Yámana.

He published, in 1767, his *Voyage around the World in H.M. Ship the Dolphin Comm. by the Hon. Commodore Byron*, which includes an account of meeting Fuegian Indians in December 1764 on Elizabeth Island. He describes coming into contact first with the "Chief," "this frightful Colossus," then with a group, "except the skins, which they wore with the hair inwards, most of them were naked" (see Hawkesworth 1785, vol. 1, 65). Byron handed out ribbon and beads and sent for tobacco from the ship. "Mr. Cumming came up with the tobacco, and I could not but smile at the astonishment which I saw expressed in his countenance, upon perceiving himself, though six feet two inches high, become at once a pygmy among giants" (Hawkesworth, vol. 1, 69).

The Admiralty was disappointed with these achievements, and within one month of Byron's return, Samuel Wallis, in charge of the *Dolphin*, and Philip Carteret on the sloop *Swallow*, were sent off to complete the mission, leading to yet another circuit of the globe—a double circumnavigation in fact. They left England in July 1766, accompanied by the *Prince Frederick*, and entered the Magellan Strait in December. They anchored at Port Famine, where the *Prince Frederick* departed for the Falklands/Malvinas, taking trees from Tierra del Fuego to be planted on those islands. Wallis and Carteret met with Tehuelches, Selk'nam, and Alacaluf Indians. The two ships separated in the Pacific soon after leaving the Magellan Strait, and they searched independently for the elusive southern continent. The captains returned separately to England in May 1768 (Wallis), with the *Dolphin* becoming the first ship to circumnavigate the world twice, and in June 1769 (Carteret). Carteret had a difficult time on the *Swallow* and lost most of his crew on the voyage. The captains formed a bad impression of Tierra del Fuego for its dangers and cold. Nevertheless, a new map of the strait resulted from the voyage.

Shortly after Wallis's return, Lieutenant James Cook embarked on what would be his first circumnavigation. He left England on HMS *Endeavour* in August 1768, and returned in July 1771. This voyage had a scientific objective: sponsored by the Royal Society of London, Cook was to observe the passage of the planet Venus over the sun, so as to measure the distance from the Earth to Venus. This was a phenomenon that could only be observed from one of the islands in the southern Pacific—and the island chosen was Otaheite.

Cook sailed through the Le Maire Strait, between Staten Island and the south-eastern tip of Tierra del Fuego, before rounding Cape Horn, which he fixed with astonishing accuracy. He landed on Tierra del Fuego, in January 1769, in the Bay of Good Success, where contact with the Fuegian Indians was friendly. Cook thought them "perhaps as miserable a set of People as are this day upon Earth" (see Collingridge 2003, 150). While Cook surveyed the Bay, the naturalist Joseph Banks spent five days collecting plants, including a night spent in the hills. Unhappily, they miscalculated their return, and two of his servants died from exposure. Banks returned to public acclamation in England for his botanical discoveries while, apart from a brief notice on the ship's arrival, Cook was hardly mentioned in the press, although well respected within the Admiralty. Exactly one year later, the second great voyage set out.

James Cook's second circumnavigation on HMS *Resolution* lasted three years, from July 1772 to July 1775. His given objective was to search for the Great Southern Continent—an obsession of the age—despite his conviction that this was a myth. Cook's expedition departed with HMS *Resolution* and HMS *Adventure* under Tobias Furneaux. Two astronomers and a naturalist named John Reinhold Forster were on board. They sailed into Tierra del Fuego from the west and examined the shores of the Magellan Strait and Cape Horn.

The exploration proper actually started at Cape Horn, from where Cook sailed almost 2,400 kilometers due south to prove there was no land there, although in fact they must have sailed to within 120 kilometers of the Antarctic continent. The two ships separated on this voyage and rejoined in New Zealand. Cook then decided to carry out a great sweep of the Pacific, during which he turned north to Easter Island and later explored the southern part of Tierra del Fuego, where he met with Yámana Indians, and Staten Island. He also met with Alacaluf Indians, who lived in canoes, and described seeing "two young children . . . at the breast entirely naked; thus they are inured from their infancy to cold and hardships" (*A Voyage towards the South Pole* 1821, 168). His verdict on the Fuegians was typical of the early visitors: "Of all the nations I have seen, [these people] seem to be the most wretched. They are doomed to live in one of the most inhospitable climates in the world without having sagacity enough to provide themselves with such conveniences as may render life in some measure more comfortable" (*The Voyages of Captain James Cook* 1821, vol. 4, 172). Passing Cape Horn, he observed, "Hardly any thing in nature can appear with a more barren and savage aspect than the whole of this country" (*Voyages* 1821, vol. 4, 160).

These two voyages had a lasting significance in the fight against the scurvy which had so decimated Anson's crews. Scurvy was the scourge of the Royal Navy, and James Cook is often credited with conquering it. The British Admiralty was determined to find a cure, and the voyages of Byron, Wallis, Carteret, and Cook were used to test various theories. James Cook read a paper at the Royal Society in March 1776 in which he lauded the value of the "malt wort" (a product from the beer brewing process) taken on the expeditions. He also took lemon juice, which was used in a few cases, but he formed a poor opinion of its effectiveness, and so contributed to the delay in its general introduction in 1795. The remarkably low incidence of scurvy on his ships is better ascribed to Cook's excellent leadership and his insistence on eating fresh vegetables at every opportunity. He noted in his journal that in Tierra del Fuego "very good celery is to be met on several of the low islets" (*Voyages*, vol. 4, 171). Cook also found "scurvy grass" in damp places in the Magellan Strait, and used this as a cure.

The second voyage was notable too because Cook took a chronometer with him to test: the Kendall K-1, a copy of Harrison's famous H-4 of 1760. This chronometer changed the nature of navigation by enabling longitude to be correctly and quickly calculated. Cook also took K-1 on his third and final voyage, and an account published at the time said that this watch stopped ticking when Cook was murdered in 1779.

On this third voyage (1776–1780), James Cook was now promoted to full post-captain. Two ships, HMS *Resolution* and HMS *Discovery*, set off on this new voyage, but Cape Horn was not rounded. Cook was killed in a confrontation on the island of Hawaii in February 1779, and the new captain, Charles Clerke, aborted the circumnavigation by returning around Africa.

One of Cook's officers who later achieved fame was William Bligh, his sailing master. The voyage of the *Bounty* started in England in December 1787, heading for Cape Horn and bound for Tahiti. Captain Bligh tenaciously battled terrible storms and contrary winds off Cape Horn for twenty-five days before reluctantly turning back toward Cape of Good Hope, adding ten thousand miles to his original itinerary. The gales "blew a Storm of Wind and the Snow fell so heavy that it was scarce possible to haul the sails up and furl them from the Weight and Stiffness," and one morning Bligh recorded in his log that "the Storm exceeded anything I had met with and a Sea higher than I had ever seen before" (see Alexander 2003, 89).

The Admiralty learned one lesson from the mutiny on the *Bounty*, and that was not to allow a ship for exploration to sail alone. So, when Captain George Vancouver was commissioned to explore and show the flag in the Pacific in the new HMS *Discovery*, he was also accompanied by the armed tender HMS *Chatham*. Vancouver had sailed with James Cook in the *Resolution* on the second voyage, as a boy of thirteen, and as a midshipman in the third voyage on the *Discovery*. Vancouver's ships left England in April 1791 on what turned out to be a five-year voyage of exploration that focused on the Pacific, but they also completed yet another circumnavigation of the globe. On the return journey in 1795, the ships visited the Juan Fernández Islands before turning to Valparaíso, despite strict instructions to keep clear of Spanish possessions in the Pacific. They did so on account of the terrible state of the ships and signs that the crew was beginning to suffer from scurvy. Vancouver stayed in Valparaíso for five weeks, carrying out repairs with the help of the Spanish authorities, and visited Ambrose O'Higgins in Santiago.

At the beginning of the nineteenth century, James Weddell undertook three voyages with the ships *Jane* and *Beaufoy* in the period 1819–1824. On Weddell's third voyage, described in *A Voyage towards the South Pole, Performed in the Years 1822–24*, he gives advice on navigating Cape Horn and writes with sadness and compassion how he made great efforts to make peaceful contact with the Yámana Indians of Tierra del Fuego. He describes resting in Wigwam Cove on Isla Hermite in 1823, close to Cape Horn, after exploring the Antarctic Peninsula and what is today called the Weddell Sea, and reaching further south than anyone ever before him—74° 15' South. Part of the Weddell Sea coincides with the Chilean territorial claim on the Antarctic, and it was in this sea that Ernest Shackleton's ship, the *Endurance*, was trapped and crushed by ice a century later, in 1915.

Weddell met with Yámana Indians, observed them over two months, and concluded, "I would willingly, for the honour of human nature, raise these neglected people somewhat higher in the scale of intellectual estimation than they have reached, but I must acknowledge their condition to be that of the lowest of mankind" (1825, 156). Weddell describes how, when anchored in Wigwam Cove, the *Jane* was approached by canoes, and how, after cautiously examining the ship, several natives came on board. The following morning, the Fuegians returned, but with different face paint, "Their appearance was as grotesque as can well be imagined; though in their estimation it was, no doubt, considered the perfection of fashion" (1825, 153).

The *Beaufoy* came to anchor, and natives also clambered aboard this ship. There then occurred an amusing incident.

A sailor had given a Fuegian a tin pot of coffee, which he drank, and was using all his art to steal the pot. The sailor, however, recollecting after a while that the pot had not been returned, applied for it, but whatever words he made use of were always repeated in imitation by the Fuegian. At length, he became enraged at hearing his requests reiterated, and placing himself in a threatening attitude, in an angry tone, he said, 'You copper-coloured rascal, where is my tin pot?' The Fuegian, assuming the same attitude, with his eyes fixed on the sailor, called out 'You copper-coloured rascal, where is my tin pot?' The imitation was so perfect, that everyone laughed, except the sailor, who proceeded to search him, and under his arm he found the article missing. (Weddell 1825, 154)

This was no exaggeration. Charles Darwin noted that the Fuegians were "excellent mimics": "They could repeat with perfect correctness each word in any sentence we addressed them, and they remembered such words for some time" (Darwin 1838, 229).

By 1826, the last royalist forces had been defeated in Chile, and over the following ten years, Spain essentially withdrew from the region that had been its South American empire since 1492. This withdrawal coincided with the carrying out of a thorough surveying and charting of Tierra del Fuego initiated by the British Admiralty, which naturally caused the government of republican Chile increasing concern.

The first to undertake this task were Captains Philip Parker King and Pringle Stokes, in a voyage to survey as comprehensively as possible the coast from Río de la Plata to Chiloé Island, a mission carried out in the years 1826 to 1830. Although Parker King was born in Australia, he was sent to England for his education, joined the Royal Navy in 1807, and was promoted to lieutenant in 1814. Captain Parker King was in overall command of the expedition, and he had an impressive flotilla—the ships *Adventure, Beagle* (a converted coaster captained by Pringle Stokes), and *Hope* (Captain Thomas Graves), as well as the *Adelaide* from Montevideo.

From January to March 1827, the *Beagle* was in Patagonia surveying the Magellan Strait. Pringle Stokes carried with him medals to give to the Fuegian Indians, with the figure of Britannia on one side and the inscription on the reverse "George IV—*Adventure* and *Beagle*—1826." In August 1828, after battling for nearly two years the storms of Tierra del Fuego, Pringle Stokes shot himself in his cabin aboard the

Beagle. The demands of the surveying work had proved too much, with scurvy affecting the crew, his maps and charts full of errors, and the rigors of working among the desolation and constant storms along the coastline. Stokes is buried in a small British cemetery at San Juan, south of Punta Arenas, near Port Famine. There is a commemoration once a year when Chilean Navy officers and representatives of the British community visit the grave to lay wreaths.

Parker King took the *Beagle* and the *Adventure* to Argentina, where Admiral Otway decided to promote his protégé Robert Fitz-Roy to command of the *Beagle*, and promptly ordered the ships back to southern Patagonia to complete the survey. This led to FitzRoy's first expedition on the *Beagle* under his command, in the period April 1829 to August 1830.

Of lasting significance was an episode involving FitzRoy and the Fuegian Indians of Tierra del Fuego. He made contact with Yámana and Alacaluf Indians, and a group of the latter stole a whaleboat, which was necessary for survey work in the shallows. FitzRoy's response was to take several hostages, all of whom escaped except for one girl and two men who seemed not to mind being on board. A fourth young man, Jemmy Button, was later added to the group.

FitzRoy named the eldest (aged twenty-six), whose real name was El Leparu, York Minster, after the headland in Tierra del Fuego discovered by James Cook and described him as "a displeasing specimen of uncivilized human nature" (1838, 2). The girl (nine), whose real name was Iocusulu or Yokchshlu, was a great favorite on board and named Fuegia Basket after the reed basket woven by the whaleboat sailors to get back to the *Beagle*. Boat Memory (twenty), was named after the stolen whaleboat. His real name was never recorded. Jemmy Button (fourteen), originally Orundellico, was exchanged for "a large shining mother-of-pearl button" (Parker King 1838, 444). FitzRoy wrote later, "Whether [the relatives] intended that he should remain with us permanently, I do not know, but they seemed contented with the singular bargain, and paddled again towards the cove from which they had approached my boat" (1838, 6). Lucas Bridges (1951, 30) describes this as "a ridiculous story, as no native would have sold his child in exchange for HMS *Beagle* with all it had on board."

Communication was naturally very difficult, but FitzRoy learned that when food was short they smoked the eldest women to death and then, if the result was sufficiently tender, would eat them. This was certainly a fabrication that FitzRoy was suitably shocked by, and the Fuegians may have been put up to this by sailors below deck. Lucas

Bridges adds, "When asked if they ate dogs when hungry, they said they did not, as dogs were useful for catching otter, whereas the old women were of no use at all" (1951, 34); this response was probably also a tale intended to astound and scandalize their listeners.

FitzRoy conceived a grand plan with great enthusiasm. He resolved to take the Fuegians with him to England, where he would provide them with an education and return them—if necessary at his own expense—with sufficient means to be the core of an Anglican mission station. FitzRoy wrote to the Admiralty on September 12, 1830, "I have maintained them entirely at my own expense, and hold myself responsible for their comfort while away from, and their safe return to their own country" (1838, 4).

The *Beagle* arrived back in Plymouth in October 1830. Robert FitzRoy misjudged or mishandled the situation, and there was little interest initially in his mission project. Tragically, one of the Fuegians, Boat Memory, died in England of smallpox. The others were sent to be educated by Rev. William Wilson in Walthamstow, near London, and there was a change of fortune when, in the summer of 1831, King William IV expressed his wish to meet the Fuegians. Queen Adelaide gave Fuegia Basket a bonnet, a ring, and some money to buy an outfit of clothes in which to return to Patagonia.

Despite the five years' work under Parker King and Stokes and Fitz-Roy, Francis Beaufort of the British Hydrographic Department was still not satisfied and wanted further work on the charts. The Admiralty recognized the potential for trade in the region and needed accurate information on southern Patagonia and the coast of Chile. The Spanish had disengaged, leaving a vacuum, and perhaps the British could establish a strong presence in the area. FitzRoy once again assumed command of the *Beagle*; the only ship to carry out the renewed surveying work on this voyage. Charles Darwin accompanied this second survey.

The voyage ended as a full circumnavigation and lasted fifty-seven months, from December 1831 to October 1836, forty-two of them spent off South America, including around seventeen months in Tierra del Fuego and on the west coast of modern-day Chile. The main objective of the Admiralty in this voyage was to arrive at a thorough geographical and hydrographical survey of Tierra del Fuego and the southern coasts of South America, with the subsidiary aim of plotting the course of a complete circumnavigation by marine chronometers—twenty-two in all. In addition, Francis Beaufort persuaded FitzRoy to experiment with the wind scale he had devised, and the *Beagle* was therefore the first ship to leave Britain able to measure with mathematical accuracy the strength of the gales it sailed through—using the now famous Beaufort scale.

In terms of the territory comprising modern-day Chile, this second survey of the *Beagle* spent two periods in Tierra del Fuego, in December 1832 and January 1833 and in May and June 1834; and it stayed along the west coast of Chile from June 1834 to July 1835. After the second stay in Tierra del Fuego, the *Beagle* surveyed Chiloé Island and southern Chile before arriving in Valparaíso in July 1834. This port served as a base for the expedition until November 1834, when the *Beagle* turned back south for more surveying in southern Chile, including Chiloé Island. An earthquake occurred in February 1835, and FitzRoy and Darwin went to investigate the effects in Concepción and Talcahuano. The *Beagle* returned to Valparaíso, where it stayed from March 11 to April 27, 1835. FitzRoy then made stops in Copiapó (June 22 to July 4) and Iquique (July 12–15), which was then part of Peru.

A key event for FitzRoy (and the expedition) occurred when he arrived in Valparaíso for the first time, in July 1834, and fell into a deep depression. The surveying work on the east coast of South America and the battling with storms in Tierra del Fuego had taken their toll, but the blow that crushed him was the news from the Admiralty that awaited him. Twelve months earlier he had decided to buy a schooner called the *Adventure* to help with the surveying work, and the Admiralty now told him to get rid of it and to decommission the crew. They added, for good measure, that he would not be reimbursed for the costs incurred. To further add insult to injury, the Admiralty criticized FitzRoy for having spent so extravagant a time on the recent surveying work on the east coast and in Tierra del Fuego. The suicides of his uncle Lord Castlereagh and his predecessor Pringle Stokes were very much on his mind. After several days in deep despondency in his cabin, FitzRoy announced that he would resign and he actually prepared a letter of resignation to Beaufort at the Admiralty. Fortunately, First Lieutenant Wickham refused to assume the captain's post and managed to persuade FitzRoy to change his mind.

FitzRoy announced that there would be no more surveying of the dreaded channels of Tierra del Fuego and that after one more look along the southern coast of Chile, they would set off across the Pacific. Their remaining time in Chile was spent in the area of Chiloé Island, in Concepción and the port of Talcahuano, with more surveying along the Chilean coast until the *Beagle* called in at Valparaíso, Copiapó, and Iquique before setting out for the Galápagos Islands.

On their return to England, FitzRoy and Darwin went their separate ways. They did have lunch together, but their last "meeting," with Darwin represented by proxy, was a pathetic affair for FitzRoy. On June 30, 1860, there was a meeting of the British Association for the Advancement of Science in Oxford dealing with "Botany and Zoology." Following a heated exchange between Bishop Wilberforce and Thomas Huxley, a figure in the audience rose, Bible in hand, to praise the works of God and belittle those of man, saying that Darwin's *Origin of Species* had caused him the "acutest pain." This was Robert FitzRoy, and he was shouted down by the crowd.

Five years later, FitzRoy committed suicide. Darwin's verdict on hearing this news was insightful: "I never knew in my life so mixed a character. Always much to love & I once loved him sincerely; but so bad a temper & so given to take offence, that I gradually quite lost my love & wished only to keep out of contact with him. Twice he quarrelled bitterly with me, without any just provocation on my part. But certainly there was much noble & exalted in his character" (Letter to J. D. Hooker May 4, 1865).

At around the time of FitzRoy's first expedition on the *Beagle*, Henry Foster commanded a British ship called the *Chanticleer* between 1828 and 1830 on a scientific expedition in the South Atlantic, to determine the force of gravity about the earth, which encompassed short stays in the region of Tierra del Fuego, including the Wallaston group of islands (which he named). While there was no naturalist on board, and Foster drowned toward the end of the voyage, the ship's surgeon W. Webster wrote up an account that included general observations on the vegetation they came across. Other British naval ships were also intent on exploring the region in the same period, although they were overshadowed in history by the successes of the *Beagle*. HMS *Samarang* was journeying round South America in 1831–1835; Captain Pendleton, on board the *Oceanic*, rounded Cape Horn from west to east in 1832; and HMS *Sulphur* surveyed the west coast of Central and South America in 1835.

The next British scientific expedition to arrive in Chile was commanded by James Clark Ross. This was the last major voyage of exploration conducted entirely under sail. The main objective was to survey the Antarctic with two ships, the *Erebus* and the *Terror*, and the voyage lasted from 1839 to 1843. On board were the surgeon-naturalist Dr. Robert McCormick, who had left the *Beagle* with hurt feelings on seeing how much FitzRoy preferred Charles Darwin, and his assistant Joseph Hooker, who became a lifelong friend of Darwin's. The two captains, Ross and Crozier, were ostensibly looking for the south magnetic pole but were really intent on breaking for the Royal Navy the "furthest south" record set by Weddell. On this voyage they confirmed the existence of the southern continent, discovered what is now called the Ross Sea and the Ross Ice Shelf, and named the Antarctic volcanoes Mount Erebus and Mount Terror. After returning to New Zealand to resupply, they set off again for the Antarctic, but after a collision between the two ships they sailed for the Falklands. After the customary stormy voyage in the southern latitudes, they stopped for a month in Tierra del Fuego in 1842 in Wigwam Cove, today called Caleta Martial. Ross wanted to take magnetic observations near Cape Horn to compare these with similar observations made at the Falklands. Ross returned to England and a knighthood and published his account of the expedition in 1847 with the title *A Voyage of Discovery and Research to Southern and Antarctic Regions.*

In 1866, Captain Richard Maine on HMS *Nassau* set out from England to spend four years studying the channels of Tierra del Fuego in order to perfect the navigation charts and so complete the survey work started by Parker King and FitzRoy. In December 1872, George Nares departed from England in command of HMS *Challenger* on a voyage of scientific discovery cosponsored by the Admiralty and the Royal Society, which some regard as representing the birth of oceanography as a discipline. At one point the expedition crossed the Pacific to Valparaíso and then surveyed south to the Magellan Strait, where they dropped anchor at Punta Arenas in January 1876. Nares had actually already been recalled by the Admiralty in mid-expedition, in 1874, to take command of the British Arctic Expedition in 1875–1876, with the *Alert* and the *Discovery*. However, in a later season, in 1878, Nares returned to the Magellan Strait in the *Alert* to carry out a hydrographical survey, which in 1879 to 1882 was completed by Captain John Maclear.

At the start of the twentieth century, the National Antarctic Expedition (1901–1904), led by Captain Robert Falcon Scott, briefly passed by Chile. This was the first voyage of the *Discovery*, with a ship's complement that included Ernest Shackleton. They sailed to New Zealand and then on to the Antarctic, where Scott, accompanied by Shackleton and Wilson, made the first ever extended journey into the interior of the then practically unknown southern continent. The *Discovery* returned to Britain through the Magellan Strait, completing her circumnavigation of Antarctica.

Shackleton was destined to spend time in Chile on a subsequent Antarctic expedition, which he commanded. Shackleton was born in 1874, in County Kildare, Ireland, of an Anglo-Irish family. He had seen Chile as a very young man. At the age of sixteen he left

Liverpool on his first voyage in a sailing ship, the *Hoghton Tower*, bound for Valparaíso via Cape Horn, which they reached in the middle of winter. It took nearly two months to get round. The ship then arrived in Valparaíso and sailed on to Iquique to take on a cargo of nitrates. Shackleton stayed with the *Hoghton Tower* for the next four years, rounding Cape Horn five times. He spent the following years sailing to the Far East and to America, and then with Scott on the *Discovery* in the National Antarctic Expedition, before being invalided home in 1903. Undaunted by the experience, Shackleton was determined to return, and he mounted and led the British Antarctic Expedition of 1908–1909 on the *Nimrod* and a second expedition on the *Endurance* with the aim of crossing the Antarctic via the South Pole. This expedition led to his return to Chile, although in a completely unplanned way.

Shackleton left Liverpool in September 1914 to join the *Endurance* in Buenos Aires, just as the First World War was breaking out. They journeyed south, and the *Endurance* got caught in pack ice in December 1914. The group drifted until their ship was finally crushed by the ice and abandoned in October 1915. They continued their drift on the ice until taking to the ship's boats in April 1916, and they arrived at Elephant Island. From Elephant Island six men sailed in an open boat to arrive on South Georgia Island on May 10, 1916. Of these six men, three, including Shackleton, crossed the glaciers of the island from King Haakon Bay to reach the whaling station at Stromness Bay on the other side. The three men left behind at King Haaken Bay were soon rescued, but two attempts to get down to Elephant Island failed. Shackleton found himself in Port Stanley in the Falklands with no further option open to him. By chance, a British mail boat called the *Orita* came in, and hearing that it was bound for Punta Arenas, he decided to go there, knowing that there was a British community to count on for help.

Shackleton gave a lecture in Punta Arenas on July 9, 1916, reporting on his odyssey to date, after being rescued from South Georgia Island, and this was duly reported in *The Magellan Times* four days later. Shackleton was accompanied at this talk by his two companions, Captain Worsley and Tom Crean, who had survived with Shackleton the 750-mile open boat journey from Elephant Island to South Georgia, and the unprecedented overland crossing of South Georgia. At the moment he was speaking to the British community, twenty-two men were waiting for rescue on Elephant Island.

Shackleton began by thanking the Chilean government for the practical and prompt help he had received: "Within twenty-four hours of my arrival, steps were taken spontaneously to equip a vessel for the rescue of my men, and only yesterday a further proof of this practical sympathy was given to me by a message from the President of Chile through the Governor of this Territory offering to put their tow boat [*Yelcho*] at my disposal" (*The Magellan Times* 1916, 3). Still uncertain as to whether the rest of his crew had survived, Shackleton continued by thanking the British Association of Punta Arenas: "I feel that we are going to rescue them, and I hope that within a fortnight or three weeks' time the twenty-two men at present on Elephant Island will be here fit and well to give you their hearty thanks themselves for the way in which your help has been forthcoming." Side by side with this text the newspaper carried several telegrams from the Western Front—a sobering reminder that a war was going on in Europe: "Paris, July 7. On both sides of the Somme the enemy attempted to oppose our offensive"; "Paris July 11. On the front to the north of Verdun the enemy's artillery replied with great violence to ours."

The actual rescue took place in two stages. First, with money raised through the British Club and a generous contribution from a Chilean named Francisco Campos, Shackleton chartered a wooden schooner called the *Emma* and sailed out of Punta Arenas on July 12, 1916, in the very middle of winter. A naval vessel called the *Yelcho* (built in Greenock, Scotland) was provided by the Chilean authorities, at no cost, to tow the *Emma* part of the journey south. Frustratingly, the *Emma* was unable to continue on account of the ice that they met about a hundred miles from Elephant Island. They pulled back to Port Stanley, and Shackleton cabled the British Association in Punta Arenas to request a tug. The British community contacted the Chilean authorities, and the *Yelcho* was obligingly sent to Port Stanley to bring the *Emma* back to Punta Arenas. Once there, Shackleton asked the naval commander to lend him the *Yelcho* for one more try at rescuing his men from Elephant Island, and after he had consulted with the naval headquarters in Santiago, permission was given. They left Punta Arenas on August 25, with Captain Luis Alberto Pardo Villalon and a crew of volunteers from the Chilean navy and successfully rescued all the men on Elephant Island. Shackleton was keen to thank the Chilean government in Santiago for their help, and he sailed together with most of the men to Valparaíso in the *Yelcho* and then traveled on to a huge reception in Santiago. In October, Shackleton went by train to Buenos Aires and eventually back to Britain. In Puerto Williams there is a monument displaying the severed bows of the *Yelcho*.

Although a failure as an expedition, the experience was seen then, and still is seen now, as an awesome achievement: Shackleton's expedition survived the worst that the southern Atlantic and Antarctica could expose them to, with not one member having died. Ironically, most of the men from the *Endurance* went off at once to fight in the Great War, and several were killed or wounded in action.

The start of the First World War coincided with the Panama Canal being opened to traffic on August 15, 1914. This signaled the end of an era for Cape Horn and the Magellan Strait. Cape Horn was on the famous clipper route, used by huge sailing ships that journeyed west to east from Europe to Australia, New Zealand and the Far East. The return journey took the ships round Cape Horn, and many vessels and sailors were lost in this endeavor. The most famous of the clippers was the *Cutty Sark*, which regularly sailed to Australia from Britain in under eighty days. However, the fastest passage from Britain to Australia, rounding Cape Horn, was made by the *Thermopylae* in 1868–1869 in a voyage of sixty-one days, London to Melbourne. From around 1890 to the 1930s, spanning the opening of the Panama Canal, the windjammer came into being—a steel-built square-rigger with between three and five masts—which competed side by side with the steam ships. These ships still hold the records for the fastest roundings of Cape Horn from 50 degrees south (Atlantic) to 50 degrees south (Pacific). Dallas Murphy (2005) gives an account of the terrible voyage of one of these windjammers, the *British Isles*, which battled for seventy-one days to round Cape Horn.

Most of the sea captains and sailors mentioned in this chapter landed briefly on Chilean land, or not at all, but there were several British visitors and travelers who did take an interest in exploring the land for knowledge about its people, its customs, its riches, and the fauna and flora—among them a novice naturalist named Charles Darwin.

Chapter 3

British Naturalists in Chile

> *Arrived at Port Famine. I never saw a more cheer-less prospect; the dusky woods, pie-bald with snow, were only indistinctly to be seen through an atmosphere composed of two thirds rain & one of fog; the rest, as an Irishman would say, was very cold unpleasant air.*
>
> —Charles Darwin, Beagle Diary *June 1, 1834*

The most famous of the British naturalists to visit Chile is, of course, Charles Darwin (1809–1882). It is well known that Charles Darwin spent time in Chile during the second expedition of the *Beagle* survey under Robert FitzRoy. Perhaps less well known is just how crucial his time in Chile was for the young naturalist in terms of the early development of the hypotheses and theories that were to have such a huge impact on his world, and ours.

On being asked to return to Tierra del Fuego in the *Beagle*, FitzRoy decided to seek a companion for the voyage, a gentleman—someone who would share his interests in science, and his expenses. This led to the appointment of Charles Darwin as the requisite Cambridge-educated, scientifically inclined, easygoing gentleman-companion (and budding naturalist) to accompany FitzRoy on the voyage.

Darwin and the *Beagle* spent roughly seventeen months in all surveying and exploring in the geography of modern-day Chile, in three periods:

1. Tierra del Fuego: December 1832 to January 1833. This was an interlude when the focus from February 1832 to May 1834 was on surveying the east coast of South America. This first visit to Tierra del Fuego on the voyage was to return the Fuegian passengers and deliver an Anglican missionary.

2. Tierra del Fuego: May and June 1834.
3. West coast of Chile: June 1834 to July 1835.

The time Darwin spent on the west coast can be divided into the following periods:

- Valparaíso: July 23 to November 10, 1834. During this stay Darwin embarked on his first expedition overland in Chile (in August 1834), from Valparaíso to Santiago.
- The *Beagle* then moved south, to undertake surveying in southern Chile, including Chiloé Island. Then, on account of an earthquake, Darwin was in Talcahuano and Concepción in February 1835.
- Valparaíso: March 11 to April 27, 1835. This stay encompassed two important expeditions overland, from Valparaíso to Santiago, then to Mendoza through the Portillo and Uspallata passes (March 18 to April 10, 1835); and from Valparaíso to Coquimbo and to Copiapó (April 27 to June 22, 1835).
- Copiapó: June 22 to July 4, 1835.
- Iquique (then part of Peru): July 12–15, 1835.

Darwin's first contact with Chile was in December 1832, accompanying FitzRoy on his cultural experiment, that of returning the Fuegian Indians to Tierra del Fuego. Darwin's first meeting with the indigenous people was in the Bay of Good Success, and sadly, he was not impressed: "Their language does not deserve to be called articulate: Capt. Cook says it is like a man clearing his throat; to which may be added another very hoarse man trying to shout & a third encouraging a horse with that peculiar noise which is made in one side of the mouth. Imagine these sounds & a few gutturals mingled with them, & there will be as near an approximation to their language as any European may expect to obtain. I believe if the world was searched, no lower grade of man could be found" (Beagle *Diary*, December 18, 1832).

Darwin was more struck by the Tehuelches of the Patagonian mainland, north of Tierra del Fuego. He recalled later that in January 1833 he had met with "the famous so-called gigantic Patagonians, who gave us a cordial reception." Darwin was able to scotch one enduring myth, that of the excessive height of these Indians: "Their height appears greater than it really is, from their large guanaco mantles, their long flowing hair, and general figure: on an average their height is about six feet, with some men taller and only a few shorter: and the women are also tall; altogether they are certainly the tallest race which we saw anywhere" (Darwin, *Journal of Researches* 1845, 232).

Notwithstanding Darwin's poor opinion of the natives of Tierra del Fuego, he still believed that the distance between uncivilized and civilized man could be crossed; he had seen firsthand the difference that FitzRoy's experiment in culturalization had made to the Fuegians taken to England. Janet Browne (1995) argues that Darwin's observations of what civilized and uncivilized peoples had in common, and where they differed, was critical to his later conviction that humans were part of the natural landscape and that there was an evolutionary bridge between the two worlds. Browne adds that of all the many and varied experiences that Darwin was subject to on this five-year voyage, what most impressed him was the realization that humans from the four corners of the earth actually shared things in common, that culture was just a veneer for humanity, and that civilization itself was something made by man, and ephemeral. This insight, Browne believes, moved him more that all the botany and all the geology, even more than the exotic tropical forest he had wandered through in Brazil.

After leaving the missionary Matthews with Fuegia Basket, York Minster, and Jemmy Button in a cove at Wulaia, FitzRoy decided to withdraw with Darwin and the crew of the *Beagle* and spend the night in Bahía Tekenika, to give their plans to establish a settlement focused on the missionary a chance to take effect. After an anxious night, they returned to find that nothing untoward had occurred, and FitzRoy decided to leave Matthews for a longer period and set off to explore the western reaches of the Beagle Channel. (Chapter 13 describes what then happened to this missionary). It was on this voyage of exploration in boats, while near the Pacific mouth of the Beagle Channel, that Darwin literally saved the expedition.

The group had left their boats and had set off on foot to have a closer look at a glacier when the same glacier suddenly calved an immense block of ice, and the resulting waves raced toward the boats they had beached. Darwin quickly realized that the boats could easily be washed away, and he raced to the spot with some other seamen just as the first of three huge waves broke over the boats and held on grimly to save their only means of getting away from the place. FitzRoy wrote, "Had not Mr. Darwin and two or three seamen run to [the boats], they would have been swept away from us irrecoverably" (FitzRoy 1838, 217). FitzRoy was so grateful that he named the waters where this happened Darwin Sound, after his friend. Not only that, FitzRoy also called the high peak where the glacier flowed

Mount Darwin, and the entire range of mountains Cordillera Darwin, names which continue in use today.

Despite such adventures, the days spent in Tierra del Fuego tended to get the crew down, and Darwin was no exception. After staying in Tierra del Fuego during May and June 1834, the *Beagle* called in at Chiloé Island and then arrived in Valparaíso in July that year. "We were all glad to leave Chiloé; at this time of year nothing but an amphibious animal could tolerate the climate. Even the inhabitants have not a word to say in its favour; very commonly I was asked what I thought of the Island; ¿no es muy mala? is it not a miserable place? I could not muster civility enough to contradict them" (Beagle *Diary*, July 13, 1834).

In Valparaíso, Darwin stayed with Richard Corfield, a school friend from Shropshire who was slightly older than Darwin and a shipping agent and merchant in the port. After resting, Darwin set off in August on horseback with his personal attendant, Syms Covington from the *Beagle*, on his first expedition in the central valley of Chile, from Valparaíso to Santiago, and climbed in the Chilean Andes for the first time. They camped out for two days in the mountains, and on the way back, Darwin was struck down with a serious fever, which he blamed on some sour wine he had drunk with the owner of an American gold mine. This was the first serious illness in Darwin's life and the only major ill health he succumbed to on the entire voyage. It kept him incapacitated for more than a month. In his old age, Darwin occasionally traced his bad health back to this illness. It has been suggested that he may have been bitten by the *benchuca* insect and contracted Chagas disease, endemic at that time in Chile, but there is no record of the characteristic symptoms appearing on Darwin.

Captain FitzRoy fell into a deep depression in Valparaíso, during which he wrote out his resignation. The effect on Darwin, homesick and in bad health, disappointed that there would be no Pacific voyage and no circumnavigation, was to galvanize him into making new plans for himself. He decided to have another look at the Andes and then return to England via Buenos Aires. Fortunately, FitzRoy was persuaded to change his mind, and he decided that there would be no return to the now detested Tierra del Fuego. Instead, the coast of Chile would be surveyed as quickly as possible, and then the *Beagle* would make a crossing of the Pacific Ocean, which encouraged Darwin to think that the much-yearned-for return to England would take place soon.

There then occurred the second marvelous "spectacle" that Darwin experienced in Chile (the first was meeting with Fuegian Indians in Tierra del Fuego)—the earthquake of February 20, 1835.

The immediate effect on Darwin was to postpone for the present any remaining thought of returning home directly to England.

The first signs that something was afoot came in January 1825, as they were surveying Chiloé Island, and they witnessed the eruptions illuminating the sky on Osorno Volcano and other nearby volcanoes in southern Chile. When the earthquake struck, Darwin happened to be lying on a forest floor in Valdivia, resting after wandering through apple orchards with Covington, when the earth suddenly moved beneath him. He described his sensations in his diary: "I can compare [the rocking] to skating on very thin ice or to the motion of a ship in a little cross ripple. An earthquake like this at once destroys the oldest associations; the world, the very emblem of all that is solid, moves beneath our feet like crust over a fluid; one second of time conveys to the mind a strange idea of insecurity, which hours of reflection would never create" (Beagle *Diary*, February 20, 1835).

The epicenter, however, was further north, and twelve days later Darwin and FitzRoy heard of the destruction in Concepción, at which news they set off in the *Beagle* for the port of Talcahuano. They anchored off the island of Quiriquina in Concepción Bay on March 4, finding that the land there had risen some three feet. They were told that the sea had drained out of the bay, leaving several ships leaning over on their sides, and that half an hour later a tremendous wave had roared in and swept into the town of Talcahuano. Two more huge waves arrived, and left behind a spectacle of destruction. Traveling on by horseback to Concepción with the British Vice Consul, Henry William Rouse, they found the city in ruins, "nothing more than piles & lines of bricks, tiles & timbers . . . there is not one house left habitable" (see Barlow 1945, 113). The six-foot thick walls of the cathedral had cracked and the roof had collapsed.

The experience of having felt the earth move, and having witnessed the destruction caused by the earthquake and the tsunami, had an enormous impact on Darwin: "To my mind since leaving England, we have scarcely beheld any one other sight so deeply interesting. The Earthquake & Volcano are parts of one of the greatest phenomena to which this world is subject" (Beagle *Diary*, March 5, 1835).

The fact that the land had risen around Talcahuano prompted Darwin to reflect on what this might mean: "The most remarkable effect (or perhaps speaking more correctly, cause) of this earthquake was the permanent elevation of the land . . . It is almost certain, from the altered soundings, together with the circumstance of the bottom of the bay near Penco, consisting of hard stone, that there has been an uplifting to the amount of four fathoms, since the famous convulsion of 1751 . . . Some of the consequences which may be deduced from the phenomena connected with this earthquake are most important in a geological point of view" (Darwin, *Journal and Remarks*, 1838, 379).

Darwin began to think "that the earth is a mere crust over a fluid melted mass of rock & that Volcanoes are merely apertures through this crust" (Beagle *Diary*, March 5, 1835). Later, when he was back in England, Darwin reflected at greater length on what he had observed and recalled how FitzRoy had come across clear evidence that the land had risen on the Island of Santa María near Concepción. The Captain had spotted "beds of putrid mussel-shells," which local inhabitants had once dived to collect, "still adhering to the rocks, ten feet above the high-water mark." Darwin's own eyes had seen that "at Valparaíso . . . similar shells are found at the height of 1,300 feet: it is hardly possible to doubt that this great elevation has been effected by successive small uprisings, such as that which accompanied or caused the earthquake of this year, and likewise by an insensibly slow rise, which is certainly in progress on some parts of this coast" (Darwin, *Journal of Researches*, 1845, 310).

Darwin concluded, "Daily it is forced home on the mind of the geologist that nothing, not even the wind that blows, is so unstable as the level of the crust of this earth" (1845, 321).

For Darwin, the earthquake and the effects he had observed constituted a practical field trip in the theories expressed by Charles Lyell in his publication *Principles of Geology* (1830–1833). Interestingly, given their later differences of opinion, FitzRoy had presented Darwin with the first volume of this work before they left England. Such was Darwin's enthusiasm for Lyell's ideas that he acquired the following two volumes during the voyage on the *Beagle*. Lyell's views were anathema to established thought at the time. Essentially, Lyell questioned the prevailing Christian concept that there was a beginning—a Creation—and that phenomena strived toward an end, toward perfection, in set-piece stages, introducing more and more complex living beings, leading up to the appearance of the human species. For Lyell, in terms of geology, mountains resulted from the surface of the earth being always in flux, working gradually, not in spurts, with the pressure exerted by the interior molten rock pushing upwards. Moreover, this explained the typical elevation of the land after earthquakes, as part of a cycle of small incremental steps, one of which Darwin had observed in Talcahuano.

Darwin was impressed too when he heard how the population had responded to the earthquake in Concepción. He was told that the people had run to the Cerro Caracol, a hill behind the city, initially confessing their sins in the belief that the end of the world had come, but then camping out quite happily on the hill. All levels of society were there, all affected by the same catastrophe to the same degree. However, in the city among the ruins, there were looters who "at each little trembling of the ground, with one hand beat their breasts & cried out 'Miserecordia' [*sic*] & with the other continued to filch from the ruins" (Beagle *Diary*, March 5, 1835).

Within a matter of days of the exhilarating experience of the earthquake, Darwin was back in Valparaíso and off on the first of two overland expeditions that year, while the *Beagle* was engaged in further surveying work. This took him from Valparaíso to Santiago, and then to Mendoza and back using different mountain passes, the Portillo and Uspallata passes. On this journey he observed that, although harder and bruised by the mountain being pushed upwards, the geology of the mountains actually seemed to consist of the same relatively recent deposits he had examined in Patagonia, on Chiloé Island, and around Concepción. Darwin came across "a petrified forest, fifty fossilized trunks in a sandstone escarpment." He could make out the tree bark and even count the growth rings on these petrified trees. This was a sight, and a discovery, that Darwin returned to later many times; this "cluster of fine trees [that] had once waved their branches on the shores of the Atlantic, when that ocean (now driven back 700 miles) approached the base of the Andes" (Darwin, *Journal and Remarks*, 1838, 332).

The conclusion was clear—there were sedimentary deposits high up in the Andes that had been laid down at a geological point of time approximately coincident with the upper-level deposits seen on the relatively flat coastal area of Chile and must have been thrust upwards from the ocean bed to make the mountain. Moreover, in the case of the Andes, this process was recent and probably still going on. This all caused Darwin, the novice geologist, several sleepless nights in Chile. His observations on geology spawned revolutionary notions, going beyond his mentor Lyell, and this is significant because the same underlying hypothesis of small and constant changes came later to inform his views on biology and on evolutionary change.

On his return to Valparaíso, FitzRoy told Darwin that the surveying in the south of Chile was finished. Heading north, Darwin spent time in Coquimbo and in Iquique, at that time part of Peru. In Coquimbo he was able to check a tentative proposition of Lyell's, that the terraces in the mountainside observed by Basil Hall in 1821 were evidence of ancient beaches, and Darwin found this to be true. In Iquique they found the port in a state close to anarchy, a reflection of the turbulence in Peruvian politics at the time.

After a visit to Callao in September 1835, the *Beagle* set off to the Galápagos Islands, and Darwin never returned to Chile. However, his experiences in Chile and the wild thoughts they provoked stayed with him all his life. His first paper on his return to England was read to the Geological Society on January 4, 1837, and dealt with his observations on Chile's coastline as an uplifted sea floor. Darwin's ideas on evolution and natural selection, on the origin of species—"that mystery of mysteries" (Darwin 1859)—owe a great deal to his observations in Chile, and culminated in the text of *On the Origin of Species*, the opening paragraph of which reads, "When on board H.M.S. Beagle as naturalist, I was much struck with certain facts in the distribution of the inhabitants of South America, and in the geological relations of the present to the past inhabitants of that continent. These facts seemed to me to throw some light on the origin of species" (Darwin 1859).

Charles Darwin remains present in Chile to this day, notably in the naming of geography, such as the Darwin Icefield, Mount Darwin, the Darwin Cordillera, and Darwin Sound. He is remembered too in the naming of Chilean fauna, such as Darwin's frog *Rhinoderma darwinii*, which is probably now extinct, and *Rhea darwinii* (Darwin's rhea) and Darwin's fox, both threatened species. There is also *Mus darwinii*, a rodent, and the marked gecko *Homonota darwinii macrocephala*.

Darwin named the *alerce* tree after Captain FitzRoy as the genus *Fitzroya cupressoides*. The names of several species of Chilean flora can also be traced to Darwin, such as *Berberis darwinii*, a species of barberry native to southern Chile and south-western Argentina discovered by Darwin in 1835. There is also *Cyttaria darwinii*, a fungus tree parasite that is common on Isla Navarino and described by Darwin as a seasonal staple food for the Yahgan Indians, as well as a cactus in Chilean Patagonia called *Maihueniopsis darwinii*. The fossil record, too: *Fusus darwinianus, Turritella darwini, Nucula darwini, Venus darwini*, and *Arca darwini*. A ground sloth which roamed Patagonia, now long extinct, is called the *Mylodon darwinii*.

Although the most famous, Charles Darwin was not the only British naturalist to visit Chile. On James Cook's first circumnavigation in HMS *Endeavour*, there was an ambitious young botanist on board named Joseph Banks, with a voyage to Newfoundland already under his belt. Joseph Banks got the Admiralty to agree to his being accompanied by an entourage of seven artists, scientists, and servants. The scientists included his Swedish friend Dr. Daniel Carl Solander, also a member of the Royal Society and a star pupil of the eminent botanist Carolus Linnaeus. Banks was destined to become the influential President of the

Royal Society (1778–1820), the shaper of Kew Gardens, and patron to generations of naturalists.

In mid January 1769, Cook anchored in the Bay of Good Success for the only landfall in Tierra del Fuego on his first circumnavigation. Cook later wrote that Banks and Solander found a great variety of hitherto unknown plants. Banks returned to England to be fêted by the public and the scientific community, leaving Cook's own achievements very much in the shade. However, when he was seen to regard the following voyage with Cook as essentially his own undertaking, and demanded (unseaworthy) modifications in the design of the *Resolution*, he was cast aside by the Admiralty, and he then set off to Iceland in a huff.

The naturalist taken on HMS *Resolution* to replace Joseph Banks in James Cook's second circumnavigation was John Reinhold Forster— a botanist, prickly and infuriating to everyone he came into contact with. He was accompanied by his son George Forster, only seventeen at the time, passionate about natural history, and a far cry from his father in personality. In December 1774, they gathered samples of plants on Tierra del Fuego that were then unknown to science.

Hugh Cuming is remembered today as a great English naturalist and conchologist, and sometimes called the "Prince of Collectors." Born in Devon, he emigrated to Chile in 1819, just as Chile was consolidating its independence, where he set up in sail making in Valparaíso. Some reports mention that Cuming was illiterate when he arrived in Chile, but he prospered sufficiently to set out on a collecting voyage in 1821. In 1826, he decided to abandon his profession and spend the rest of his career exploring the southern Pacific Ocean, with a particular focus on the collection of shells. He custom-built a yacht called *Discoverer* and engaged in collecting expeditions along the coast of Chile and to islands in the southern Pacific, including Easter Island. In 1831, he returned to England, where his enormous collections of shells and plants quickly became very famous among naturalists. Part of this collection survives today as the Cuming Collection of Brachiopods (marine animals with hinged upper and lower shells) in the Natural History Museum, London.

Alexander Caldcleugh arrived in Chile in 1821 and traveled extensively, making observations on the commercial potential offered by recently independent Chile, as part of his duties as private secretary to the British Minister in Rio de Janeiro. Caldcleugh also collected plants in Chile, which he sent to the British botanist Aylmer Bourke Lambert. The genus *Caldcluvia paniculata* is so named in his honor. He was a member of the Royal Society by the time Charles Darwin met him in Valparaíso in 1835. In a similar category, John Miers was in Chile from

1823 to 1825 for business (in which he failed) and as a botanist who studied the flora of the country. Following his return to Britain in 1825, he published his *Travels in Chile and La Plata* (1826), became a Fellow of the Royal Society, and later wrote *Illustrations of South American Plants* (1846–1857) and *Contributions to Botany* (1851–1871).

In 1828, the English explorer and plant collector Thomas Bridges sailed for the first time to Chile. His accounts show that he worked mainly in Colchagua, south of Santiago, although the collections that have survived show that he also explored other parts of central Chile, including the lowlands of Valparaíso. On his second trip to South America, Thomas Bridges landed at Cobija, went on to Antofagasta, and then traveled into Bolivia via Calama.

Not long after Darwin's visit to Chile, James Clark Ross's scientific expedition with the *Erebus* and the *Terror* visited Tierra del Fuego in 1842. They carried with them the surgeon-naturalist Dr. McCormick (who had left FitzRoy's *Beagle* in a huff), and his assistant Joseph Hooker, who hoped that the expedition would, as with Darwin, make his reputation. He was right in this, and Hooker went on to become an internationally famous plant geographer. While on board the *Erebus*, Hooker had read proofs of Darwin's *Voyage of the Beagle* and was impressed by the evident skills Darwin displayed as a naturalist.

Joseph Hooker's observation that most plants in Tierra del Fuego were surprisingly similar to the species he was acquainted with in England made him ponder on "that interesting subject—the diffusion of species over the surface of our earth." On his return to England he became a life-long friend of Darwin's and a confidant during the long period of Darwin's work on the *Origin of Species*. Darwin gave him his collection of plants from the Galápagos Islands to examine and classify, and in a letter written on January 11, 1844, Darwin shared with Hooker his early ideas on the transmutation of species and natural selection: "I am almost convinced (quite contrary to opinion I started with) that species are not (it is like confessing a murder) immutable." Hooker remembered later of this letter, "I believe that I was the first to whom he communicated his then new ideas on the subject [of evolution and natural selection]" (see Francis Darwin 1887, vol. 2, 384). Hooker encouraged Darwin to pen down his ideas in a book, and, when it turned out that Alfred Russel Wallace had come to similar conclusions, it was Hooker who arranged for the two scientists to have their papers read jointly. Hooker was present at the famous Oxford meeting of the British Association and spoke for Darwin, with Samuel Wilberforce (and Robert FitzRoy in the audience) speaking against.

Later in the nineteenth century, Robert Oliver Cunningham came to Chile as the naturalist on board HMS *Nassau*. The ship left Plymouth in 1866 to continue the survey of the Magellan Strait and the west Patagonian channels that had been started by Philip Parker King, Pringle Stokes, and Robert FitzRoy. His task was to describe the flora and fauna of that region, while Captain Mayne improved on the hydrographical charts. He published a narrative of the expedition in 1871, describing stops he made at Punta Arenas in December 1866, as well as at Ancud on Chiloé Island, collecting plants and animals along the way.

Another British naturalist to visit Chile was John Ball, known to history as an Irish politician, a naturalist (a pupil of Henslow), and an Alpine traveler. He was influenced by Joseph Hooker, who accompanied him on an expedition to Morocco. In a later expedition, John Ball examined the west Patagonian channels and the Magellan Strait in 1882, and several of his specimens are to be found at Kew Gardens. This expedition was written up as *Notes of a Naturalist in South America*, published in 1887. The Scottish traveler and botanist George Francis Scott-Elliot spent four months in Chile and Argentina in the early twentieth century collecting specimens, and in 1907 he published his account as *Chile: Its History and Development, Natural Features, Products, Commerce and Present Conditions.*

The first British naturalist of international repute to actually settle in Chile was Edwyn Charles Reed. He was born in 1841, in Bristol, and died in Concepción in 1910. He started his career as a naturalist at the Bristol Museum before leaving on an expedition to Brazil. He returned from Brazil to England in 1869 in poor health—he had probably contracted malaria—and his doctors recommended that he move to a drier climate. Reed decided to emigrate to Chile, and in 1869 started as an entomologist in the National Museum, where he worked for seven years studying Chilean fauna and flora. In 1876, he became curator of the Natural History Museum of Valparaíso, working alongside the founder, Eduardo de la Barra.

His health remained poor, and he resigned after a year to teach natural history and physical geography at the naval academy in Valparaíso during the following seven years. In this period he founded an observatory in the port, and a School Museum at the seminary of San Rafael Arcángel. Once again, for health reasons, he resigned and relocated to towns in the mountains, to Baños de Cauquenes, where he established a regional natural history museum (in 1895), and to Los Andes, where he dedicated himself to writing about entomology. In 1902, he was appointed director of the new Museum of Concepción, where he worked until his death in 1910. With his eldest son, Carlos Samuel Reed Rosa, he began to turn rooms in his house into exhibition displays when the museum proved too small for his exhibits. Reed worked enthusiastically on building up his collection, and the fishermen of Talcahuano, Lota, Tomé, and Penco became accustomed to his delving into their nets for new specimens.

Reed was a member of the prestigious Société Scientifique du Chili and published in the Society's journal, as well as the *Anales de la Universidad de Chile*, the *Boletín de la Sociedad Nacional de Agricultura*, and the *Revista Chilena de Historia Natural*. He is remembered for his work on Chilean fauna, including catalogs of insects, birds, and fish. One of his insect collections was sent to the Washington DC Natural History Museum. His son Carlos followed his father's footsteps, and became section head at the Chilean Museum of Ethnology and Anthropology, and Director of the zoo in Santiago.

Finally, there are the remarkable stories of two British anthropologists, Richard Latcham and Katherine Routledge. Richard Latcham was self-taught, but his contributions to the field of Chilean anthropology are still honored today. He was born in Bristol, graduated in civil engineering in London in 1888, and left in the same year for Chile with a post in the Chilean government's Department of Colonization. This work involved surveying and constructing roads in the south of the country, in Araucanía, where the Mapuche Indians had, a few years before, signed a peace treaty with the central government. Richard Latcham settled down in Temuco—a rough frontier town at that time—and spent the next five years among the Mapuche Indians, during which he learned their language. This close contact with the Mapuches, coupled with his powers of observation and intellect, led him to study the indigenous culture and, later, to publish accounts of his findings. In 1893, he departed for Santiago, where he taught English, and then for La Serena, where he also taught English and worked as an engineer in the mining industry. Following his return to Santiago in 1902, Latcham started to publish his anthropological studies, which began to appear from 1903. Recognition for his pioneering work came later, beginning with his appointment as Professor of Indigenous Art at the *Escuela de Bellas Artes* in Santiago in 1927, Director of the National Museum of Natural History in 1928, Dean of the Faculty of Fine Arts at the University of Chile in 1929, and Professor of American Prehistory in 1935.

Richard Latcham's attention turned from the Mapuches to anthropology and archaeology in northern Chile, with a special focus on excavation in *Norte Chico*, the region which extends from the Atacama

Desert to just north of Santiago. Although there is doubt today about his main assertion—that there are similarities in the anthropology and archaeology (especially the pottery) of this region and the pre-Colombian cultures over the mountains in Argentina—the name he coined for this culture, *Diaguitas*, is still in use. Artifacts excavated by Latcham can be viewed in Santiago's *Museo de Ciencias Naturales*. His publications include *Los changos de las costas de Chile* (1910); *La organización social y las creencias religiosas de los antiguos araucanos* (1924); and *La prehistoria Chilena* (1928). For his contributions to anthropology, the Chilean government awarded Richard Latcham the Order of Merit in 1939. Known today in Chile as Ricardo Latcham, he spent the rest of his life in his adopted country, apart from visits to neighboring countries, and died in Santiago in 1943.

Chile's Easter Island has fascinated British visitors with scientific interests. In 1868, John Linton Palmer, a surgeon aboard HMS *Topaze*, provided a description of the island in his *A Visit to Easter Island, or Rapa Nui, in 1868* published in the *Journal of the Royal Geographical Society* of London. But the most famous and enduring account was published by Katherine Routledge (née Pease), born in Darlington in northern England, who undertook a survey of the archaeology and anthropology of Easter Island from March 1914 to August 1915. Her book, *The Mystery of Easter Island: The Story of an Expedition* (1919), tells of how she set out in a custom-built schooner called the *Mana* with her husband William Scoresby Routledge and the support of the Royal Geographical Society, the British Association for the Advancement of Science, and the British Museum.

Her intention was to catalog and explore the origins of the famous statues on Easter Island and to study the inhabitants' culture. During their stay on the island, the German East Asia Squadron refitted off Hanga Roa (prior to the Battle of Coronel), and the couple discovered that Britain was at war with Germany. This was not the only difficulty; Katherine Routledge was also embroiled in a native uprising against sheep ranchers led by a charismatic visionary named Angata. On her return to England, she showed signs of suffering from schizophrenia, and this worsened from 1925 and developed into what would today be diagnosed as delusional paranoia. Katherine evicted her husband from their home in London and locked herself inside. Four years later, her family forced her into a mental institution, against her will, where she died in 1935. Katherine Routledge's legacy lives on in the field notes given to the Royal Geographical Society, and her findings are still today regarded as essential reading for students of the ethnography of Easter Island.

Chapter 4

Chile's Wars

I do not hesitate in asserting, that but for his assiduity and unremitting attention, his military knowledge, and determined valour, the western shores of America would have still been in the possession of Spain; her fleet would have now commanded the Pacific, and "British Commerce" would have been excluded from the extensive market which it enjoys.

—W. B. Stevenson, Lord Thomas Cochrane's secretary, 1825

There is a monument in Valparaíso called the *Arco Británico*, or British Arch, which was erected in 1911 to celebrate one hundred years of Chilean independence. It is the work of the Chilean architect Alfredo Azancot. The monument is faced in white marble and carries at the top the figure of the Victorian British Lion, and on its sides the effigies of Cochrane, O'Higgins, Simpson, and O'Brien—all heroes in the War of Independence. This O'Higgins is Bernardo, whose name is most closely connected with the victories of the patriot army in Chile. He was the Chilean-born son of an Irishman, Ambrose O'Higgins. The other three names relate to the naval war—Thomas Cochrane, a Scotsman; Robert Simpson, an Englishman; and George O'Brien, an Irishman.

The first declaration of independence was on September 18, 1810, which is celebrated every year as a national holiday in Chile. This early revolt was principally aimed at the colonial government in Lima, since Chile as a captaincy-general was subordinated to the Viceroyalty of Peru, and Spain had been overrun by Napoleon's armies. The declaration was motivated by Napoleon forcing his brother Joseph on to the Spanish throne. The National Junta in Chile declared itself an autonomous republic in the name of Ferdinand, heir to the deposed King of Spain, suppressing the office of the captain-general but professing "to hold

Figure 4.1 Arco Británico (British Arch) in Valparaíso

the country for the legitimate sovereign, resisting French usurpation" (Maria Graham 1824, 197). Effective independence from Spain came later, with the Battle of Maipú in 1818.

British government policy in Latin America during the several wars of independence against Spanish colonial rule was crucial to their eventual success. When these conflicts broke out, Britain offered to mediate between Spain and her colonies in 1812, but Spain turned down this offer. Later, Spain offered Britain special commercial advantages in exchange for naval support against the rebels, but British Foreign Secretary Castlereagh declined to give any help.

Robert Stewart, Viscount Castlereagh, was Foreign Secretary in the period 1812 to 1822, spanning the defeat of Napoleon in Europe. He was pressured by British commercial interests, who were favorable to independence after so many years of Spanish monopoly on trade in the Americas, and faced opposing pressure from conservative elements in the government, for whom the granting of independence was anathema. In his famous and pivotal memorandum of August 1817, Castlereagh declared Britain's neutrality in the conflicts but urged Spain (and Portugal) to consider reforming the colonial systems if they wanted to achieve peace and see their colonies become loyal once again. Significantly, he made it clear that Britain would not allow any other European power to intervene in the region on behalf of Spain. He also secured a guarantee from the nations in Europe that the only forces that would be sent to Latin America would be Spain's. This policy was enforceable, since Britain had a navy that controlled the Atlantic.

Castlereagh also dragged his feet when Spain complained at the recruitment of British mercenaries for the wars, especially for the armies of Bolívar in Venezuela and, later, New Granada (Colombia, Ecuador, and Venezuela). The result was that when the restrictive Foreign Enlistment Act was finally passed in Britain in 1819, more than five thousand British soldiers had already traveled to the region. As time went by and it became clear that the rebellions would be victorious, Castlereagh decided on a policy of de facto commercial recognition by extending the Navigation Acts in 1822 to permit Latin American ships to call into British ports.

George Canning succeeded Castlereagh in September 1822, after the latter committed suicide. He too was favorable to Britain's recognition of the new republics and continued with Castlereagh's policy toward the region. However, the domestic and international political situations made him act cautiously. In foreign affairs, Canning had two main concerns. The first was that France would take the opportunity to interfere in Latin America—the Royal Navy had spotted

French ships off the Island of Chiloé. Maria Graham wrote in her *Journal* on July 7, 1822, "I confess that a French invasion (for I will not think England so wicked) would be a most fearful misfortune to these rising states, and one from which nothing but a naval force could defend them."

Canning had the "naval force," and when he met in October 1823 with the French Ambassador to London, Prince Jules de Polignac, the outcome of these discussions was the "Polignac Memorandum." This committed France to noninterference in Spanish America. In the same month, Canning secured the Cabinet's agreement to send consuls and special commissioners to Spanish America to assess firsthand the reality of the declarations of independence. Christopher Nugent was appointed in 1823 as the first Consul to Chile, in Valparaíso.

Canning's second concern was the United States. His initiatives in Latin America predated the Monroe Doctrine (declared in December 1823) and in fact gave it teeth, since the United States at that time was in no position to enforce this statement of regional policy on its own. In January 1824, Canning declared that the independence of the Latin American nations was a consummate fact and deserving of formal recognition. In July, Canning persuaded a reluctant cabinet to recommend to the king that a commercial treaty be negotiated with Buenos Aires, and then in December 1824 he informed the government of Spain that he had decided to immediately recognize Colombia, Mexico, and Argentina as independent states. This recognition came at the cost of commercial treaties being imposed by Britain on these new countries, and, indeed, it does seem that Canning had his eyes on building up trade for the Britain with the region. Leslie Bethell (in Bulmer-Thomas 1989, 4) quotes from a letter Canning wrote to his friend Lord Granville, British Ambassador to Paris, in December 1824: "Spanish America is free and if we do not mismanage our affairs sadly, she is English." In December 1826, Canning summed up the situation to Parliament: "I resolved that if France had Spain, it should be not Spain with the Indies. I called the New World into existence to redress the balance of the Old."

George Canning is remembered positively for his role in consolidating the newly independent republics and, in the words of Agustín Edwards (1937, 5), for following a policy that became "the cornerstone of the splendid relations that Britain has had with Latin America and, by extension, with Chile." Edwards tells the story of how King George IV resisted this policy of recognition; after all, the monarchy had been overthrown in Spanish America and republics installed. Canning prevailed in his policy—even threatening to resign in December 1824—and prepared the speech from the throne for the opening of Parliament in February

1825 that laid out the policy. The King refused to read this statement and gave as an excuse that he had lost his false teeth!

There is a statue of George Canning near the Los Héroes Metro Station in Santiago. The foundation stone was laid by the Prince of Wales on his visit to Chile in 1925. In London, Canning's name continues in close association with Latin America in the naming of Canning House, founded in 1943 to encourage understanding between Britain, Spain, Portugal, and Latin America.

Henry John Temple, third Viscount Palmerston, was foreign secretary during most of the years between 1830 and 1851 and continued with Canning's policies toward the New World. Palmerston too recognized the need to forestall French and North American meddling in the region. However, Britain's full recognition of Chile as an independent republic came quite late, in 1841, when Britain's consul general in Santiago, John Walpole, was given the additional title of chargé d'affaires. This formal recognition was cemented in 1854, during Manuel Montt's government, when the Treaty of Friendship, Commerce and Navigation was signed between the two countries.

British connections with the political landscape of Chile actually go back to the period before independence from Spain. Ambrose O'Higgins was for a time the Governor of Chile before becoming Spain's viceroy in Lima, with oversight of Chilean affairs. O'Higgins was born in 1720 in County Sligo, Ireland, during the time of the Protestant Ascendancy. Control of Ireland was exercised from Westminster during the eighteenth century, and the best positions went to English Protestants prior to the 1800 Act of Union and the joining of the Kingdoms of Ireland and Great Britain.

O'Higgins was the son of a peasant farmer and was educated in Cádiz by an uncle who was a chaplain at the Court in Madrid. Little is known for certain about his early years, but he may have left Ireland because as a Catholic under Anglo-Irish hegemony he saw no future for himself in public service. In Cádiz, O'Higgins began to work for the Irish merchant firm of Butler, and it seems that he went to Peru on their behalf for commercial reasons in 1756, arrived briefly in Chile in 1757, and returned to Cádiz in 1761, where he joined the army as an engineer draftsman. He was back in Chile in 1763 or 1764 as the personal assistant of Irish-born John Garland, who was the military governor of Valdivia. O'Higgins' first employment in Chile was building weatherproof shelters in the Andes to help couriers in their journeys over the mountains to and from Argentina, and he spent two years at this work. He returned to Spain in 1766 and was back again in Chile, in Santiago, in 1769 or 1770.

Ambrose O'Higgins is next seen serving in the war against the Mapuche Indians in the period 1770 to 1777, starting as a dragoon captain and finishing as a cavalry colonel, and it was said that no one knew the Araucanía region better than he did, despite the fact that he remained a foreigner and spoke Spanish badly. By 1778, when his son Bernardo was born, Ambrose O'Higgins was still in the service of the Spanish authorities and living in Chillán. This town was close to the "frontier," loosely marked by the River Bío-Bío, that divided lands to the north colonized by the Spanish from the southern region occupied by the Mapuche Indians.

O'Higgins had now come to the attention of his Spanish masters as someone successful in taking on the Indian rebellions. He later became Governor of the Province of Concepción (in 1786), then Governor, Captain-General, and President of the Royal Audience of the Kingdom of Chile from 1788 to 1795; and in 1796 he was appointed Viceroy of Peru in Lima. When he died in 1801, he had still not mastered the Spanish language, despite the many years spent in South America.

As Captain-General of Chile, O'Higgins founded several settlements, including San José de Maipú, Linares, and the port of Constitución, and he was also responsible for repopulating Osorno, which earned for him the title of Marquis of Osorno. His other achievements include the road from Valparaíso to Santiago, the first pavements in Santiago, and a drainage system for the River Mapocho to reduce flooding. O'Higgins was the first Governor of Chile to attempt personally to visit every part of the country, traveling on horseback and on foot in the north and south of Chile, and crossing the Andes by the track between Santiago and Mendoza—all of this to become familiar with the territory he was governing. Despite his earlier military incursions into the Mapuche territory of Araucanía, as Governor, O'Higgins was able to build friendly relations with the indigenous leaders, which culminated in the Parliament of Negrete. Relations were so cordial that the Mapuches agreed to have the royal road go through their territory to Osorno, and, ironically for his son Bernardo, the Araucanians were among the very last royalist faithful to resist independence from Spain.

Ambrose's son was Bernardo O'Higgins, the Chilean soldier, revolutionary, and liberal dictator of Chile in the period 1818–1823. He was born in 1778, the illegitimate son of Ambrose O'Higgins and Isabel Riquelme, the eighteen-year-old daughter of Simón Riquelme, at whose estate near Chillán Ambrose had briefly stopped. Maria Graham met Bernardo in 1822 and described "his blue eyes, light hair, and ruddy and rather coarse complexion, [which] do not bely [*sic*] his Irish extraction; while his very small and short hands and feet belong to his Araucanian pedigree" (Graham, August 26, 1822). It seems that Ambrose promised to marry Isabel, but this promise was not kept, and Ambrose set off on a military campaign south of the "frontier" against the indigenous Mapuche Indians.

Meanwhile, Isabel was kept away from public gaze, and when the baby was born, he was given to a local matron. Historians say that for Ambrose the fact that he had a son, albeit an illegitimate son, soon became an obsession, and he took the baby away from the Riquelmes and gave him into the care of a friend in Talca. Bernardo did return to Chillán to attend school but was then moved on to Lima for further education. When his father was appointed Viceroy of Peru, Bernardo was once again on the move—the presence of an illegitimate son in Lima was not in keeping with the important position—this time to Cádiz in Spain and then to England for five years where, for reasons that are unclear, he lived in Richmond-upon-Thames in the care of two watchmakers, Spencer and Perkins.

Bernardo returned to Chile in 1802, after the death of his father, and assumed the surname of O'Higgins, a matter which his father had stubbornly refused to consider while he lived. In June 1811, Bernardo attended the first republican congress as the deputy representing Chillán and soon became embroiled in the early stages of the War of Independence. He did not impress as a military officer, although he showed his personal courage and tenacity during the siege of royalist forces at Chillán. The siege did not succeed in its aim, and this meant that José Miguel Carrera, the leading force until this setback in the conflict against Spain, lost support in Santiago.

The Battle of El Roble followed, which was a turning point for O'Higgins and for the revolution. Carrera fled the battlefield in the middle of the fighting, leaving O'Higgins in command, and—to everyone's surprise—O'Higgins won. He famously proclaimed, it is said, "To die with honor or live with glory!" In recognition of this victory, the ruling committee in Santiago gave command of the army to O'Higgins. Carrera met O'Higgins in Concepción and surrendered his command, upon which he left for Santiago, only to be captured by the royalists and imprisoned in Chillán.

The early years of the revolt against the Spanish were dominated first by José Miguel Carrera and his brother and then by the division that emerged between the O'Higgins and Carrera factions. The two men came to hate each other. While Carrera was still in jail, the patriots and the royalists had both come close to exhaustion, and a treaty was signed to end hostilities in May 1814. Curiously, it was Captain Hillier of HMS *Phoebe* (who had engaged USS *Essex* off Valparaíso in March that year) who acted as guarantor of the conditions underlying the peace between the Spanish forces under General Gaenza and the patriots.

O'Higgins was one of the signatories to the treaty. All prisoners were released, but in July 1814 Carrera carried out a coup d'état. O'Higgins brought his troops north to Santiago to face off with Carrera, but the worst was avoided when they discovered that the viceroy in Peru had disembarked soldiers from Lima and royalist volunteers from the south of Chile in the port of Talcahuano. Carrera and O'Higgins hastily patched up their differences but in 1814 were defeated at the Battle of Rancagua—according to Maria Graham's *Sketch of the History of Chile* (1824), Carrera's troops never arrived—and they went with their remaining forces across the Andes to Mendoza. This was the year of the restoration of the Bourbon monarchy in Spain, and the royalists now took back control of Chile for another two and a half years.

In Mendoza, O'Higgins and Carrera joined forces with the leader of the independence movement in Argentina, José de San Martín. In 1814, Argentina was in the vanguard of the independence movement in South America and had already declared itself an independent republic. San Martín sided with O'Higgins, whom he recognized as the leader of the émigré forces from Chile. They spent the next two years preparing the logistics for the impressive crossing of the Andes by their army, with O'Higgins in charge of two battalions. The Spanish forces were defeated at the Battle of Chacabuco in 1817. Santiago was taken and independence proclaimed on January 1, 1818, in the Plaza de Armas in Concepción. The march into Chile by San Martín and O'Higgins in 1817 was significant in the regional context since, together with Bolivar's victories in the north in 1819, this heralded the domino-like fall of Spanish dominion in Latin America, region by region.

After the Battle of Chacabuco, San Martín declined the title of Supreme Director of Chile, which went instead to Bernardo O'Higgins. There were still a number of engagements with royalist forces to contend with, culminating with the Battle of Maipú in April 1818, and with this decisive victory Chile was now effectively independent. Royalists held out in the south of Chile but could never again mount a significant threat on land to the new republic, although they remained a thorn in the side of government until 1826, when the last royalists were defeated on Chiloé Island.

Bernardo O'Higgins ruled as an autocrat, albeit with liberal views, in a way that bordered on dictatorship, and public discontent increased as a result of the continuing war, economic stagnation, and the absence of effective political institutions. Despite these problems at home, O'Higgins decided that his priority was to unseat the viceroy in Peru, and to this end he took out a loan in 1822 of one million pounds, contracted in Britain, to finance an attack on Lima with a force under Admiral Cochrane and troops under San Martín.

This was not a popular move, and in 1823, with civil war threatening, O'Higgins resigned from government and went into exile in Peru. Before he left, a British visitor named Robert Proctor met with O'Higgins—at that time "a kind of state prisoner"—in the house of the governor in Valparaíso. Proctor came away not entirely impressed: "O'Higgins is an undoubtedly brave man, and a tolerable general-officer; but his character seems to be too open and undesigning for times of intrigue and revolution" (*Narrative of a Journey* 1825, 108). Bernardo O'Higgins left no descendants. He is remembered today in the naming of one of Chile's fifteen administrative regions, the VI Región del Libertador General Bernardo O'Higgins, and countless streets, avenues, and parks throughout the country.

Several British men took part in the independence campaigns on land, both as officers and as soldiers of fortune. Rodriguez (2006) estimates that around two hundred British mercenaries fought in San Martín's armies. A significant name is that of General John Mackenna, born in 1771 in Drogheda, Ireland. He went to Spain with his uncle, Count O'Reilly, to study at the Royal School of Mathematics. In 1787, Mackenna graduated from the Royal Academy of (military) Engineers, entered the Irish Brigade of the Spanish army, and saw fighting in northern Africa, where he was promoted to second lieutenant. Returning to Spain, he was promoted again (in 1792) to lieutenant in the Royal Regiment of Engineers and fought in Spain's war against the French.

In recognition of his services, the Spanish army promoted him to captain in 1795, and it was on an assignment in the service of Spain that he went to Peru in 1796, via Argentina and Chile, where he served under Viceroy Ambrose O'Higgins. The viceroy appointed him Governor of Osorno in Chile, where he convinced a number of families to move to Osorno from the Island of Chiloé in order to start a colony. Mackenna built a storehouse and two mills, together with the road south from Osorno to present-day Puerto Montt. This activity worried the Captain-General of Chile, Gabriel de Avilés, into thinking that perhaps O'Higgins and Mackenna were planning to settle an Irish colony on Osorno. When Ambrose O'Higgins died in 1801, Avilés was named his successor as Viceroy of Peru, but despite his animosity and this position of authority, he was unable to remove Mackenna from Osorno, who remained in that post until 1808.

In 1809, John Mackenna married a Chilean woman whose family had connections with the revolutionary movement, and in the following year, he joined the defense committee of what was now declared the Republic of Chile. In 1811, during the first phase of the war for independence, he was appointed Military Governor of Valparaíso. Mackenna broke with the faction supporting Carrera, and for this reason he was dismissed from this post and taken prisoner. His support was all for O'Higgins, and on his release Mackenna became one of O'Higgins' officers fighting the Spanish forces. His greatest military honor was at the Battle of Membrillar, where he provoked the temporary collapse of the royalist army. O'Higgins appointed him commandant-general in recognition of this important action. He also fought in the battle of San Carlos and the siege of Chillán. When the Carrera faction carried out the coup d'état, Mackenna was banished to the Argentinean province of Mendoza. Sadly, while in Buenos Aires in 1814 reorganizing the Chilean-Argentinean army after the Cancha Rayada disaster, he died in a duel with Carrera. Among his descendants is his grandson, the Chilean historian Benjamín Vicuña Mackenna.

Another key figure in the republican army was William Miller, born in Kent in 1795. In 1811, he joined the British army and fought in the campaign against Napoleon until his defeat in the Battle of Waterloo in 1815. Miller arrived in Buenos Aires in 1817 and soon joined an artillery regiment. He crossed the Andes to Chile with the patriot forces and was involved as head of artillery under Manuel Blanco Encalada in the disaster and retreat of Cancha Rayada, where he drew attention to himself by keeping calm and saving two valuable pieces of cannon. He missed the decisive Battle of Maipú because he was in Valparaíso with the mission of capturing the merchant ship *Windham*. Miller was successful, the ship was renamed the *Lautaro*, and he was responsible for fitting out and crewing what became the patriots' first warship.

Following a naval campaign in Talcahuano, William Miller returned to Valparaíso and then led the Chilean marines disembarked by Cochrane in Valdivia. This was a victorious enterprise, but when he subsequently led two hundred marines in an attack on the island of Chiloé, they were routed, and he was wounded. When the battle was taken to the Spanish in Peru, Miller set off for Callao in Cochrane's expedition as commander of the squadron's military force. Following the victory in Peru, he was promoted to lieutenant-colonel. Once the royalist resistance in Chile was overcome, Miller served as a general with Sucre and Bolívar and became Mariscal del Perú in 1861. His memoirs were published by his brother John Miller in 1828.

John Thomond O'Brien was born in Wicklow, Ireland, in 1786. In 1811, he was sent to Buenos Aires with a commission to trade, only to discover a vocation for military matters. He joined a cavalry regiment and fought against royalist Spanish and Portuguese forces in Uruguay. In 1816, he moved to Mendoza and placed himself under the command of San Martín. O'Brien was ordered to lead a group of troops to garrison the Mal Paso—a pass high in the Andes near Portillo. They spent the entire winter there, but when they emerged, eleven of the troop of twenty-five had died from cold and exposure. On his return to Mendoza, San Martín named O'Brien his aide-de-camp and later described him as "the gallant comrade who fought so many years by my side in the cause of South America." He took part in the cavalry charge at Chacabuco, and in the Battle of Maipú. He then went off to help in the battles for independence in Peru, becoming a general, and later in Bolivia. He died in Lisbon in 1861.

William de Vic-Tupper was born in Guernsey and arrived in Chile in 1821, where he became a lieutenant colonel during the War of Independence. He directed the final charge that helped in the defeat of royalist forces in Chiloé and later became director of the Chilean Military Academy. Vic-Tupper was appointed Governor of Coquimbo in 1829 and was murdered in 1830 in Lircay by rebellious Indians after the Battle of Maule.

Samuel Haigh was a man of many parts—doctor, businessman, and soldier. He was born in London in 1787, arrived in Chile in 1817, and served throughout the closing years of the War of Independence. He had the honor of taking the message from San Martín to Bernardo O'Higgins in which the triumph at Maipú was announced. It is said that Haigh entered the Alameda in Santiago shouting, "Viva Chile! Viva la patria!" and was seen waving the blood-stained message from San Martín. In 1829, he published his account of these experiences, *Sketches of Buenos Ayres and Chile*.

James Paroissien was born in Barking, Kent, in 1784. He came to Chile with Lord Cochrane and became Chief Surgeon in San Martín's Army of the Andes. He was present at the disaster of Cancha Rayada, where he ministered to Bernardo O'Higgins, who was wounded in the arm, and at the victorious Battle of Maipú, where San Martín ordered him to write down the message giving news of the victory, the one that Samuel Haigh took to Santiago. In 1820, Paroissien became one of the two aides-de-camp to San Martín and accompanied the General in the land campaign in Peru.

Numerous other British names appear in the history of this confrontation. Arthur Wavell was designated second commander-in-chief of the patriot army under Blanco Encalada and later sent by O'Higgins as a Chilean delegate to help the Mexicans in their fight for independence. Incidentally, this Arthur Wavell was the grandfather of Field Marshall Archibald Wavell, who for a time commanded British forces in the Middle East during the Second World War. Charles O'Carroll played a major role in the campaign against the royalist forces and was taken prisoner and executed. Colonel Thomas Sutcliffe held important posts during the War of Independence and later became Governor of the Juan Fernández Islands. On his return to England, he published *Sixteen Years in Chile and Peru from 1821–1839*.

Thomas Leighton was head surgeon with O'Higgins on several campaigns. W. B. Stevenson was a traveler who arrived in Chile in 1803 and was taken prisoner by the Spanish. Later, he joined the patriot forces and became one of Cochrane's secretaries. He published his experiences in *Twenty Years' Residence in South America* (1825). John Thomas was a companion and secretary to Bernardo O'Higgins in exile. Dr. Hannah served as a surgeon in O'Higgins' army, and Maria Graham (June 19, 1822) refers to "the physician of the O'Higgins, Dr. Craig . . . who seems peculiarly to possess the information concerning all I want to know." Michelle Prain (2007) tells the story of another British physician, Nathaniel Miers Cox, who was born in Grosmont, England in 1785 and died in Valparaíso in 1869. While visiting a friend in Chile in 1814, he was caught up in the War of Independence and joined O'Higgins' army as first surgeon of the patriot army. He was at the Battles of Cancha Rayada and Rancagua and endured the exile in Mendoza.

According to Derrick-Jehu (1965), there was also an "English brigade," which formed part of Bernardo O'Higgins' patriot forces in San Martín's Army of Liberation. This must be the company of around one hundred *cazadores ingleses* (English hunters), or riflemen, referred to by Rodriguez (2006) as being led by Captain John Young. This company was made up chiefly of officers who had served in the Peninsula War against Napoleon.

There were not only officers who took part in the independence struggle; there were of course many British soldiers too, now mostly anonymous, who were attracted to fight with the patriot forces as mercenary "soldiers of fortune" when they found themselves unemployed following the final defeat of Napoleon in 1815. Gilbert Mathison met a number of them in Santiago in 1822 and found that they all agreed on one thing, "namely, in expressing unqualified regret at having ever left their own country to enter into the Patriot service. Their health had been wasted, and their expectations, for the most part, disappointed: but, having gone so far, it was too late to recede, and they felt obliged to pursue their career in South America to the end" (Mathison 1825, 202).

The war was also fought against the Spanish at sea, and without question, the leading figure in Chile's naval struggle for independence was Thomas Cochrane, tenth Earl of Dundonald, born in 1775 in Culross, Scotland. A short account of his early career is important for understanding why Cochrane should turn up in Valparaíso in November 1818, at a crucial juncture in the war against Spain. He joined the Royal Navy as a midshipman on board the frigate HMS *Hind* in 1793, the year that France declared war on England and Holland. Then he commanded HMS *Speedy* at the age of twenty and fought Spanish forces in the Mediterranean. Over this time, Cochrane built himself a reputation for imperturbable self-confidence, tremendous courage, cool audacity, intelligence, taking the initiative, and doing the improbable, the unexpected, the outrageous, and even the unthinkable in taking on superior forces. Another quality of Cochrane's was his care and concern for the men who fought under him, which made him much loved. But to many in the establishment he was arrogant, impudent to authority, and bad tempered.

In 1803, Cochrane served on HMS *Arab* to help blockade Napoleon Bonaparte's invasion forces at Boulogne. In 1805, he captained HMS *Pallas* and was later involved in harrying the French navy and merchant ships on HMS *Imperieuse*. This ship carried a young midshipman named Frederick Marryat, who later became the popular novelist Captain Marryat. Cochrane's exploits won a grudging respect from his foreign enemies—Napoleon called him the "sea wolf." But he made enemies in high places in his own country and was not helped by getting himself elected to Parliament (in 1806), where he spoke for naval reform and railed against the corruption and abuses in the Royal Navy. Cochrane won reelection to Parliament, and as an independent he attacked the two political parties of the day, the Whigs and the Tories. This upset the establishment, and he became the victim of official and vindictive reprisals.

Then, in early 1814, with Napoleon's army in retreat but far from beaten, Cochrane was accused of participating in a hoax that became known as the Great Stock Exchange Fraud. While it seems very likely that his uncle Cochrane-Johnstone was involved, it is almost certainly the case that Cochrane was innocent. However, he was found guilty, expelled from the House of Commons, and then summarily dismissed from the Royal Navy. On his release from prison, Cochrane harried the government on the side of the Reformers and goaded the establishment from Parliament.

The Chilean representative for the new republic in London, José Alvarez Condarco, had been sent there to raise funds and look for help. In 1818, he approached Cochrane and offered him command of the rebel naval forces. Chile recognized that winning battles on land was all very fine, but control of the sea remained in Spanish hands and was protracting, even jeopardizing, the war for independence. The Spanish military forces had been defeated decisively in the Battle of Chacabuco in 1817, and Bernardo O'Higgins was already installed as Supreme Director, but the Spanish fleet and garrisons along the coast remained and threatened any successful outcome for the revolution.

Cochrane was seen as having clear advantages to the Chilean patriots: he was obviously a very able seaman and leader of men, and he was a man of principle and an outspoken supporter of liberty. Moreover, he was available. In August 1818, Cochrane left England discretely, and set off for Boulogne. His plan was to take delivery of the steamship *Rising Star*, which was being built for the Chilean navy at Deptford with money raised by his brother William. Cochrane's idea—bizarre and improbable as it now seems—was to collect Napoleon from St. Helena and then make for Valparaíso. But progress on the ship's construction was slow (it actually arrived in Chile in July 1822, when the major sea battles had been won). The Spanish in Chile were regrouping their naval forces in Valdivia, and the Chilean authorities prevailed on Cochrane to set off for Chile immediately on a sailing ship called the *Rose*.

However, Cochrane did not forget his plan to put Napoleon on the postindependence throne of South America; he merely put it on ice for the time being. Two years later, it seemed to Cochrane that independence was now a foregone conclusion. So, while arrangements were being made for the patriot navy and army to leave Valparaíso for the assault on Spanish forces in Peru, Cochrane sent a confidential messenger, Lieutenant-Colonel Charles, to St. Helena to interview Napoleon. When Charles arrived in St. Helena, he found that the exiled Emperor's health had deteriorated, and he returned to Valparaíso empty-handed. Napoleon in fact died soon afterwards, in 1821.

Cochrane arrived in Valparaíso in November 1818. The Chilean naval commander, Blanco Encalada, resigned in favor of Cochrane, who received the title of Vice-Admiral of Chile, and Commander-in-Chief of the Naval Forces of the Republic. The "navy" consisted then of just seven ships captured from the Spanish or bought from Britain.

There was the *O'Higgins* (the flagship), the *San Martín* and the *Lautaro*, as well as four smaller ships, the *Chacabuco*, the *Araucano*, the *Puyrredon*, and the *Galvarino*. The *Galvarino* had been brought to Chile in a speculative move as the British ship *Hecate* by two Englishmen, Martin Guise, a veteran of Trafalgar, and Captain John Spry, and sold to the new Chilean government. Guise and Spry had their eyes on promoting themselves through their service in Chile and were to become Cochrane's enemies in the war. The Spanish could deploy a much larger force, fourteen ships and twenty-eight gunships, including the formidable forty-four gun *Esmeralda*.

Cochrane's first move was to take the battle to the Spanish where they were strongest, in Peru, and in 1819 he attacked Callao, the port and naval base of Lima, taking his four largest ships. The naval engagement was inconclusive, and Cochrane set about blockading the port and intercepting Spanish ships. Nevertheless, these early actions were a wake-up call for the Spanish. They now knew who they were up against and "on becoming acquainted with this fact, bestowed on me the not very complimentary title of 'El Diablo,' by which I was afterwards known amongst them" (Cochrane 1859, vol. 1). By June 1819, Cochrane was back in Valparaíso for refitting, and in September, he was again off Callao but unable to dent its improved defenses. He then turned to Spain's other great fortress on the west coast—Valdivia in Chile.

A morale-boosting victory against the Spanish was needed, as much for the new republic as for the new naval commander, and Valdivia was the natural choice. This is where the Spanish would launch an offensive if they decided to take on the new republic in the capital Santiago. But this would be no walk-over. Cochrane later described Valdivia as "a fortress previously deemed impregnable" (Cochrane 1859, vol. 1). The Chilean government reduced Cochrane's chances of taking the garrison when they declined to provide soldiers for the assault. True to his previous form against the French, Cochrane sailed off undaunted with just his flagship, the *O'Higgins*, and lots of self-confidence. On board was Major William Miller, who commanded the Chilean marines.

On arrival off Valdivia, on January 18, 1820, Cochrane raised Spanish colors and requested a pilot. He knew that he had a good chance to be mistaken for the Spanish frigate, the *Prueba*. The pilot duly arrived, came on deck, was made Cochrane's prisoner, and "persuaded" to help the patriot forces. The *O'Higgins* then did a tour within the bay of the approaches and positions of the battlements, and, to the bafflement of the Spanish on shore, exited out to sea. Cochrane learned that the Spanish ship *Potrillo* was expected, carrying pay for the garrison in Valdivia. The *Potrillo* was captured, with the bonus of dispatches detailing Spanish dispositions and tactics.

Cochrane then sailed north to Concepción, where Governor Freire provided 250 men for the assault on Valdivia. They returned south, now with a schooner, the *Montezuma*, and a brig, the *Intrepido*, to augment his small naval force. There was a near calamity on the voyage back to Valdivia, when the *O'Higgins* went aground on a reef during the night off the island of Quiriquina. Typically cool and levelheaded in an emergency, Cochrane gave the orders that released the ship from the reef, and then, when the water entering the hull threatened disaster, went down himself to mend the pumps. This was sufficient to keep the ship afloat, although still leaking badly.

The Spanish fortifications at Valdivia were seemingly insuperable. The harbor was set in a small bay with a mouth just three quarters of a mile across. On either side of the mouth were the forts of Niebla and Amargos, and there were, in addition, fortifications on the island of Manzanera in the center of the bay. Although the state of currents and tides made any thought of landing anywhere in the vicinity very difficult, Cochrane looked at a place called Aguada del Inglés, lying a little to the west of the mouth of the bay. This spot seemed to offer an option for landing at low tide, although guarded by a fortification called (ironically) Fort Inglés. The place also fitted with Cochrane's maxim, "an attack where least expected is almost certainly crowned with success" (1859, vol. 1).

The *O'Higgins* was in no state to take part in the attack, so the Chilean marines under Major Miller and the soldiers taken from Concepción were disembarked onto the schooner and brig. Cochrane turned to his usual deceit, hoisting the colors of Spain, and on February 3, 1820, he approached the spot he had chosen, right under the guns of Fort Inglés. The boats for landing his marines on the beach were in the water, but hidden from view behind the brig. Spanish troops appeared and challenged the ships. Cochrane had an officer who was born in Spain explain that they had come from Cádiz with the *Prueba*, but had suffered badly in storms rounding Cape Horn, getting separated and losing their ship's boats. The Spanish were unconvinced, and late in the afternoon, when they spotted one of the small boats that had drifted into view, the guns of Fort Inglés began to fire on Cochrane's small flotilla.

The *Intrepido* was hit. Retreat was out of the question, so Cochrane ordered an immediate assault on the beach, which took place in a hail of musket fire. Once on the beach, Miller led his marines with bayonets drawn—they had little choice, since much of their gunpowder had been lost when the *O'Higgins* ran aground. Darkness fell, and Cochrane's forces set upon the fort, with one group advancing at the front, making as much noise as possible, and a second group edging round silently to the rear of the fort. Caught between the two flanks, the Spanish defenders panicked and ran from their positions in a rout that led to the capture of the nearby Fort San Carlos, followed by Fort Amargos. During the following day the last stronghold on the western side of the bay, Corral Castle, was abandoned by the Spanish. Despite the considerable odds against the mission being successful, Cochrane's force had so far lost only seven dead and nineteen wounded.

The eastern forts, in particular Fort Niebla, were still intact, but on the following day Cochrane sent in the *Intrepido* and the *Montezuma*, and—as ever, the master of deceit—brought up the *O'Higgins* to give the impression that new troops were about to land. The Spanish withdrew from the eastern shore of the bay and took off to the town of Valdivia, about fourteen miles up the River Valdivia. The invaders set off upstream in their two ships to assault the town but were met by townspeople with the news that the Spanish governor and his soldiers had fled. Cochrane's force of 250 men had taken Spain's major military base in southern South America, estimated by Maria Graham (1824) at two thousand men, and at a final cost of only twenty-six casualties.

Valdivia was a major turning point in the War of Independence. Cochrane wrote in his *Narrative*, "The annexation of this province [Valdivia], at one blow conferred on Chili complete independence, averting the complicated necessity for fitting out a powerful military expedition for the attainment of that object" (1859, vol. 1). Back in Valparaíso toward the end of February 1820, Cochrane discovered that the Ministry of Marine had assumed that his attack on Valdivia would be defeated and, according to Donald Thomas (2001), had in his absence prepared accusations of his having acted without their authority. The government now announced its congratulations.

But all was not well. Cochrane was keen to get hold of the "prize money"—a natural expectation in early nineteenth century naval warfare. There were promises, and nothing more, so Cochrane resigned on May 14. Nevertheless, to show his commitment to the country, if not to the government, Cochrane bought a hacienda at Herradura, about eight miles from Valparaíso. The O'Higgins government then offered sixty-seven thousand dollars, which was not paid.

Cochrane had another headache—his two rivals for preeminence in the navy, Captains Guise and Spry, were openly in revolt against him. Zenteno, the Minister of Marine, unwisely tried to force Spry on him as the flag-captain in the coming enterprise against the Spanish in Peru. Cochrane's secretary, W. B. Stevenson, wrote that Cochrane simply announced that "Captain Spry should never tread the quarter-deck of the flag-ship as captain of her, so long as he held command of the squadron" (1825, 247). (Maria Graham called Spry "a low-minded man"; he later deserted and became one of San Martín's aides-de-camp). San Martín had to agree with Cochrane, who chose instead Thomas Crosbie as the flag-captain.

Cochrane then had Captain Guise put under arrest for neglect of duty and insubordination, and when the government would not agree to a court-martial, he resigned once again, in July 1820. This whipped up a storm of written support from every one of the squadron captains (except Guise and Spry) and all twenty-three of the officers. As a result, letters came to Cochrane from San Martín and O'Higgins entreating him to reconsider and to fight on for Chile's freedom, and these made him change his mind. (Martin Guise was given a staff appointment by San Martín and, after Cochrane left Chile, he became in 1823 Commander of the Peruvian Navy. He died in 1829 while attacking Guayaquil, and he is honored today as an independence hero in Peru).

The situation now was that Spain was defeated in Chile but still had significant forces in Peru and in principle could strike south and reverse all the recent gains. The strategy decided on was for Cochrane to lead the naval force against Callao and for San Martín to assault Lima on land, using ships as much as possible to leapfrog ahead and hasten their arrival. Once in Peru, Cochrane was infuriated by San Martín's exaggerated caution and procrastination in committing his troops to battle. So, true to form, Cochrane went ahead regardless, and in an action that was as reckless as it was audacious, he managed to cut out the *Esmeralda* in the harbor of Callao and sail her away—the most powerful warship that the Spanish had on the Pacific coast. There followed, for Cochrane, raids along the coast from Callao to Arica, and Lima surrendered after three months of this continual harrying of the Spanish forces.

In Lima, San Martín at last arrived and announced that he was taking over as the Supreme Head of Peru. Cochrane saw this as an act of treachery to Chile and to Bernardo O'Higgins—becoming the ruler of another country while still subject to Chile as commander of the allied forces—and he said so. San Martín's response was to order Cochrane to hand over the Chilean squadron, and Cochrane refused. San Martín said that in that case he would buy the squadron, and failing that, the men would not be paid. There was then a huge row in the Royal Palace in Lima, which San Martín closed by entreating Cochrane to renounce Chile and take up a command in Peru. Cochrane of course would have nothing to do with this offer, and when the pay still had not arrived for his Chilean men, he went after San Martín's yacht, the *Sacramento*, and removed the gold and silver loot the Liberator had acquired in his campaigns. With this he paid off the men but took nothing for himself. (Maria Graham [1824] wrote that Cochrane seized the money from the *Lautaro*.)

Cochrane was back in Valparaíso in June 1822, and by the end of the year had resigned his command in Chile and agreed to a new assignment, that of commanding the Emperor of Brazil's fleet to fight for independence from Portugal. He invited Maria Graham to accompany him, and they left Chile in January 1823 for the Juan Fernández Islands, Cape Horn, and Rio de Janeiro. Following the conflict in Brazil, Cochrane took part as the first Admiral of Greece in that country's war of independence against Turkey.

Sadly, his relations with the new republic in Chile were soured for the rest of his life on account of money he felt he was owed. There was an award of six thousand pounds made by the Chilean government in 1845, but this amount was docked against the claims made by neutrals who insisted on recompense for the damages they received in the course of the conflict. Cochrane complained that his being shortchanged was the new government's way of appeasing the British business community in Valparaíso. His sense of injury was against the government and never against the people of Chile, and he never doubted the principles for which he had fought. When he was leaving Chile in January 1823, Cochrane issued a proclamation (printed by Maria Graham) that concluded,

> Chilenos! You know that independence is purchased at the point of the bayonet. Know also, that liberty is founded on good faith, and on the laws of honour, and that those who infringe upon these, are your only enemies, amongst whom you will never find COCHRANE. (Graham, January 3, 1823)

Today, Cochrane is remembered in Chile with a statue (inaugurated 1873) and the Casa de Lord Cochrane (which he never in fact occupied), both in Valparaíso, and in several street names the length and breadth of the country. There is also a Lake Cochrane and the town of Cochrane in southern Chile. Over time, Chile has also named five ships in his honor as the *Cochrane* or the *Almirante Cochrane*. The first took part in the War of the Pacific; the second was a dreadnought battleship laid down in Britain in 1913, acquired unfinished by the Royal Navy during the First World War, and converted into the carrier HMS *Eagle* in 1918. The most recent is a frigate, formerly

HMS *Norfolk*, commissioned into the Chilean navy in 2006. There is no statue to Cochrane in London—the establishment had been too much offended—but his tomb in Westminster Abbey carries the arms of Chile, Peru, Brazil, and Greece. Nor is there any reminder in Brazil, where his exploits are today almost entirely forgotten.

Cochrane is also remembered in fictionalized accounts of his exploits. C. S. Forrester used Cochrane as the model for his hero Horatio Hornblower, and he can be identified in the books published by Captain Marryat, the midshipman who served under Cochrane. There is also the character of Jack Aubrey in Patrick O'Brian's novels, translated into film in Peter Weir's *Master and Commander* (2003), who is inspired by Lord Cochrane. The episode in the film where Cochrane launches a decoy with lanterns at night to lead his pursuers astray is based on one of Cochrane's exploits.

In the patriot navy, Cochrane had under his command several British captains and officers. The names include captains George O'Brien, Robert Simpson, John Pascoe Grenfell, Martin Guise (described by Maria Graham as "a good-natured gentlemanlike man"), Cochrane's flag captain Thomas Sackville Crosbie, Henry Cobbett (nephew of William Cobbett, the writer, and described by Maria Graham as "polite, intelligent, and communicative"), Admiral James George Bynon, Robert Forster, Cladius Charles, Richard Vawell (who joined Cochrane from Bolívar's Albion battalion in 1822), James Ramsey, James Shepherd, and William Wilkinson (who arrived in Valparaíso in 1818 as first mate on the *Cumberland*, renamed the *San Martín*, which he captained). Grenfell, Crosbie, and Shepherd were among the officers who followed Cochrane to fight for Brazil's independence.

Even before Cochrane became commander-in-chief of the patriot navy, there were already many British names among the top officers. Most of these naval officers were available because they were out of work following Napoleon's defeat at Waterloo and the virtual demobilization of the Royal Navy, and they were targeted by Chilean recruiters. Sources suggest that as many as 90 percent of the commissioned British naval officers at that time were unemployed and on half pay, while the midshipmen had no income at all.

The navy list in 1818—the year that Cochrane arrived in Chile—was dominated by British names, and in 1820 the majority of the estimated fifty officers and 1,600 sailors in the new Chilean Navy were from Britain. For example, Charles Fletcher Hillman (1900) gives the names of the sailors who participated on November 14, 1820 in the key capture of the *Esmeralda* in Callao Bay, and the majority are British.

There had been a previous attempt to take the *Esmeralda*, on April 27, 1818, when George O'Brien was killed leading a boarding party from the *Lautaro*, and for this act of bravery he is remembered as the first naval hero of the Chilean navy. O'Brien was born in Ireland and started a career in the British navy, where he reached the rank of lieutenant but was dismissed for acts of indiscipline. Apparently, he had a quick temper. He arrived in Chile as the pilot of a merchant ship, and by chance he was in Valparaíso when the British squadron and the United States' *Essex* were in the port in 1814. He volunteered for duty on HMS *Phoebe* and participated in the subsequent action against the *Essex*. He then continued in merchant shipping along the coast of Chile. However, his action on board the *Phoebe* had not gone unnoticed, and when in 1818 Chile captured the frigate *Windham*, renamed the *Lautaro*, O'Brien was made captain of this ship.

Spanish ships were blockading Valparaíso, and O'Brien sailed out in the *Lautaro* flying British colors with the order to check on the blockade, but, given his innate impetuousness, he raised the Chilean flag, fired off three salvoes, rammed the *Esmeralda*, and led the boarding party. Major Miller's marines kept up a covering fire, and O'Brien was able to bring down the Spanish flag. The two ships became separated in this combat, leaving O'Brien and a few men alone on the *Esmeralda*. Lieutenant Turner on board the *Lautaro* supposed that the *Esmeralda* was taken, now that there was no Spanish flag flying, and after sending over a boat with eighteen men to reinforce O'Brien, he set off to engage another Spanish ship. But the Spanish on the *Esmeralda* overran the boarders in fierce hand-to-hand fighting, during which O'Brien was one of the first to fall. It is said that while dying he muttered the words: "Never leave her my boys; the ship is ours." The *Esmeralda*, however, escaped to Talcahuano. O'Brien had served the new republic for just twenty-three days.

Another significant figure in the naval conflict was Robert Winthrop Simpson, born in England, in 1799. He probably arrived in Chile as a midshipman with Lord Cochrane on the sloop *Rose*, contracted to fight in the War of Independence. In 1821, he was already a lieutenant in the Chilean navy, and took part in the conflict in Peru, being promoted to captain in October the same year. Cochrane gave Simpson command of the brig *Araucano* and sent him to Acapulco to harass Spanish shipping. While Simpson was on land in California buying provisions, the foreign crew took over the brig and set off for Australia.

Despite this setback, on his return to Chile in 1824, Simpson was given command of the *Voltaire* and helped in the blockade of Chiloé.

In 1825, Simpson took part in the blockade of Callao, under Admiral Encalada, and he continued into 1826 heavily involved in the wars of independence in both Peru and Chile, including the defeat of the royalists on Chiloé Island. In 1826, the Chilean fleet was dispersed, and Simpson took charge first of a Peruvian ship, the *Congreso*, and then a Mexican ship that had the same name. On returning to Chile in 1829, he became the Naval Governor of Coquimbo, and then from 1830 to 1836 he commanded the *Aquiles* and carried out the first hydrographical survey conducted by an officer in the Chilean navy. In 1836, he commanded the *Valparaíso*, flagship of Admiral Encalada, until the declaration of the War of the Confederation in January 1837, when he returned to the command of the *Aquiles*. He operated off the Peruvian coast to disturb trade and captured the *Confederación*, which he then captained.

In January 1839, the Chilean squadron under Simpson's command was attacked by the larger Peruvian-Bolivian privateer fleet under the command of the French sailor Juan Blanchet. This resulted in the Naval Battle of Casma—the only significant naval battle of the war—which Chile won decisively, and was left in dominion over the southeastern Pacific. Simpson was rewarded with the title of commodore in May 1839. Following the dissolution of the confederation at the Battle of Yungay, Simpson returned to Chile with his fleet and, in the years 1840 to 1852, enjoyed a successful career in the Chilean navy, rising twice to become General Commander of the Navy. In 1852, he became naturalized as a Chilean citizen and traveled to Europe to supervise the construction of the *Esmeralda*, becoming its first captain. In 1853, he was promoted to rear admiral and continued his career in the Chilean navy until retiring in 1871. He died in Valparaíso in 1877.

Other British names were prominent in the war at sea. John Pascoe Grenfell was born in Battersea and came to Chile in 1819 to fight with Cochrane, after service in the East India Company. He took part in many of the naval conflicts of the War of Independence, including the cutting out of the *Esmeralda* in Callao harbor, and rose to the rank of lieutenant.

James George Bynon was born in England in 1789, disembarked in Valparaíso in 1818, and took part in Cochrane's first offensive in 1819 against Callao. The following year Bynon was with Cochrane in Valdivia, and later he took part in the liberation of Chiloé from royalist forces. He then retired from the Chilean navy and participated in the War of the Plata Republic against Brazil. On his return to Chile he was involved actively in the War of the Peruvian-Bolivian Confederation, in which he helped capture the *Confederación* and was for a time in charge of the blockade of Callao. After this war, Bynon became Maritime Governor of Valparaíso, then of Concepción, and finally of Atacama. In 1852, he was named interim General Commander of the Navy; in 1860, he became head of the squadron's general staff, and in 1880 he rose to Vice Admiral.

Robert Forster was born in Northumberland and was contracted in England by José Alvarez Condarco to fight in the War of Independence. He served under Cochrane and captained his flagship, the *O'Higgins*. He saw action in the first campaign of 1819 against the Spanish in Peru, where he commanded the *Independencia*, and took part in the second campaign against Callao. Forster left Chile on the demobilization of the navy and rejoined the Royal Navy in 1832.

John Williams was born in South Wales, entered the Chilean navy in 1824, took part in the liberation of Chiloé in 1826, and became the maritime governor of this island. He supported General Ramón Freire Serrano when he rose against the government of Joaquín Prieto Vial and was consequently dismissed from the navy. He returned to duty in 1838, in time to participate in the second campaign of the War of the Peruvian-Bolivian Confederation. In 1843, having taken up duties again as the Maritime Governor of Chiloé, he took the *Ancud* to the Magellan Strait to establish Chile's presence in Patagonia, a feat still celebrated in the naming of Puerto Williams on Tierra del Fuego. Later, John Williams became the Maritime Governor of Talcahuano, in the years 1849 to 1855.

The Chilean Navy was, therefore, modeled from its beginnings on the British Royal Navy, and it still is. Having achieved independence, Chile recognized that with the tremendous length of their coast along the Pacific they would need a strong navy, and they looked to Britain as the pattern to follow. A practice developed whereby Chilean midshipmen served their apprenticeships on British warships.

As we have seen, there were British officers involved in the War of the Peruvian-Bolivian Confederation (1836–1839), but in Chile's naval conflicts later in the nineteenth century, although there were still British names in prominence, they were by now Chilean-born descendants. This was the case in the second war with Spain, the War of the American Union (1864–1867), in which Chile, Peru, Ecuador, and Bolivia joined forces against Spain, and in the War of the Pacific (1879–1883), when Chile took on Peru and Bolivia.

Juan Williams Rebolledo was one of John Williams' three sons, born around 1826. He distinguished himself in the second war against Spain and was designated naval commander at the outset of the War of the Pacific. Other British descendants took part in this war, such as

Carlos Condell, Enrique Simpson Baeza (the Admiral Simpson who served with Arturo Prat on the *Esmeralda*), Manuel Thomson (killed in 1880 while commanding the *Huáscar*), and Patricio Lynch.

Carlos Arnaldo Condell de la Haza was born in Chile in 1843, the son of a Scottish merchant seaman and Manuela de la Haza, of Peruvian descent. Condell took part in the naval battle of Papudo during the war with Spain in the 1860s, and he then joined the captured *Covadonga* under the command of Manuel Thomson. When the War of the Pacific broke out in April 1879, Condell was charged with the blockade of Iquique, and as captain of the *Covadonga* took part in the Naval Battle of Punta Gruesa, which led to the capture of the Peruvian *Independencia*.

Patricio Lynch was born in Santiago in 1824. He descended from an Irish family who came from Galway and settled first in Buenos Aires. (This is the same influential family to which Ernesto "Che" Guevara Lynch belonged.) Patricio Lynch entered the Chilean Military Academy in 1837, and he served in the Royal Navy from 1840 to 1874, when he returned to Chile as a first lieutenant. Following the fall of Iquique in 1879 to Chilean forces in the War of the Pacific, he was appointed *Comandante de Armas* of the city, and soon afterwards he became the political head of Tarapacá. In 1881, the Chilean Senate made him a rear admiral in recognition of his campaign in Peru, and in May that year he became head of the army of occupation in Peru, a post which he held for three years and two months.

The cornerstone of the naval war between Chile and Peru in the War of the Pacific was an armored iron-hull warship called the *Huáscar*, built at the Laird Brothers shipyard in Birkenhead. This warship was state of the art in its day and was equipped with a revolving turret that housed two three-hundred-pounder guns. Before the war with Chile, Peru had commissioned the *Huáscar* for the conflict in the mid 1860s with Spain—the War of the American Union. The *Huáscar* departed for Peru in January 1866, but it had a difficult crossing and arrived after hostilities at sea had ceased.

When the War of the Pacific broke out in 1879, Peru had a seemingly invincible asset in the ironclad *Huáscar*. In May of that year, this warship led the actions that lifted the blockade by the Chileans of the port of Iquique. In an act of supreme valor, the Chilean corvette *Esmeralda* set upon the *Huáscar*, and the Chilean Captain Arturo Prat was killed on the deck of the iron warship while leading a boarding party. The *Esmeralda* was sunk by repeated ramming. The *Huáscar* continued to harass Chilean ports and ships in a series of engagements that saw sixteen Chilean ships sunk and several others captured or damaged. The artillery batteries of Antofagasta were also destroyed. All of this held up the Chilean invasion on land for nearly six months.

In October 1879, the Chilean Navy captured the *Huáscar* in the Battle of Angamos, in a battle in which the first shots were fired by the *Cochrane*, killing the Peruvian Admiral Grau and then disabling the ship. Thereafter the tables were turned in favor of Chile, since Peru was unable to prevent the invasion of its territory. The *Huáscar* became a heritage ship in 1924 and was berthed in Talcahuano, where she remains today. Major renovation work was carried out in 1951 and 1952, and the ship was declared a shrine to the glory of both navies, the Peruvian and Chilean. The *Huáscar* is now a floating museum, and as the last of her class still afloat she is certainly worth visiting.

After achieving independence in 1818, Chile defined its geographical boundaries in very general terms, essentially as comprising the land encompassed by the Atacama Desert, Cape Horn, the Pacific Ocean, and the Andes. Excepting the Chilean province of Mendoza, on the other side of the cordillera, which was handed over in 1776 to the Viceroyalty of Río de la Plata, these boundaries were very similar to the area covered by the captaincy-general of Chile in colonial times. The sometimes unknown and entirely unmarked land borders were no cause for concern for many years, since the frontiers were inhabited by Indians, and there were the natural boundaries of desert to the north, the mountains to the east, and the inhospitable lands of the extreme south.

The first decades of the newly independent state were focused instead on organizing government and dealing with the royalists. When the Constitution was successfully promulgated in 1833, the Chilean government turned to the question of its boundaries and immediately became alarmed by British activity in Tierra del Fuego, especially with the surveying work from Magellan Strait to Chiloé undertaken from 1826 to 1836 by Philip Parker King, Pringle Stokes, and Robert FitzRoy.

Chile's response was to send John Williams in the *Ancud* to establish a strong presence in 1843 at Fuerte Bulnes in the Magellan Strait. Argentina became alarmed at what might be meant by Chile's sudden interest in Patagonia. The frontier between Chile and Argentina was far from clear, but the two countries agreed in a treaty of 1855 on the boundary between them, which essentially provided for the maintenance of the status quo of 1810.

In 1878, with the threat of war with Bolivia and Peru looming in the north, Chile agreed to the terms of the Fierro-Sarratea agreement, by which she essentially abandoned her claims to most of Patagonia, and Argentina carried out a conquest of the region in 1879–1880, moving the Tehuelche Indians into reservations and herding them across the frontier into Chile. The region was then divided between Chile and Argentina by a new treaty, in July 1881, agreed to during the War of the Pacific.

This treaty defined the frontier between the two states as following the main cordillera of the Andes southward to latitude 52 degrees south and included consideration of the boundaries in Patagonia, the Magellan Strait, and Tierra del Fuego. Chile's President Aníbal Pinto wanted to ensure Argentina's neutrality and to avoid any squabble that might also lead to war in the south. So he authorized his envoy, Diego Barros Arana, to make whatever concessions were necessary, and this led to Argentina receiving the Atlantic coast of Patagonia and Chile the Pacific coast.

However, there was disagreement over exactly where the line fell, and a supplemental protocol was drafted in 1893 stating that Argentina was to hold in perpetuity all territory to the east of the line of the highest peaks that divide the waters, with Chile holding all territory to the west. Unfortunately, this accord erroneously equated the main Andes ridge line with the water divide, which is not always the case in high mountain terrain, and a new treaty was negotiated in 1896 to deal with the differences between the two lines. The treaty provided for arbitration by Queen Victoria, and this proved to be the start of a long period during which Britain was involved in arbitration between the two countries. Four sectors were submitted to the consideration of the British Crown's arbitration commission in 1899. The ruling on one of the sectors, 41° 12' 18" South to 48° 53' 10" South, proved particularly difficult, but the commission duly reported and demarcation pillars were set up along the frontier.

Regrettably, the distance between each pillar turned out to be rather long—of special concern were the forty kilometers between pillars 16 and 17—and this led to frequent disputes between the two countries. The two sides agreed to submit once again to British arbitration, and one of the British arbitrators, Sir T. H. Holdich, spent eight months in Patagonia, leading to an award signed by King Edward VII in 1902. One intriguing aspect of the arbitration was that it affected a small, and recently established, settlement of mainly Welsh colonists in the area known originally as Colonia 16 de Octubre and renamed in 1918 as Trevelín, "the place of the mill" in Welsh. Settlers had migrated from Puerto Madryn to the banks of the River Percey and the upper reaches of the Chilean River Futaleufú in 1888, in valleys high in the

Andes, and at a place where the ridge and watershed did not coincide. The British commission enquired of the inhabitants which country they belonged to (there was no formal referendum), and both countries offered land titles. Some 94,000 square kilometers were in dispute. Chile was awarded 54,000, but Argentina kept most of the productive valleys in the region, including the Welsh colony.

The statue of Christ the Redeemer of the Andes was unveiled in March 1904 at the highest point on the old road between Mendoza and Santiago to commemorate the settlement of the long dispute. It is commonly believed to have been cast from the bronze of melted-down cannon used in skirmishes between the two nations, although this claim is doubtful. However, this accord also proved to be contentious, and in 1964 the Chilean government invited the British government to intervene as an arbitrator. The final decision was handed down in 1966 and agreed to by both countries, and this led to twenty-one intermediary pillars being established along the disputed boundary.

There was one final bone of contention—the three islands of Picton, Lennox, and Nueva in the Beagle Channel—which were the source of a recent serious border dispute involving Chile and Argentina. The two countries agreed in 1967 to submit themselves to arbitration by Britain's Queen Elizabeth II, and in May 1977, the judgment given in the name of the Queen ruled that these islands and all adjacent formations belonged to Chile. Argentina refused to accept this ruling, and relations between the two countries worsened almost to the brink of going to war. This was averted by the Act of Montevideo in 1979, which provided for the mediation of Pope John Paul II and culminated in the ratification of a treaty to settle the dispute in May 1985.

Chapter 5

Visitors and Explorers on Land

> *We only took one servant with us, knowing that English servants inevitably prove a nuisance and hindrance in expeditions of the kind, when a great deal of "roughing it" has to be gone through, as they have an unpleasant knack of falling ill at inopportune moments.*
>
> —*Florence Dixie*, Across Patagonia, *1880*

Arguably, the first British travel-writer on Chile was Thomas Falkner. He was born in Manchester in 1707 and studied at Manchester Grammar School before going on to become a surgeon. His health proved to be delicate, and his doctors recommended that he take a sea voyage. This led to his taking a position as a surgeon on board a slave ship that arrived in Buenos Aires in 1731. Once arriving there, Falkner became seriously ill. The Jesuits there nursed him back to health, and he was so overcome by this experience that he converted to Catholicism and became a Jesuit.

In 1734, now as Father Thomas Falkner, he was sent to do missionary work in the immense and largely unexplored lands south of the Rio de la Plata, where he lived for the next thirty-eight years, traveling extensively. When Charles III ordered the expulsion of the Jesuits from South America in 1768, Falkner went back to England (in 1771) and then in 1774 an account of his travels was published entitled *A Description of Patagonia, and the Adjoining Parts of South America*, which was prefaced as "containing an account of the soil, produce, animals, rivers, lakes etc. of those countries; the religion, government policy, customs, dress, arms and language of the Indian inhabitants, and some particulars relating to the Falkland's Island."

This was not Falkner's original text, but the work of others who had access to his papers. The book not only detailed and mapped what he had seen but also recommended that the authorities in England should establish a port and settlement on the coast of Patagonia. Naturally, the Spanish Court took fright, realizing that they had little first-hand knowledge of the region and that the English might occupy territory in the south, as had happened in the Falklands/Malvinas in 1765. The publication coincided too with James Cook's second circumnavigation, which included stopping at Tierra del Fuego. This all made the Spanish take the region more seriously. Following in the tradition that included John Byron, Falkner described the tremendous height of the "Patagonian giants," but he was the last to do so.

Following Falkner, few British visitors came to Chile until the time of the War of Independence early in the next century. Samuel Haigh is an example of the several travelers-cum-businessmen who were attracted, and he added soldiering to his curriculum once he arrived in Chile. Haigh was drawn to Chile in 1817 by the chance to make his fortune since, according to a "rich relation," "great news had just been received from South America, no less than the opening of Chile to foreign trade, in consequence of the victory of Chacabuco, gained by the patriots; that this was the time to make a push for a fortune" (1829, vii). He left England as discretely as he could with a cargo to sell in Chile. His account, *Sketches of Buenos Ayres and Chile*, describes meeting the small British community in Santiago in 1817: "All the English, then in Santiago, did not amount to twelve, and as they were comparatively strangers in this place . . . they associated constantly with each other" (1829, 132). He also met with General San Martín and "was much struck at the appearance of this Hannibal of the Andes . . . He received me with much cordiality, for he is very partial to the English nation" (1829, 133). Traveling on to Valparaíso, Haigh attended a ball at the Governor's home. "The ladies were not such as would be found in first-rate society in Santiago, but as it would have been impossible to have made up a ball without them, a rather extended invitation had been issued" (1829, 178).

Haigh unloaded his cargo from the port, returned to Santiago to sell his products, then journeyed to Mendoza, Buenos Aires, and back to England. Convinced that there was money to be made, he then chartered a brig, the *Enterprise*, "loaded with goods consigned to myself," and sailed round Cape Horn toward Valparaíso. But just when the ship expected to emerge into the Pacific the following day, a great storm blew in from the northwest and it was only twenty-two days later that they saw the land of Diego Ramirez again. He arrived in Valparaíso in December 1820, 135 days after leaving England. Haigh found more evidence of British immigrants, including one who had put up an ambiguous sign reading: "*Acomodación*: Good beds for a gentleman and his horse" (1829, 309).

Also encouraged by the opening up of Chile to international trade, Alexander Caldcleugh arrived in Chile in 1821 and traveled extensively throughout the country, commenting on the commercial prospects. His observation on Chilean wine stands out: "The grape has always been cultivated with success, but the wine is of indifferent quality. That kind which is made near Conception [*sic*], and called 'vino de penco,' is considered the best" (*Travels in South America*, vol. 1, 349).

Caldcleugh was living in Santiago in 1835 and met Charles Darwin prior to his overland expedition from Santiago to Mendoza. Caldcleugh observed the same earthquake as Darwin, and in 1836 he published in the *Philosophical Transactions of the Royal Society of London* "*An Account of the Great Earthquake Experienced in Chile on the 20th of February 1835; With a Map.*" His paper begins by musing on the reported links between earthquakes and observable phenomena, many of which he concludes are "fancied signs," so that while some "place great confidence in rats running violently over the ceilings of the room, others prepare for a shock when they observe the stars twinkling more than usual, and all fears are removed when much lightning coruscates in the Cordillera" (1836, 21). His own observation was that large flocks of birds were seen to fly from the coast toward the Andes a few hours before the earthquake hit.

The most famous British traveler-writer on Chile, Maria Graham, also arrived during the closing stages of the War of Independence and also experienced a devastating earthquake. Maria Graham was born near Cockermouth, in Cumberland (now Cumbria), as Mary Dundas in 1785. Maria was adopted as a kind of literary pen name. Maria was proud of belonging to a Scottish family of long lineage, the Dundas clan. Her father, George Dundas, spent a career in the Royal Navy that led up to his appointment as Commissioner of the Navy in Bombay. George took Maria with him to his new assignment, and on the long voyage in 1809, Maria met and fell in love with a young Scottish naval officer named Thomas Graham. They got married in India, and on their return to England in 1811, Maria published her first book, *Journal of a Residence in India*.

In 1821, Maria received an invitation to accompany her husband on the frigate he commanded, HMS *Doris*, which was sent to Chile with the aim of giving protection to British trade interests in that region. Soon after rounding Cape Horn, however, in April 1822, Thomas Graham died of a fever on board ship. Maria was naturally distraught when the ship docked in Valparaíso with the flag at half mast, but she decided to defy the conventional expectation that she return to Britain on the next available ship and instead determined to stay on in the port. Her published *Journal of a Residence in Chile* (1824) begins, "His Majesty's ship *Doris*, Valparaiso harbour, Sunday night, April 28th, 1822. Many days have passed, and I have been unable and unwilling to resume my journal. To-day, the newness of the place, and all the other circumstances of our arrival, have drawn my thoughts to take some interest in the things around me. I can conceive nothing more glorious than the sight of the Andes this morning on approaching the land at day-break."

That she decided to stay in Chile was remarkable, since, in her own words, she was "a widow, unprotected, and in a foreign land; separated from all my natural friends by distant and dangerous ways, whether I return by sea or land!" (May 20, 1822).

Maria Graham rented a small cottage in Valparaíso. "I took possession of my cottage at Valparaiso; and felt indescribable relief in being quiet and alone"; "My house is one of the better kind of really Chilean cottages" (May 9, 1822). She spent the next nine months living among Chileans in a period which coincided with civil war and an earthquake. Royalists still held out on the island of Chiloé, and while she was in Chile General Freire marched northwards from Concepción to threaten Bernardo O'Higgins in Santiago.

She wrote articulately, and with wide-ranging intellectual curiosity, about everything she saw and experienced, while shunning the British community. She wrote in her *Journal*, "There is a sad proportion in the English society here of trash" (June 19, 1822), adding later, "I say nothing of the English here, because I do not know them except as very civil vulgar people, with one or two exceptions" (September 5, 1822). While she was in Valparaíso there occurred one of Chile's worst tremors on record, on November 19, 1822. Her immediate problem was that she had to pack up and leave her cottage "because my house is let over my head to some persons who, seeing how well it has stood, have bribed the landlord to let it to them. *They are English!*" (November 25, 1822. Italics in the original). She moved to Quintero, thirty miles from Valparaíso.

Maria Graham was the first to provide a written account of the effects on the landscape of an earthquake in her *Journal*, published in 1824: "Never shall I forget the horrible sensation of that night. In all other convulsions of nature we feel or fancy that some exertion may be made to avert or mitigate danger; but from an earthquake there is neither shelter nor escape" (November 20, 1822). Aftershocks continued to the end of December, always inducing "that utter helplessness which is so appalling" (November 21, 1822).

Of lasting significance are the observations she made about the land having risen: "The whole shore [of Valparaíso] is more exposed, and the rocks are four feet higher out of the water than before" (November 22, 1822). The shore near Quintero "is raised about four feet," exposing mussel-beds which were now dry, and: "Above these recent shells, beds of older ones may be traced at various heights along the shore; and such are found near the summits of some of the loftiest hills in Chile, nay, I have heard, among the Andes themselves" (December 9, 1822).

Her observations were summarized in the *Transactions of the Geological Society of London* in 1824, and this was the first publication by a woman in this journal. The article contributed to the polemical debate about geology that came to boiling point in the 1830s. Science was then caught between two conflicting views on the link between earthquakes and the process of mountain building. She had seen for herself that large areas of land had risen from the sea and had come to the conclusion that "the coast had been raised by earthquakes at former periods in a similar manner," as shown by "several ancient lines of beach, consisting of shingle mixed with shells, extending in a parallel direction to the shore, to the height of 50 feet above the sea" (*Transactions* 1824, 413–15).

The geologist Charles Lyell—soon to be so influential on Charles Darwin—included Graham's observations in his work *Principles of Geology* published in 1830, and mentioned her name in the text. This was too much for the President of the Geological Society in Britain, George Bellas Greenough, who resolved to attack Lyell's notions on geology, but instead of confronting Lyell head-on, he instead publicly made ridicule of Maria Graham's observations (in 1834).

Greenough was especially dismissive of her contention that the land had risen. How could a nongeologist have any credence in understanding the complex forces of geology? This must be a deliberate lie. It is said that Maria's husband and her brother offered to challenge Greenough to a duel, but Maria was made of sterner stuff and, according to her nephew, John Callcott Horsley, she responded by saying: "Be quiet, both of you, I am quite capable of fighting my own battles, and intend to do it." Her answer was to publish a crushing reply to Greenough, entitled *On the Reality of the Rise of the Coast of Chili* (1835). Maria Graham's views were not long afterwards corroborated by Charles Darwin, who observed for himself the same phenomenon in 1835 on visiting Talcahuano and Concepción after the earthquake of that year.

Maria Graham remarried in 1827, to Augustus Wall Callcott, and when he was knighted in 1837, Maria became Lady Callcott. She contracted tuberculosis, and the last eleven years of her life were spent as an invalid. She died in 1842, at the age of fifty-seven. Maria Graham remained the only woman to visit and write about Chile in the period of the independence conflicts. She was way ahead of her time, since women travelers began to appear only half a century later; in the case of Chile, with the formidable Annie Brassey (1876) and Lady Florence Dixie (1878). Maria Graham also wrote by far the most detailed, comprehensive, and accurate account of the customs and politics of the new nation. Her *Journal* has been translated into Spanish, and, in recognition of her contributions, the Chilean government paid for the restoration of the Callcotts' grave in London's Kensal Green Cemetery. In a ceremony that took place on September 4, 2008, the Chilean Ambassador, Rafael Moreno, unveiled a commemorate plaque that praises Maria Graham as "a friend of the nation of Chile."

In the same year that Maria Graham arrived in Valparaíso, Gilbert Farquhar Mathison also paid a visit and wrote up his observations in his *Narrative of a Visit to Brazil, Chile, Peru and the Sandwich Islands during the years 1821 and 1822*, published in 1825. Mathison estimated the population of Valparaíso at around five thousand: "English and Americans . . . appeared to constitute the bulk of the population of the town; and so many naval officers, mates of merchantmen, sailors, and men of business, were every where seen, that, but for the mean and dirty appearance of the place, a stranger might almost fancy himself arrived at a British settlement" (1825, 176).

Mathison went on to Santiago on horseback and was able to make comparisons. Santiago impressed him by "the tranquility and absence of all bustle during the busiest hours of the day, which makes it seem more like a provincial town than the capital of a large State. The port of Valparayso is, in fact, the place where all foreign business is transacted" (1825, 195).

Later in the century, another intrepid British traveler named George Chaworth Musters achieved the first nonindigenous complete crossing of Patagonia from south to north. Musters was born in Naples of English parents in 1841. He followed a career in the Royal Navy and later became a member of the Royal Geographical Society. After trying his hand at sheep-rearing in Uruguay, Musters arrived in the Falklands in 1869 and decided to explore continental Patagonia.

Starting in Punta Arenas, he traveled to Isla Pavón, where he joined a group of Tehuelche Indians. They journeyed mainly along the eastern edge of the Andes and arrived in Carmen de Patagones (today in the south of the Province of Buenos Aires) after just over a year, having covered 2,750 kilometers. His book *At home with the Patagonians* was published in London in 1871 and has recently been reprinted. There are two appendices to his book; the first is a glossary of words and expressions in the Tehuelche language, and the second is a discussion of the stories surrounding whether the Patagonian Indians were giants. His conclusion was that they were taller than most Indians, but not giants. At that time, the Tehuelches were already on their way to extinction, and Musters estimated that there were only about 1,500 natives left in the several nomadic groups. Lake Musters exists today, on the Argentinean side of Patagonia—one of the two large lakes in the Patagonian interior.

A British traveler to Chile in the more recognizable mould of a modern tourist was Annie Brassey, whose account, *A Voyage in the* Sunbeam, was published in 1878. The *Sunbeam* (a steamship) left England in July 1876, and in October the passengers were taking in the geographical wonders of Patagonia. Annie Brassey noted in her journal after docking in Punta Arenas, "We went to see three Fuegian females, who are living in a house belonging to the medical officer of the colony. Their skin is slightly copper-coloured, their complexions high-coloured, their hair thick and black; and, though certainly not handsome, they are by no means so repulsive as I had expected from the descriptions of Cook, Dampier, Darwin, and other more recent travellers" (1878, 126).

The group invited Dr. Fenton to dinner, and prodded him with questions about the "Patagonians" or "Horse Indians," and the "Fuegians" or "Canoe Indians." Her summary of the evening's conversation is worth quoting at length:

> The former inhabit, or rather roam over, a vast tract of country. They are almost constantly on horseback, and their only shelter consists of toldos, or tents, made of the skins of the old guanacos, stretched across a few poles. They are tall and strong, averaging six feet in height, and are bulky in proportion; but their size is nothing like so great as old travellers have represented. The Fuegians, or Canoe Indians, as they are generally called, from their living so much on the water, and having no settled habitations on shore, are a much smaller race of savages, inhabiting Tierra del Fuego—literally Land of Fire—so called from the custom the inhabitants have of lighting fires on prominent points as signals of assembly. The English residents here invariably call it Fireland—a name I had never heard before, and which rather puzzled me at first. Whenever it is observed that a ship is in distress, or that shipwrecked mariners have been cast ashore, the signal-fires appear as if by magic, and the natives flock together like vultures round a carcase. (1878, 130–32)

Charles Darwin's prejudicial comments on the Fuegians leap out of her description—"They are cannibals, and are placed by Darwin in the lowest scale of humanity" (1878, 132). Still on the subject of the natives of Tierra del Fuego, Brassey continues, "An old author describes them as 'magpies in chatter, baboons in countenance, and imps in treachery.' Those frequenting the eastern end of the Straits wear—if they wear anything at all—a deerskin mantle, descending to the waist: those at the western end wear cloaks made from the skin of the sea-otter. But most of them are quite naked. Their food is of the most meagre description, and consists mainly of shell-fish, sea-eggs, for which the women dive with much dexterity, and fish, which they train their dogs to assist them in catching" (1878, 132).

In the following year, 1877, Julius Beerbohm came to Patagonia and published two years later a book entitled *Wanderings in Patagonia, or, Life among the Ostrich-Hunters*. Beerbohm had worked in Argentinean Patagonia as an engineer prospecting for coal and other minerals, and when his mission finished, he decided to cross the pampa to Punta Arenas and then board the first steamer going to Europe to arrive there. He set off from Buenos Aires in August 1877, crossed Patagonia, and came out at Punta Arenas, which he called Sandy Point. On this journey, he joined up with a small group of gaucho hunters who spent their lives hunting rheas (the "ostriches" in the book title) and guanacos.

He met with the native Indians of the Patagonian pampas and formed a positive impression:

> The Tehuelches are divided into two tribes, the Northern and the Southern. The Northerners are the least numerous, but on the other hand, they have the advantage of being less "civilised" than their Southern kindred, who, being frequently in contact with the settlers of Sandy Point, have assimilated not a few of the pleasant vices of "los Christianos," as all white men are called by them. . . . I must say that in general intelligence, gentleness of temper, chastity of conduct, and conscientious behaviour in their social and domestic relations, they are immeasurably superior not only to the other South American indigenous tribes, but also, all their disadvantages being taken into consideration, to the general run of civilised white men. (1879, 89–90)

On his way, he became separated from his companions, except one, and finally arrived in November 1877 at Punta Arenas completely exhausted and stumbled into a mutiny by the convicts and the soldiers, the Motín de los Artilleros.

Two years later, Julius Beerbohm was back in Tierra del Fuego, having accepted an invitation to join an expedition as an "expert" and to provide illustrations for the eventual publication of the account. This "party" was led by Lady Florence Dixie, a formidable woman in the Annie Brassey mould. She was the only woman in a very aristocratic group that included Lord Queensberry; Lord James Douglas; her titled husband, Sir Alexander Beaumont Churchill, eleventh Baronet Dixie; and Julius Beerbohm, whose book had just been published when they departed from England.

Florence Dixie's history is very interesting. She was born as Florence Douglas in London in 1855. Her father was Archibald Douglas, seventh Marquis of Queensbury. He accidentally shot himself when Florence was three years old, as he was cleaning his gun, although this may have been suicide. His wife, Caroline, wanted to change her religion after her husband's death, to Catholicism, but his family refused to accept this, and so she packed up and moved to France with her children. These headstrong ways were apparently passed on to her daughter Florence. Florence had a twin brother named James, and an elder brother named Francis, who died in a climbing accident when she was eight. Distraught once again, Florence's mother dragged the family from country to country in Europe. Almost certainly this fostered in Florence the restlessness (and love of travel) that blossomed in adulthood. In 1875, Florence married Alexander Dixie, and in December 1878, the couple left Liverpool on board the *Britannia* set on exploring Patagonia for six months.

In her best-selling book *Across Patagonia* (1880), Florence Dixie explains the motivation behind the expedition: "Precisely because it was an outlandish place and so far away, I chose it. Palled for the moment with civilisation and its surroundings, I wanted to escape somewhere, where I might be as far removed from them as possible" (1880, 2). The published narrative shows that most of their time in Patagonia was spent hunting, but in the interludes between shooting guanaco there are insightful descriptions. For example, she describes the geography seen as they journeyed through the Magellan Strait:

> After passing the Second Narrows, Elizabeth Island, so named by Sir Francis Drake, came in sight. Its shores were covered with wild-fowl and sea-birds, chiefly shag. Flocks of these birds kept flying round the ship, and the water itself, through which we passed, literally teemed with gulls and every imaginable kind of sea-fowl. We were soon abreast of Cape Negro, about fourteen miles from Sandy Point. Here the character of the country suddenly changes, for Cape Negro is the point of

the last southerly spur of the Cordilleras, which runs along the coast, joining the main ridge beyond Sandy Point. All these spurs, like the Cordilleras themselves, are clothed with beech forests and thick underwood of the magnolia species, a vegetation, however, which ends as abruptly as the spurs, from the thickly-wooded sides of which, to the completely bare plains, there is no graduation whatever. (1880, 30)

Florence Dixie was excited when canoes with Fuegian Indians paddled out to meet their ship. Unfortunately, she persisted in the myth of the natives' cannibal ways—"They are reputed to be cannibals, and no doubt justly so. I have even been told that in winter, when other food is scarce, they kill off their own old men and women," and she adds a novel detail, "though of course they prefer a white man if obtainable" (1880, 30).

Florence Dixie was taken by the general appearance of the "pure bred" Tehuelches and provided a detailed description of their clothing and manners.

> They have naturally little hair on the face, and such growth as may appear is carefully eradicated, a painful operation, which many extend even to their eyebrows. Their dress is simple, and consists of a "chiripa," a piece of cloth round the loins, and the indispensable guanaco capa, which is hung loosely over the shoulders and held round the body by the hand, though it would obviously seem more convenient to have it secured round the waist with a belt of some kind. Their horse-hide boots are only worn, for reasons of economy, when hunting. The women dress like the men except as regards the chiripa, instead of which they wear a loose kind of gown beneath the capa, which they fasten at the neck with a silver brooch or pin. (1880, 67)

This account is important because, tragically, Florence Dixie was among the last Europeans to see the Tehuelches exhibit their natural lifestyle and culture. She noted that they were well on their way to extinction as a race and that there were only around eight hundred of these nomads alive at the time of her visit. This soon became rather more a matter of genocide, following the introduction of sheep-farming in the 1880s, not long after her visit. The Tehuelches (and Fuegians) found the flocks of sheep very much to their taste, and they were easier to hunt than the traditional guanaco and rhea. This brought them into conflict with the farmers, and there was a deliberate "ethnic cleansing" of natives in the immense grazing lands of Patagonia from the mid 1890s.

Florence Dixie tells a wonderful story of the experience of camping out on a hunting expedition into the pampa and being overtaken by a group of Tehuelches. The first to arrive was an Indian woman, followed some fifteen minutes later by two men who

> came crashing unceremoniously through the bushes; and wheeling their horses about the camp, careless of our crockery, after a short examination they dismounted, and coolly sat down by our fire, answering our angry looks with imperturbed stares of stolid indifference. Five minutes later another party arrived, followed shortly by a further batch, and presently we were quite inundated by a swarm of these unbidden guests. Of course our work was stopped, all our attention being required to look after our goods and chattels. Over these we kept guard in no very good humour, breathing fervent prayers the while for speedy relief from our friends, who on their part evinced no particular hurry to go away. They had made themselves comfortable at our fire, and were passing round the social pipe in evident good humour with themselves and their present quarters. To complete the irony of the situation, one of their number who could speak Spanish came and asked me for a little coffee, which he purposed to cook in our kettle, which was still simmering conveniently on the fire. As may be imagined, he met with an indignant refusal; however, it only appeared to amuse him and his friends, and by no means influenced them in hastening their departure. Meanwhile time went on, and some expedient for getting rid of them had to be devised unless we wished to lose a whole day. It occurred to us that they might possibly be bribed to go away by means of a small offering of whisky; and through Gregorio we accordingly intimated to them that if they would leave us they should be rewarded for their kindness with a glass of that spirit. To our relief they accepted this offer, and we presently had the satisfaction of seeing them ride leisurely away. To do them justice, I must say that, contrary to our fears, they did not steal any of our effects, though possibly the strict watch we kept over them may have had something to do with this unusual display of honesty. (1880, 82–83)

It is somewhat uncanny that so many British visitors to Chile experienced severe earthquakes during their stay, and Florence Dixie was no exception. In chapter 9 of her narrative, she describes the sensation of an earthquake that struck while the group was in the pampa: "A loud rumbling sound rose on the air; and, before I had time to wonder what it could mean, a heaving of the ground, resembling a sea-swell, sent me flying on my back, and, as by magic, the silent camp became alive with shouts of fear and wonder, as everybody rushed out of the tents in dismay. The shocks occurred again and again, but each time weaker, and in about five minutes they had ceased altogether, but it was some time before we recovered our equanimity" (1880, 102).

When they got back to Punta Arenas (which Dixie called Sandy Point) they discovered that the earthquake had caused considerable damage to the settlement. "As may be imagined, the earthquake provided us with matter for conversation for some time, and in that respect, at least, was a not unwelcome occurrence" (1880, 103).

The last notable British visitor to Chile in the nineteenth century was the veteran *Times* journalist William Howard Russell. He came in 1889 at the invitation of the "Nitrate King," John Thomas North, and wrote up his observations as *A Visit to Chile and the Nitrate Fields of Tarapacá*, published the following year. Colonel North and his entourage sailed from England on the SS *Galicia* of the Pacific Steamship Navigation Company and arrived at the port of Coronel in Chile in March 1889. Russell came down with a bad cold while in Coronel, and from the cabin where he was confined he formed his first impressions of Chile: "I am obliged to confess that they were not favourable. There was no 'atmosphere', no limpid light on the mountain front, no play of shade and colour on the plain" (1890, 44).

Just the features that another group of British visitors to Chile—artists—found very much to their liking.

Chapter 6

British Artists in Chile

And behold, just over my head, a great group of the noble flowers, standing out like ghosts at first, then gradually coming out with their full beauty of colour and form in every stage of growth; while beyond them glittered a snow-peak far away.

—Marianne North

Marianne North (1830–1890) visited Chile in 1884, despite suffering from ill health, in what turned out to be her last great journey overseas. She was keen to paint the monkey-puzzle tree in its natural environment and the blue paya flowers in the Chilean Andes. The scene of suddenly coming across the flowers is captured in a painting that now hangs in the Marianne North Gallery at the Royal Botanic Gardens as part of the collection of 832 of her paintings, which represent over nine hundred plant species, including one genus and four species named in her honor.

There are two other outstanding British names in the history of art in Chile. The first is Charles Chatworthy Wood (1792–1856). Ricardo Bindis Fuller, in his study of Chilean painting (1984), describes him as the first artist of importance among the Europeans in Chile. Charles Wood was born in Liverpool in 1792, and Bindis Fuller believes that certain difficulties with his taxes made him emigrate to the United States in 1817. He went to work in Boston as a landscape painter, and later he was contracted by the American government to join a scientific expedition as an artist.

In this capacity, Wood arrived in Chile in 1819 on board the American frigate *Caledonia* (or *Macedonia*, according to one source). Bindis Fuller says that Captain Downes invited San Martín, the Argentinean liberator, and his general staff to a ball on board the frigate and that the ballroom was adorned with paintings by Charles

Wood. San Martín said that he would like to meet the artist, and it is possible that he was presented by Captain William Miller. Having met the artist, San Martín offered Wood a post in the patriot army, which he was compelled to decline because of his commitments to the American expedition.

Still according to Bindis Fuller, Charles Wood was back in Chile in mid-1820 and had thought more about the offer. James Paroissien, an English officer with San Martín's forces, broached the subject again, and this time Wood accepted, becoming an artillery lieutenant in August 1820. He joined the patriot navy on board the *San Martín* and set about making strategic drawings of the places where the navy would expect to face action. He was on hand in November 1820 in Callao, Peru, to witness the taking of the *Esmeralda* of the Spanish navy, which inspired him to paint *La Toma de la Esmeralda*.

Wood participated in the later campaigns of the War of Independence, and was appointed an engineer in the army. It is not clear what prompted Wood to stay on in Chile after the war was over, but we know that he became in 1830 the first teacher of drawing at the Instituto Nacional, and that he designed the Chilean coat of arms, still in use today, and the stamp of the gold coins—the *onza* and the *cóndor*. Bernardo O'Higgins and the Senate had designed a coat of arms in 1819 that needed replacing; for one thing, the country no longer consisted of just three provinces.

In 1832, President Joaquín Prieto invited a group of Chilean artists to a meeting at which the model proposed by Charles Wood was approved. The President signed off the new design, and a new law was sent to Congress, which gave its sanction in June 1834. The new design incorporated several new features, including the figures of a *huemul* (a Chilean deer-like animal) and a condor on either side of the shield, both set with "a naval crown of gold." The crowns carried echoes of monarchy, and they were polemical for a while.

Wood's original sketch was unfortunately lost in a fire, and anyway it proved difficult to standardize the new design. There was not then the printing technology to disseminate the coat of arms, and there was also the fact that the *huemul* was largely unknown to most Chileans. Wood's drawing of this animal had been made, apparently, based on a description written down some fifty years previously. This led to a number of different interpretations, and in 1918, the Chilean Army General Staff conducted a full review that led to agreement on the definitive design, which now incorporated the phrase *Por la razón o la fuerza* ('By reason or by force') in homage to Bernardo O'Higgins.

Charles Wood also worked later as an engineer on Chile's first railway line from Caldera to Copiapó, constructed between 1849 and 1851, and in Valparaíso he worked as an engineer and also produced topographical maps of the port in collaboration with John Searle. Wood clearly developed a love for Chile, and married a Chilean lady, Dolores Ramírez de Arellano. They had two children, Carlos and Jorge, both of whom served in the Chilean army and saw action in the War of the Pacific.

Charles Wood excelled at drawing, and he was an accomplished watercolor artist, a talent that he passed on to his son Jorge. His only known work in oils is the *Naufragio del Arethusa* (the *Shipwreck of the Arethusa*), painted in 1826, which shows with great drama and accuracy the sinking of this ship off the coast of Valparaíso. This painting is perhaps his best-known work and is found today in Santiago's Museo Nacional de Bellas Artes, along with his pencil drawings *Castillo de San Antonio* (1846), *Buques en Valparaíso* (1847), and his pencil and watercolor *Carenando buques* (1848).

Antonio Romera (1976) classifies Wood's work into two groups. The first group is of paintings that describe the customs of the places he saw. His watercolor *Vista panorámica de la ciudad de Santiago* is perhaps the most characteristic of this category, where we see in the foreground the details of a colonial soldier and a dog. Another painting that belongs to this group is *Tajamar del río Mapocho*. The second group, according to Romera's study, *History of Chilean Painting*, consists of his narrative works, such as *Marcha del ejército de Chile*, *La toma de la Esmeralda*, *Niebla en Valparaíso* (1832), *El faro de Eddystone* (Eddystone Lighthouse: 1833), and *Mañana* (1841)—paintings that are reminiscent of Turner's style.

Unlike other foreign artists who took up residence in Chile, Wood did not form disciples, presumably on account of the variety of his activities and his apparently restless nature. He lived in Chile until 1852 and died in London in 1856.

The other outstanding British artist who lived in Chile was Thomas Jacques Somerscales (1842–1927). Somerscales was born in Kingston-upon-Hull, the son of a shipmaster. He was educated at Christ Church School until he was thirteen and then studied education at the Cheltenham College in Gloucestershire. In 1863, he joined the Royal Navy as a naval instructor on the training ship *Cumberland*, teaching mathematics, geography, and drawing, and over the following five years he continued with this teaching on four other Royal Navy ships, traveling the world, including a three-month visit to Valparaíso in 1864. In 1869, he caught malaria while he was visiting Panama on HMS *Zealous* and came down with a bad fever. The Admiral agreed to his being landed at Valparaíso to recuperate. However, his illness was so severe that the doctors recommended that he not return to the tropics, and he left the Royal Navy.

Somerscales was contracted as a teacher of drawing and calligraphy at the Valparaíso "Artizans School," which had opened in 1857. He lived in the school building on Cerro Concepción until 1877, when disagreements over the role of religion in the school led to his resignation and that of the head teacher and his assistant—Peter Mackay and George Sutherland—who all left to start a new school, the Mackay and Sutherland School.

When he was young, Somerscales had often sketched but had no formal training as an artist. Once in Chile he started to paint landscapes of the countryside around Valparaíso. Three of these landscapes were displayed at the 1872 National Exhibition in Santiago, where Somerscales won a silver medal. In 1874, he took a view of Valparaíso to a similar exhibition in Santiago. He also got married in this year, to Jane Trumble Harper.

A turning point came in 1875 when he witnessed a storm in the bay of Valparaíso and the struggle over several hours of the captain of the corvette *Esmeralda* to save his ship. This must have had a big impact on him, for he now devoted himself as an artist almost exclusively to marine art. The War of the Pacific broke out in 1879, and a number of Somerscales' paintings of the Chilean naval engagements with Peru became very popular. Later on, he took up painting scenes of merchant shipping, mainly off the coast of South America, as well as landscapes, which include views of Valparaíso, Santiago, Chillán, Lota, and the Aconcagua Valley.

From around 1884, Somerscales took part in national competitions in Chile and gave classes in his workshop, which later became known as the "Somerscales School." Several of the young Chilean artists who studied with him became famous later, such as Alfredo Helsby (1862–1933), who painted Chilean landscapes and has works in the Museo Nacional de Bellas Artes in Santiago, and Álvaro Casanova Zenteno and Manuel Aspillaga. Alfredo Helsby is considered to be one of Chile's greatest painters and was the son of British-born William Helsby, the pioneer of Chilean photography.

Thomas Somerscales' daughter Alice died in 1890, which led to tensions within the family. His eldest sons were coming up to university age, and Somerscales was thinking of his mother, who had never met the children or his wife. So, at the age of fifty, and after thirty years away from England, he decided to return home. It seems that he took up work as a teacher in Manchester. The following year he exhibited his first painting at the Royal Academy, where it was awarded a medal. In 1898, he painted one of his most famous and popular paintings, *Off Valparaíso*, which was shown in 1899 at the Royal Academy and purchased for the Tate Gallery. In all, he exhibited twenty-eight paintings at the Royal Academy over the years. In 1911, the Chilean Congress commissioned a painting from Somerscales that relates to the first national squadron of Chile, where it remains today.

Somerscales regarded Chile as his second home and came back four times, in 1903, 1907, 1909 and 1912, returning to England with his family for the last time in 1915. His house in Cerro Alegre in Valparaíso has now been converted into a hotel, the Hotel Thomas Somerscales. He died in Hull in 1927. His work amounts to around six hundred paintings, which can be found in several galleries—the Tate Gallery, the National Maritime Museum at Greenwich (two works), the Ferens Art Gallery in Hull (four works), and the Museo Nacional de Bellas Artes in Santiago.

His paintings include:

- *Combate naval de Iquique*, oil on canvas, on display in the *Museo Nacional de Bellas Artes* in Santiago;
- *Zarpe de la primera escuadra libertadora*, which is found in the Congress building in Santiago;
- *Muerte de Prat*, in the *Pinacoteca de la Armada de Chile*;
- *Hundimiento de la Esmeralda*, in the *Pinacoteca de la Armada de Chile*;
- *Combate naval de Punta Gruesa*, in the *Club Naval de Valparaíso*;
- *Combate naval de Angamos* (1889), in the *Museo Histórico Nacional* (on loan from the Museo Nacional de Bellas Artes);
- *Off Valparaíso* (1899), at the Tate Gallery in London;
- *A Barque Running Before a Gale* (1910), in the National Maritime Museum, Greenwich;
- *Sinking of the* Scharnhorst *at the Battle of the Falkland Islands, December 8, 1914.* (ca. 1915), in the National Maritime Museum, Greenwich;

Other British artists who were inspired by Chile include those who accompanied explorers and visitors. Augustus Earle was the artist on the second voyage of the *Beagle*. He left the expedition in late 1833, due to ill health, and was replaced by Conrad Martens as the ship's artist. Martens was discovered in Montevideo and left the *Beagle* in 1835 to travel and finally to settle in Australia. The first lieutenant of the *Beagle*, John Clements Wickham, was also a talented artist, and his sketch of Concepción in ruins after the 1835 earthquake was published in FitzRoy's *Narrative*. Other narratives of travel in Chile have sketches to bring to life the events and observations. Florence Dixie's *Across Patagonia*, for example, was illustrated by her companion and fellow-traveler, Julius Beerbohm. Maria Graham included sketches of Chile in her *Journal*, published in 1824, and also painted scenes encountered on her journeys into the countryside in watercolor and oil. Colonel John Thomas North took with him to Chile in 1889 two journalists, including William Howard Russell, and a celebrated artist from *The Illustrated London News* named Melton Prior (1845–1910). Melton Prior provided sketches for Russell's book *A Visit to Chile and the Nitrate Fields of Tarapacá* (1890), and several were published from August 1889 in *The Illustrated London News* and were seen by readers all over the world.

John Searle (1783–1837) was born on the Isle of Wight and visited Valparaíso for the first time in 1822 on a voyage to India. He returned to Chile in 1830, possibly when the ship he was traveling on was shipwrecked off the coast, and settled down in Valparaíso, where he took up painting as a means to make ends meet. Searle became a friend of Charles Wood, with whom he carried out studies of the topography of the region. He was talented in drawing and watercolor and is known for his paintings of the old port of Valparaíso. He has left descendants to this day in Chile. These include Edmundo Searle Lorca who, under the name Mundo Searle, is remembered as one of Chile's best cartoonists; and two painters—Edmundo's daughter Perla Searle Artaza and his grand-daughter Angela Wilson Searle.

While James Whistler (1834–1903) was born in the United States, he spent most of his adult life in England and France. His painting entitled *Nocturne in Blue and Gold: Valparaíso Bay* is justly famous and was inspired when Whistler visited Chile during the 1866 war against Spain. Sources also mention Henry Swinburn (1859–1929), the Santiago-born son of Charles Swinburn, an immigrant from Liverpool, and Dorotea Kirk Echazarreta. Henry (Enrique) Swinburn was Benjamín Vicuña Mackenna's private secretary, and in this capacity he helped organize the first Exposición de Bellas Artes in 1880. He is best known as a painter of landscapes, especially in the Valley of Santiago. There is mention too of work by William Walton, a portrait artist at the close of the nineteenth century in Valparaíso.

In photography, an Englishman named William Glaskell Helsby introduced the daguerreotype, and the first commercial use of photography, into Chile. In 1846, just seven years after its invention by

Louis Daguerre, Helsby was already offering daguerreotype portraits in a studio in Valparaíso. His brother, Thomas Columbus Helsby, joined him in 1853, after three years' pioneering experience with photography in Buenos Aires, where his studio was considered the best in the city. A third brother, John Stephens Helsby, arrived in 1854 and took charge of the gallery that William opened in Santiago. While the Helsby name lived on in Chile, most notably in his son, the painter Alfredo Helsby, it seems that William Helsby left Chile around 1860 never to return.

Finally, Bernardo O'Higgins had a talent for painting that is not well known. There are two watercolors by O'Higgins in the Museo del Carmen de Maipú in Chile: a self-portrait of 1822–1823, and a miniature portrait of his half-sister, Rosa Rodríguez Riquelme (Rosa O'Higgins). Two other watercolors, dating from 1823–1824, can be seen in Lima, in the Museo Nacional de Antropología, Arqueología e Historia del Perú. One is entitled *El Batallón Numancia recibe la bandera del Ejército Libertador al momento de pasar el puente de Huara* (*The Numancia Battalion receives the flag of the Liberation Army while crossing Huara Bridge*), and the second is of the same Battalion swearing an oath of allegiance to the flag.

Chapter 7

British Communities in Chile

English tailors, shoemakers, saddlers, and inn-keepers, hang out their signs in every street; and the preponderance of the English language over every other spoken in the chief streets, would make one fancy Valparaiso a coast town in Britain.

—Maria Graham, Journal of a
Residence in Chile, *May 23, 1822*

Bernardo O'Higgins considered the possibility of bringing British colonists to Chile to contribute to economic development but did not pursue the idea in the face of the opposition of certain priests who feared this would open the door to Protestantism in Chile (see Prain 2007). However, once independence for Chile was secured, the government's early policy was to facilitate selective immigration, and with this in mind a law was passed in 1824 to encourage Europeans to establish businesses in urban centers and to settle in the sparsely populated regions in the south. Those who came were mainly German, Swiss, and British. Other laws followed. In 1845, a decree was passed aimed at enticing settlers from Europe by providing, under certain conditions, the passage to Chile and an allotment of land with seed and tools on their arrival. This was the Law of Selective Immigration, passed during the presidency of Manuel Bulnes, and it focused on colonizing lands south of Valdivia toward modern-day Puerto Montt.

In 1872, when Federico Errazúriz was President, the Sociedad Nacional de Agricultura was given the responsibility of managing the General Office of Immigration. A decade later, in 1882, during the War of the Pacific, the General Colonization Agency in Europe was established, headquartered first in Paris. Following Chile's victory in the north and the addition of two new provinces to her territory, there was a need to consolidate the territorial gains and ensure

Chile's sovereignty by increasing population in this region, and there were not enough Chilean nationals to achieve this quickly.

At the same time, Chile now looked south to the lands beyond the River Bío-Bío, dominated by the Mapuche indigenous peoples. The colonization agency's main objective was to offer uncultivated land in southern Chile to immigrants. And in the far south there was another worry over sovereignty—Argentina had taken advantage of the War of the Pacific to revive the question of her border with Chile, and in 1881 Chile had given in to many of Argentina's territorial claims in Patagonia. However, there were still unresolved issues relating to their common border, and, as a result, the Chilean government made the question of populating the south with European settlers a matter of urgency.

The colonization agency introduced a change in immigration policy, attempting to avoid the concentration of immigrants of a single nationality, as in the previous phase with Germans in the south. Between 1883 and 1901, around 36,000 European immigrants came to Chile. Two-thirds of this number were contracted through the colonization agency, including 2,074 British immigrants, slightly more than the number of Germans. This agency closed in 1904.

From 1886, President Balmaceda pursued this policy of encouraging immigration from abroad, especially from Europe. In July 1887, Chile's Foreign Minister told the British Minister-Resident that the republic was keen to encourage British settlers to help populate the south of Chile. This is not well documented, but it seems that early the following year several British families arrived in Valparaíso prior to going south. Cecil Levis (1988) writes that most of these immigrants traveled by train from Talcahuano to Angol and then continued by cart to Victoria and Traiguén.

Each settler received forty hectares, plus an additional twenty hectares for each son over eighteen. They were also given a pair of oxen, a cart and plough, seed, and sufficient wood to build a simple house. In exchange, they undertook to work the land for five years and then pay back this investment. However, this was not a successful enterprise, and J. G. Kennedy, the Minister-Resident in Santiago, was plagued with complaints in 1888, and throughout 1889, that the reality was not exactly the picture painted by the Chilean colonization agent in Britain. This was indicative of a general problem with immigration policy in the late nineteenth century; much of what was promised to the immigrants was not delivered. Some of the lands given were either infertile or too small to be profitable, and the communications infrastructure did not exist and took a long time to develop. By 1911, most of these British settlers had left Chile, many for new lives in Australia.

The British representative was driven to prepare a British Foreign Office report to Parliament in 1890, "European Emigration to Chile," in which he referred to the "nearly 1,000 British subjects (inclusive of women and children) already established in the Province of Traiguén" (Foreign Office 1890, 3). Kennedy was alarmed at the conclusion of a contract the previous year between the Colonization Agent-General in Europe and the Belgian firm of L. de Llanos, Keats, and Company, whose British headquarters were in Glasgow. This contract was for the recruitment and transport to Chile of twenty-five thousand emigrants during 1889, to which the British vice-consul responded (in a memorandum included in the Report), "There is not room for one-tenth of this number in this country, nor will there be such room for many years hence" (Foreign Office 1890, 18).

The contract also signaled a change of policy for the Chilean government. No longer would colonists be brought out with few questions asked under a comprehensive assisted scheme. They would now be screened, on departure, and on arrival in Chile, to ensure that they corresponded to stated norms, including these: "They must all be healthy and strong, and must produce certificates of their trade and of good conduct. Single women, or those without families, are excluded" (Foreign Office 1890, 4). Additionally, they were required to make a financial contribution to costs before the voyage and were committed to repaying the balance of the passage in half-yearly installments over two years. In return, on their arrival, the emigrants were "at perfect liberty to engage themselves to anyone, and to make their own bargain for wages."

Kennedy reported that the first batch of British emigrants had arrived under this new scheme and that these aspiring colonists had complained of "the misleading information contained in a pamphlet supplied to intending emigrants by the firm of Llanos and Keats" (Foreign Office 1890, 2). His anxiety increased with the knowledge that another group of six hundred British emigrants was on its way. Kennedy's main allegation was that the real value of Chilean currency was inflated at around double its real buying power. For this reason he "would not encourage British subjects to try emigration to Chile," and he concluded the preface with these words: "I earnestly desire to beg Her Majesty's Government to warn British men and women against so-called free emigration to Chile" (Foreign Office 1890, 3).

Nevertheless, British colonists continued to arrive, although in smaller numbers. There is a fascinating document available at www.patbrit.org ("The British Presence in Southern Patagonia"), consisting of a contract drawn up in 1895 between Nicolas Vega, "Agent in Europe of the Chilian Government for Colonization," and David Dobson, "a subject of Great Britain," married with seven children. The immigrant was contracted to settle in the Province of Chiloé, "at the place which shall be allotted to him by the Inspector General of Colonization, or by the official acting on his behalf." The agency contracted to "furnish him at the port of Liverpool a third class passenger ticket to Chili, for himself and for every member of his family," and stipulated the luggage entitlement, the subsistence on arrival, and the right to seventy hectares of land (plus thirty hectares for each male child over eleven). In addition, the settler was to be provided with a pair of oxen, a cart, equipment (including "an American plough"), and "an uprooting machine for every twenty families" if the land should turn out to be wooded. In return, David Dobson had to commit himself to working the grant for at least six years and "during that time, not to leave the settlement without permission from the Director of the Colony." At the end of this period, the settler would receive the title deed as owner of the land. There is a warning too, that if he "should leave his grant clandestinely, he will be prosecuted according to the law."

These measures were aimed at settling uninhabited agricultural land, especially in the south, but there was another, and later, focus for assisted immigration. This was the growth of Chile's incipient industry, and between 1893 and 1898, the Sociedad de Fomento Fabril (Industrial Promotion Agency) in Chile brought around 1,200 immigrants to the country, not counting family members, in an effort to import their education and their technical skills for the growing needs of industry. Incidentally, the first President of this agency was Agustín Edwards Ross, himself the grandson of a British immigrant. The Sociedad was instrumental in persuading the government to exchange immigration for agricultural purposes by a stronger focus on the industrial needs of the country.

Assisted immigration of this kind, however, accounted for only a fraction of the British who came to reside in Chile. Most came on contract, with money in their pockets, or at least the prospect of income on their arrival, not fleeing persecution or abject poverty. And most settled in the urban environments, not in the countryside.

According to national censuses, there were 4,267 British nationals living in Chile in 1875, making up 25 percent of all Europeans living there, and only the German community was larger. Numbers rose over the following thirty years, but percentage shares decreased, through 1885 (5,310 immigrants, 20 percent of the total), 1895 (6,838, 16 percent), until a peak in numbers in 1907 (9,845, 14 percent). The numbers then decreased, as did the proportion they represented among the European immigrant population—in 1920 (7,220, 10 percent), and 1930 (5,369, 8 percent). Many left Chile, but others stayed and started families. One estimate (Derrick-Jehu 1965) is that by 1900 there were around twenty thousand people of British descent living in Chile.

Carl Solberg (1970) shows that the greatest impact of immigration on the social structure of Chile (and of Argentina) was the rapid emergence of a middle class in the second half of the nineteenth century, composed mainly by foreigners and their descendents, disproportionate to their numbers in the overall population. The 1895 census in Chile shows that 4,120 out of the 6,555 members of the Chilean middle class were Europeans. Carl Solberg estimates that 29 percent of the immigrant population in Chile in the late nineteenth century corresponded to the middle class, while in Argentina the figure would be around 15 percent.

However, unlike Brazil and Argentina, where the growing foreign-born middle class was generally absorbed and accepted, in Chile there was some resentment, and there were protests against immigrants, especially in the period leading up to the First World War. This arose in part because economic expansion was initially slower in Chile and therefore there was greater competition for posts in the bureaucracies that accompanied this growth, and in part because the native population was less cosmopolitan and more inclined to resent the wealth and status which the immigrants obtained.

At the same time, another difference is that immigrants in Argentina and Brazil were only exceptionally accepted into the upper social classes by the landowning oligarchies, while in Chile several foreigners did attain this status. This was especially true of the British immigrants, generally those who had arrived in the first half of the nineteenth century and who benefited from marriages contracted between successful tradesmen and the daughters of the Chilean landowning class. This merging of the traditional agrarian oligarchy with the immigrant traders, mining entrepreneurs, and farmers who prospered during the nineteenth century led to a social transformation in Chile—the creation of a ruling class that was both bourgeois and traditional, backed by a middle class of professionals and government bureaucrats. However, as time went on, this became less and less true, and the later generations of British to visit Chile tended not to settle down there—the Gibbs and Williamsons resided occasionally in Chile, as did Henry Fox (although David Duncan of the firm Duncan Fox never came), but Britain was always their home.

There were two early watersheds for British immigration to Chile, which was initially to Valparaíso. The first was the decree of the first republican Junta de Gobierno in 1811, which ushered in free trade after centuries of Spanish monopoly. The second was the victory against the Spanish forces in the Battle of Chacabuco on February 12, 1817. This victory brought with it the reassurance, after the earlier defeat of the patriot forces at Rancagua in 1814, that independence was truly on its way, as the Battle of Maipú was to confirm in 1818.

Strangely enough, one of the first events involving the British in Valparaíso happened not on land, but at sea, and related not to commerce with Chile, but to war with another nation. During the War of 1812 between Britain and the United States, the frigate USS *Essex* under Captain Porter left Delaware in October 1812, rounded Cape Horn, visited Valparaíso in May 1813, and then attacked the British whaling fleet in the Pacific. The British responded by sending a squadron after the *Essex*, and the *Phoebe* (a frigate) and the *Cherub* caught up with the corvette when she returned to Valparaíso on March 28, 1814.

The port lay of course in neutral waters, and the British squadron leader, Commodore James Hillyar, had to wait. Mackenna (1884) reports, "It is said that both captains frequently met at the festive house of the governor-general, saluting politely and even conversing on indifferent matters, but keeping each of them, through the neutral windows of the castle, a sharp eye to their respective ships lying one next to the other in the bay" (Mackenna 1884, 22).

Eventually Captain Porter slipped out of the harbor, quickly followed by the English ships, and the *Essex* was engaged off Punta Gruesa. Porter surrendered after a short, uneven, and vicious battle, at the close of which an English officer went aboard to receive Porter's sword and promptly fainted; such was the scene of carnage that he encountered. On the American side fifty-eight sailors were dead, sixty-five wounded, and thirty-one missing, while the British had five killed and ten wounded. There is a monument in the Dissidents' Cemetery No. 1 in Valparaíso to the memory of the American sailors who died in this engagement.

The British businessman (and soldier in the independence conflict) Samuel Haigh first visited Valparaíso in 1817. He commented on the British community in Valparaíso in his *Sketches of Buenos Ayres and Chile* that eleven years previously there were only two English residents in the port, and now there were about two thousand out of a total population he estimated at nearly twelve thousand. In these eleven years, six British companies had established themselves in Valparaíso: James Powditch, Bunster, Andrew Brest, John Callon, William Taylor, and William Forbes.

Arriving a little later in Valparaíso, Alexander Caldcleugh also gave his impressions in his book *Travels in South America during the Years 1819–20–21*. "The houses are generally mean, even the governor's house and the custom-house are of poor appearance; but all the symptoms of great increase of trade are visible in many new erections for warehouses" (1825, vol. 2, 45). He judged Valparaíso's population to be around five thousand, much less than Samuel Haigh's estimate.

Maria Graham arrived in Valparaíso in 1822 and described her first impressions of the port: "It is a long straggling place, built at the foot of steep rocks which overhang the sea, and advance so close to it in some places as barely to leave room for a narrow street, and open in others, so as to admit of two middling squares, one of which is the market-place, and has on one side the governor's house, which is backed by a little fort crowning a low hill" (Graham 1824, May 9, 1822).

Later in her *Journal of a Residence in Chile*, Maria Graham commented on the improvements made by the Governor to the roads and streets, adding, "These things seem little to Europeans. But they forget that this Valparaiso, one of the greatest ports on this side of the vast continent of South America, is little more in appearance than an English fishing town. SIDMOUTH is a capital city in comparison" (capitals in original, Graham 1824, June 27, 1822).

Gilbert Farquhar Mathison also visited in 1822 and described in his *Narrative* (1825, 176–77) how he arrived in "Valparayso,"—"a dirty sea-port, composed of small mud houses seldom more than one story high." Clearly, he was not impressed, not even by the countryside around Valparaíso, which "whether viewed near or at a distance the appearance of the place is equally unattractive. How a name, which literally signifies 'Paradise vale' could be applied to it, is not very obvious."

The following year, 1823, John Miers was in Valparaíso and also came away with a poor opinion of the port. In his *Travels in Chile and La Plata*, Miers reported estimates given to him of the population of Valparaíso, which had increased from fewer than three thousand in 1817 to fifteen thousand in 1823, of whom three thousand were British, although he thought these numbers were exaggerated and believed truer figures would be six thousand inhabitants with, no more than four hundred British-born.

Robert Proctor wrote about Valparaíso in his *Narrative of a Journey across the Cordillera of the Andes, and of a Residence in Lima, and Other Parts of Peru, in the Years 1823 and 1824*. "[Valparaíso] consists of one long straggling street, situated on a narrow strip of land between the sea and the almost perpendicular hills." He was in the port soon after a devastating earthquake: "When we arrived, Valparaiso exhibited a most melancholy spectacle, in consequence of the Late Earthquake. The Almendral suffered most severely, scarcely a house having escaped" (1825, 106–7).

Ten years later, Charles Darwin made his first visit to Valparaíso, in July 1834, and described the town in his Beagle *Diary* (July 31, 1835) as "a long straggling place" (the same phrase used by Maria Graham in 1822); "wherever a little valley comes down to the beach, the houses are piled up on each other, otherwise it consists of one street running parallel to the coast." He added on August 15, 1834, "Whoever called Valparaíso the 'valley of Paradise' must have been thinking of Quillota."

From the early 1820s, British involvement in commerce grew exponentially, with several companies established in Valparaíso over the rest of the century, mainly in wholesale and representation of national and foreign companies. These firms included names that became famous in Chile, such as Gibbs, Duncan Fox, and Williamson Balfour. As evidence of the increase in British trade with Chile, in 1825 there were around ninety British ships anchored in the Bay of Valparaíso, against seventy from the United States. Fifteen years later, this number had increased to 166, against 56 from the United States, 48 from France, and 17 from Hamburg, and Valparaíso was by 1840 transformed into a significant trading port.

With the growth in foreign trade, there came the installation of commerce and industry in the port. The *Matrícula Comercial de Valparaíso* for 1866, where all industrial and commercial activity in the port was registered, shows that of the twenty-five factories in the port only one was Chilean, when the total number of foreigners in the 1865 census was just 6.63 percent of the overall population, including 1,014 British citizens. These arrivals settled from the 1820s on Cerro Alegre—known by the British as Mount Pleasant—to escape from the hustle, misery, and smells of the port area. Later in the century, a British community also established itself on Cerro Concepción.

Immigrants from Europe continued to stand out in commerce in the second half of the nineteenth century, as shown in the 1895 census for Valparaíso, where 32 percent of those working in commerce were foreign-born, as well as 27 percent of those working in industry, when the immigrant population was only 7.45 percent of the total. The British dominated among these foreigners, and many of the retail shops, wholesale companies, services, and banks that appeared in Valparaíso in the second half of the nineteenth century and early twentieth century were run by British businessmen and contracted personnel. (See Chapters 8 and 10.)

British commercial interests in Valparaíso supported the creation of a telegraph service between Valparaíso and Santiago (inaugurated in 1852), the setting up of the first telephone service in Chile in 1880, and the beginnings of communications by cable from 1875. These initiatives were carried out by British industrial firms backed by their shareholders and involved the importing into Chile of British technologies and engineers.

The British Chamber of Commerce in Valparaíso was established in 1917—as a response to the special situation of the First World War—with around thirty companies as members. This was Consul Maclean's initiative to draw British companies away from the Valparaíso Chamber of Commerce and to better apply the blacklists to German commerce. By 1927, the British Chamber had grown to more than two hundred members, with branches established in Antofagasta, Iquique (the Tarapacá Chamber of Commerce, 1918), Concepción, and Valdivia. However, the influence of British business and of the British community in Chile in general, and in Valparaíso in particular, started to decline by the end of the 1920s, and the chamber relocated to Santiago in 1932.

The growing community of British residents in the nineteenth century stimulated a demand for churches for the non-Catholics among them. The Union Church was founded by David Trumbull in 1847 (heavily influenced by the United Free Church of Scotland), and St. Paul's Anglican Church was established in 1858. (See Chapter 13.)

David Trumbull set up the Valparaíso Seamen's Mission in 1846, focused on improving the social conditions of the British seamen on ships anchored in the bay, which gained official support from the Missions to Seamen in London from 1906. In September 1925, the Prince of Wales laid the foundation stone for a new building. The Mission closed in 2007. The Salvation Army was established in Valparaíso in 1912, aimed at helping sailors and foreigners who were destitute, and the local population too. Other institutions were created to provide help when it was needed to members of the British community—the British Benevolent Society, and the St. Andrew's Society (founded by Scottish residents in 1918).

British residents in Valparaíso founded Freemasonry lodges that functioned in English, starting with the Star and Thistle No. 509 (1871) under the Grand Lodge of Scotland, and Harmony No. 1411 (1872) dependent on the Grand Lodge of England. (See Juan Ricardo Couyoumdjian's research into English-speaking freemasonry in Chile, 1995). There was a need too for a social club, and the Union Club was founded in 1842, followed by the Junior Club in 1883 for younger members. The two clubs merged later for reasons given by William Russell Young in his reminiscences: "The members of the Union Club had eaten themselves into poverty, whilst those of the Junior had drunk themselves into prosperity" (1933, 20). An alternative association, the Albion Club, was founded in 1897, only to amalgamate in 1906 with the Union Club to form the English Club. Not surprisingly, members who were not English were unhappy with this name, and this changed to the British Club, but only in 1920. Another name change came after World War II, when it became the British-American Club.

There was also a need for fire vehicles and the volunteers to run them, especially after a destructive fire in December 1850, and the Association of Voluntary Firemen (the first of its kind in Chile) was set up in the following year. One of the first companies of firemen was made up by British and Anglo-Chilean residents, and in 1901 the 11th Company of Firemen was founded with the name of *George Garland* to pay homage to the British immigrant who helped found the Valparaíso Fire Corps and had been a volunteer in the 1st Company of Firemen.

The census of 1875 shows that around two-fifths of the British nationals living in Chile were resident in Valparaíso. In fact, this percentage was never less than one quarter in the period 1854 to 1885. Baldomero Estrada's study (2006) of the British community in Valparaíso reproduces census statistics which show that in 1875 there were 1,785 British citizens in the port, the largest group among the foreign communities, and a position they maintained in the 1885 census. Naturally, such numbers meant that the port took on a very British character. Scottish-born residents made up a considerable proportion of the British community in Valparaíso. Baldomero Estrada's research (1987) into the wills posted by British citizens in that city between 1850 and 1900 shows that while 48 percent were born in England, 34 percent came from Scotland. However, the number of British had been overtaken by Italians in 1895, by Italians and by Germans in 1907, and by Italians and by Spanish in 1920, with a sharp decline during and after the Second World War, until in 1952 there were just 419 British residents remaining.

Early British visitors, as we have seen, were not particularly impressed by Valparaíso, but later in the century, the "one long straggling street" (Proctor) and the "long straggling place" (Darwin and Graham) had by 1876 grown into "two interminable streets, running along the edge of the sea, at the foot of the hills, which rise immediately behind them, and on which are built all the residences and villas of the gentlemen of the place. Very few live in the town itself, which is composed almost entirely of large warehouses and fine shops, where you can get almost anything you want by paying between three and four times as much for it as you would do in England" (Annie Brassey 1878, 188–89).

In 1889, William Russell spent several days in Valparaíso and "was surprised and pleased at the appearance of the city"—"There is a long semicircular curve of white buildings, church spires, warehouses, and public edifices bordering the bay behind a forest of masts" (1890, 67). Russell commented that Valparaíso, clearly by then a thriving port, was "the resort of ships of all nations, the majority, however, flying the British flag."

The British community in Valparaíso was flourishing by the mid-1920s. The following snapshot of British institutions in that decade is collated from Aníbal Escobar (1923), and a commemorative album published in 1925 in honor of the Prince of Wales' visit to Valparaíso and Santiago. There was the British and American Hospital, founded in 1913 and closed around 1945. According to Michelle Prain (2007), this hospital had a long history, starting as a facility called Resident Patients in the house of Dr. Ancrum, who arrived in Chile in 1848. Later came the British Naval Hospital, and then the British Hospital founded in 1897 in Cerro Alegre. This building was seriously damaged in the 1906 earthquake, and the British and American communities joined forces for a new hospital, which opened in 1913.

Escobar lists the Anglican Institute, the Assembly Hall (in Viña del Mar), the British Club, the Valparaíso Seaman's Institute, the Salvation Army, the St. Andrew's Society, the Union Church (and the Union Church Young Men's Club), the British Benevolent Society (from 1876), the Valparaíso Learners Institute (founded 1906 and aimed at British and North American sailors), and the British Social Musical and Dramatic Society. Of particular interest is the British Women's League, founded 1915 during the Great War, with the aim of helping the Red Cross and raising funds for the war effort. In 1923, the League was helping soldiers and sailors wounded in the war and their families and providing shelter for British seamen. The several schools and sports clubs with British links in Valparaíso (and nearby Viña del Mar) are named in separate sections of this book.

There are several physical reminders today in Valparaíso of the important British stamp on the history of the port. There is the Arco Británico (British Arch), erected in 1911, and the Casa de Lord Cochrane (Lord Cochrane's House)—a semicolonial mansion dating from 1842, which Cochrane never actually lived in. It is situated above the Plaza Sotomayor, and houses the Museo de Valparaíso. There is a statue to Lord Cochrane— the first public monument to be erected in Valparaíso—inaugurated in 1873 in the Plaza Sotomayor but moved in 1920 to its present location at the intersection of Avenida Brasil and Bellavista. Other reminders include the Valparaíso Sporting Club, which still exists; Avenida Gran Bretaña; Plaza Waddington, in memory of Joshua Waddington, the copper and shipping magnate who arrived in Chile in 1818; and the imposing building that once housed the Anglo-South American Bank.

The rest of the British lived mainly in the export provinces, increasingly in the northern nitrates region, while the capital, Santiago, never accounted for more than 10 percent of the total number of Britons living in the country. Nevertheless, it was in the capital that the British institution of scouting was founded in Chile, in 1909, with no less a person than Robert Baden-Powell as the first honorary president. Baden-Powell made a brief visit to Chile in March of that year, during which he lectured on scouting in the Universidad de Chile. This led to Chile being the first country outside British dominions to have a recognized program. Scouting remains popular in Chile today, under the guidance of the Association of Guides and Scouts of Chile (AGSCH).

Returning to Escobar's 1920s snapshot, there existed in Santiago during that decade several associations focused on British residents and descendants. The Club House was set up for the English speaking community's recreational needs, "with the absolute exclusion of games of chance." This association brought together the activities of the British Society, the British Athletic Club, the Cricket Club, the English Football Club, the Los Leones Tennis Club, the Hockey Club, and the Santiago Golf Club. The British Society (founded 1921) resulted from the amalgamation of the British Benevolent Society, the British Patriotic Committee, and the British Nursing Home Committee. The Queen Mary's Needlework Guild had been active in the First World War, and joined the British Society (Ladies Section).

The Prince of Wales Country Club, which is still in existence, was started in 1925 by a provisional committee made up of the Presidents of the British Society of Santiago, the British Athletic Club, and the Los Leones Tennis Club. Land was purchased with loans from the British Society and members of the British business community, such as Duncan Fox, the Pacific Steam Navigation Company, and Gibbs & Company. The committee decided to take advantage of the visit to Chile in 1925 of the Prince of Wales, who agreed for his name to be used and to lay the foundation stone.

Gradually, then, the center of gravity for the British community began to move from Valparaíso to Santiago in the 1920s. The Chamber of Commerce's move in 1932 is a watershed in this process, and it was consolidated in later decades. The 14th Fire Company of Santiago, for example, was established in 1958, with the formal name of The British and Commonwealth Fire Rescue Company *J. A. S. Jackson*, in homage to John Alfred Stewart Jackson, founder of the Grange School.

In the very south of Chile, a substantial British community established itself in Punta Arenas and the Territory of Magallanes. The naming of the place as Sandy Point—translated later into Spanish as Punta Arenas—derives from John Narborough's voyage in 1669–1671. His *Account* provides this description: "Sand-point [*sic*] is a mean low Point, lies out more than the others Points of the Schore, and a few trees grow on it" (see Dooley 1993, 36). Nearly a century later, in late December 1764, John Byron landed at Sandy Point in search of drinking water and later wrote a very flattering report on the place, with its good hunting and fishing, and "clean air"! In the next century, the hydrographical work carried out by Captains Parker King and FitzRoy between 1826 and 1836 was instrumental in drawing attention to the possibilities of settlement in what later became known as Punta Arenas.

Although not paramount on the new government's agenda following the declaration of independence from Spain in 1818, there was a worry over how to exert Chilean ownership over its claim on Patagonia and how to effect settlement there, particularly given the interest shown by other countries in this region (especially Britain) and the later fractious border disputes with Argentina. Bernardo O'Higgins, for example, promoted the idea of having steam tugs in the Magellan Strait to help with the passage of ships.

But the prospects were not immediately inviting, as shown in Parker King's comment in 1839 on the Spanish failure to establish a settlement at Port Famine: "This was the first, and perhaps will be the last, attempt made to occupy a country, offering no encouragement for a human being; a region where the soil is swampy, cold and unfit for cultivation, and whose climate is thoroughly cheerless" (Parker King 1838, 34).

Nevertheless, Chile determined in 1843 that its sovereignty in the region was predicated on actual occupation, and an expedition under John Williams was sent from Ancud on Chiloé Island to the Magellan Strait to carry the flag. He landed at Sandy Point in October 1843, accompanied by the naturalist Bernardo Philippi and some sailors. They found deposits of coal, which they felt might make a settlement economically viable in the future. However, they did not consider the place as suitable for their purposes, since it would be difficult to fortify.

So, the first settlement was founded on Punta Santa Ana near the site of the infamous Port Famine, with just eleven colonists, and became known as Fuerte Bulnes after the President who had prompted the initiative. While the site chosen on a prominent headland at the halfway point in the strait was strategically attractive, it proved difficult to sustain, despite being reinforced with a military garrison of sixty men in 1844. The site was also not suitable as the base from which colonization could spread. The land was too poor and too rocky for cultivation; there were no meadows for cattle to graze on; the weather was very changeable; and there was little drinking water.

A new Governor of Magallanes, José de los Santos Mardones, surveyed the region in 1847 for a better site and settled on Sandy Point, just thirty-six miles to the north of Fuerte Bulnes. From this exploration we know that the indigenous name for the site was *La-Colet*, but the name did not prosper, and in Chile it became known as Punta Arenosa (literally, Sandy Point), Punta de Arena, and only later as Punta Arenas. The advantages of the site included a better supply of water, space for expansion of the population, warmer in summer (but colder in winter), and overall a much drier climate. The move was effected in 1848, and Fuerte Bulnes was finally abandoned by December of that year.

While the original idea was to establish a military garrison alongside a civilian settlement, Punta Arenas very quickly assumed the character of a penal colony, presumably on account of its isolation, and as such it was affected by two major mutinies. The first was in 1851—the *Cambiazo* Mutiny, named after the lieutenant who led the uprising. It lasted for five weeks and destroyed the settlement. The British ship *Elisa Cornish* happened to be at Punta Arenas and was robbed of the gold and silver it was carrying and then commandeered with another ship to carry away the entire population of over four hundred people. Two days later the PSNC steamer *Lima* called in to find just three men, who had been hiding in the woods. By April 1852, Punta Arenas was a ghost settlement, empty of inhabitants and abandoned. The second mutiny, in 1877, was witnessed firsthand by the British traveler Julius Beerbohm.

In the first years of its existence, few ships bothered to put into Punta Arenas. Martinic (*Punta Arenas*, 1988) reports that between April 1849 and December 1850 only sixteen ships—steam and sailing—called in, out of 149 ships that were seen. This was actually an unusually large number of ships making through the Magellan Strait, motivated by the California gold rush. Nevertheless, for many years only one in three ships in the strait would anchor at Punta Arenas.

Colonization was also slow in getting off the ground, and clearly, the disastrous abandonment of the settlement in 1852 was not an auspicious start. However, President Manuel Montt decided that Punta Arenas was to be repopulated, but this time as a settlement and not as a penal colony, although the latter function continued for several years. Bernardo Philippi was engaged as the new Governor to return there with a group of German colonists on the Chilean ship *Infatigable*, under the command of Juan Williams Rebolledo, son of the Welshman who had led the first Chilean expedition to the region nine years previously.

In November 1867, President Pérez issued a decree intended to encourage settlement around Punta Arenas, offering land grants to families who settled there, whether Chilean or foreign. Robert Cunningham, a naturalist on board HMS *Nassau*, landed at Sandy Point in that year and described seeing wooden houses and three main constructions: the church, the Governor's house, and the Fort, which was christened irreverently by some of the English officers the Punch and Judy House.

In 1871, a British ship was involved in an incident in the Magellan Strait with international ramifications. This was the *Elgiva*, caught by the Chilean authorities illegally extracting guano on the coast of Tierra del Fuego, but with an authorization given by the Argentinean government in Buenos Aires. This brought into relief just how uncertain Chile's dominion was over Magallanes and strengthened the role of Punta Arenas as the natural jumping off point for asserting this sovereignty.

Other early British visitors have left their observations on Punta Arenas. Annie Brassey wrote of visiting Sandy Point in 1876—"the only civilized place in the Straits. It is a Chilian settlement, and a large convict establishment has been formed here by the Government." She found a settlement with a population of around 1,200 inhabitants, "composed entirely of one-storied log huts, with slate or tile roofs, and with or without verandas. They are all arranged in squares, separated from each other by wide roads; and the whole settlement is surrounded by stockades" (Brassey 1878, 125).

One year later, in November 1877, Julius Beerbohm arrived in Punta Arenas, exhausted from his "wanderings" in the Patagonian pampa. What he did not immediately realize was that the settlement was a powder keg about to explode. His sleep that first night was broken by cannon fire, which turned out to be a mutiny by the convicts and the soldiers known as the Motín de los Artilleros. While the mutineers pillaged, Beerbohm escaped to the woods, with inhabitants from the settlement, and on his return to Punta Arenas he saw that "the better portion had been burned down; of the fort, the hospital, the Government buildings, and a great many private houses, nothing remained but a smoking heap of charred timbers" (1879, 275). Among the wounded were the Governor and an Irish doctor, Thomas Fenton. Order was restored by Chilean soldiers who arrived on the warship *O'Higgins* and later on a British steamer, the *Iberia*.

Two years later, in 1879, Florence Dixie visited Punta Arenas and was not impressed. "I suppose there possibly may be drearier-looking places than the town of Sandy Point, but I do not think it is probable. . . . We all agreed that the epithet of 'God-forsaken hole' was the only description that did justice to the merits of this desolate place, nor did subsequent and fuller acquaintance with it by any means induce us to alter this unfavourable opinion" (*Across Patagonia* 1880, 33).

A great tragedy occurred at Punta Arenas in 1881. HMS *Doterel* had sailed from England in January 1881 en route to join the British Pacific Fleet, and soon after she moored off Punta Arenas in April, an accidental explosion in the forward magazine ripped her apart, killing a total of 143 men. There were only twelve survivors, among them the ship's captain. Lucas Bridges describes hearing the explosion and remembers how, when Captain Richard Evans was rescued and taken into the cabin of his father's boat, the *Allen Gardiner*, he was so tall that "his scorched head blackened the ceiling of the cabin, leaving marks we children looked at with awe when they were pointed out later" (1951, 92).

Three weeks later HMS *Garnet* arrived with a group of divers and was soon followed by the *Penguin* and the *Turquoise*, which helped in finding the wreckage. The dead were buried in the old town cemetery, which closed in 1894. In 1936, the municipality of Punta Arenas was given permission by the Royal Navy to relocate the *Doterel* burial to its current site, in the municipal cemetery. A bronze memorial was commissioned, and it records the names of all those who died. There is a second memorial plaque in the Old Royal Navy College Chapel, at Greenwich.

The first British immigrants to Chilean Patagonia (Magallanes) arrived after President Pérez's decree of November 1867. Statistics quoted by Mateo Martinic (2002) show that in 1875 there were an estimated thirty British nationals in the region, which grew successively in the National censuses of 1885 (291 British), 1895 (378), to

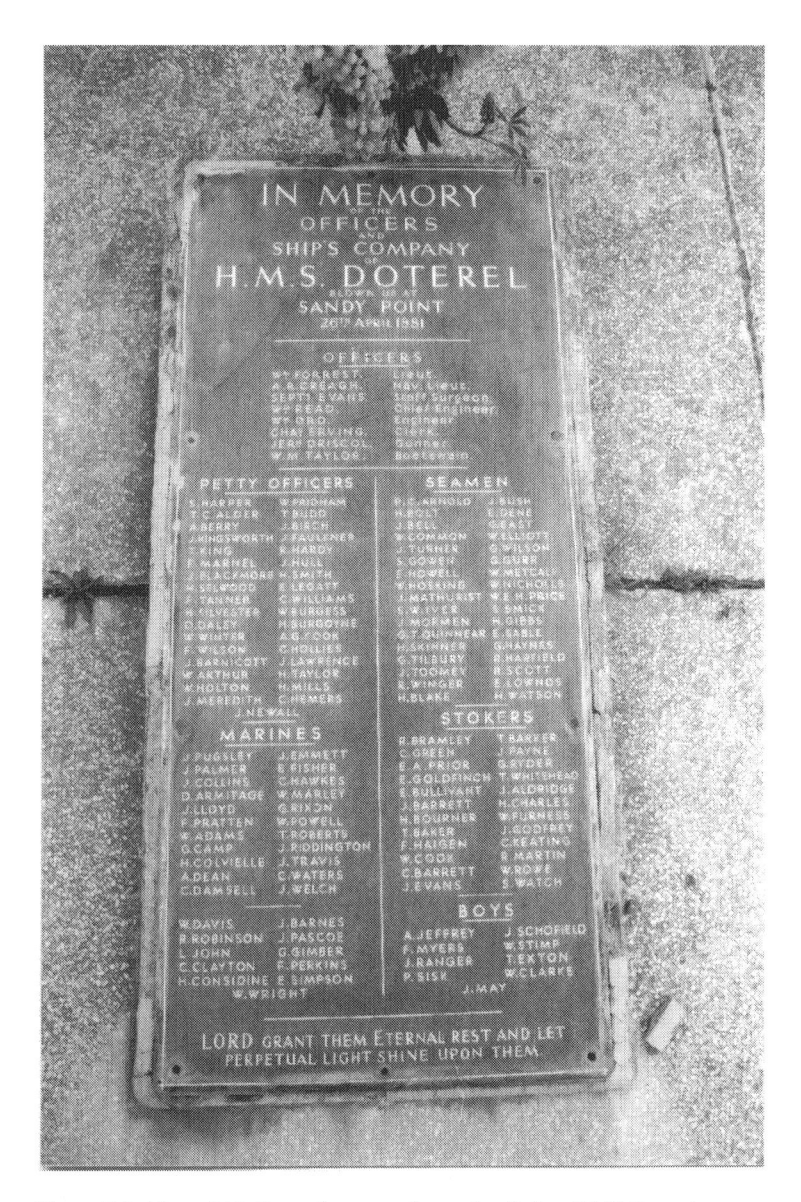

Figure 7.1 Memorial in Punta Arenas to those who died on HMS Doterel

reach a peak of 1,190 British nationals in the year 1907—about 37 percent of all the foreigners in Magallanes.

Sheep-rearing proved to be the economic salvation of Punta Arenas, after the collapse of other ventures, such as coal and gold prospecting. Butland (1953) reports that in 1875 there were no more than three hundred sheep in the region. Overtures were made to farmers on the Falklands/Malvinas, but interest was initially low, on account of the uncertain frontier with Argentina. In 1878, Henry Reynard, an immigrant from the Channel Islands and British Consul in Punta Arenas, was the first to take the risk of introducing sheep-rearing on a large scale in this region. However, it was the Governor of Magallanes, Diego Dublé Almeida, who took the first step by traveling to the Falklands in 1876, where he purchased three hundred head of sheep. Arriving back in Punta Arenas, Dublé sold the sheep to Reynard and ceded Elizabeth Island for their acclimatization, in the Magellan Strait near Punta Arenas. They survived, and the realization dawned that the huge territory of pampa around the city was ideal grazing land. Slowly, sheep were introduced from 1878 to 1879 along the coast between Cabo Negro and Punta Dungeness, and this process speeded up when Chile and Argentina agreed their boundary south of 52 degrees south in the treaty of July 1881.

Several of the pioneer sheep farmers were immigrants from the Falklands who arrived in the 1880s, such as Thomas Saunders, a Scotsman from Fifeshire. Saunders had seen the potential in Patagonia for rearing sheep, and in 1883, with his partner John Hamilton, he sent to the Falklands for a boatload of sheep, who all arrived dead. Undaunted, Saunders brought another flock of sheep overland from Buenos Aires—a trek of 2,250 kilometers that lasted a year. In 1898, the company of Hamilton & Saunders owned three *estancias* (ranches) totaling forty thousand hectares, including the famous Otway Station.

Other entrepreneurs were, like Henry Reynard, already resident in Magallanes, and this group included the Wood brothers (Henry, William, and Stanley), and Dr. Thomas Fenton. Fenton was a doctor in practice in Punta Arenas from 1874 and is the same man who was wounded in the insurrection in Punta Arenas of 1877. He later volunteered as a surgeon in the Chilean army in the War of the Pacific, with the rank of Sergeant Major.

By 1885, there were already forty thousand sheep, a figure that grew exponentially, so that by 1906 there were close to two million sheep in southern Chile, and 153 of the 249 shepherds in the region were British (mainly Scottish). British investment grew, and official figures furnished by the governor in 1893 show that ranches owned by British farmers, or part-owned in partnership with other foreigners, covered 48 percent of the land use in Chilean Magallanes and Tierra del Fuego and accounted for 70 percent of the territory's total number of sheep. The human population also grew, and the 1895 census shows that 3,227 people lived in Punta Arenas, together with just over 5,000 inhabitants in the territory. In the same year, the first bank opened in Punta Arenas—the Bank of Tarapacá and London.

Martinic (2002) emphasizes that the British contribution to the successful development of sheep farming in Magallanes was crucial, especially in the period between 1880 and 1920. The English and Scottish who came had the knowledge, technology, and experience, backed by investment capital, which in time positioned the region's wool production as reaching among the best standards in the world.

Over time, the land grants and the sheep-farming ranches got larger, and this was especially true of Tierra del Fuego, where large concessions were rented out in the period up to 1913, unlike the generally smaller and individually run ranches on mainland Patagonia. These concessions were funded mainly by British capital. The following summary is based on Martinic (2002):

The first of these concessions, of 123,000 hectares, was exploited by Wehrhahn, Hobbs & Company, with about one-third of its capital being British (Martinic's estimate). This became later the Gente Grande (literally, "Big People") Farming Company.

Another concession was given to Nogueira, Wales & Company, which later became the Tierra del Fuego Sheep Farming Company. This company was set up in London expressly to exploit one of the concessions given to José Nogueira, a Portuguese businessman. In 1898, this *estancia* comprised 180,000 hectares, and four-fifths of its capital was British, managed by the Waldron & Wood group.

A third concession of 170,000 hectares was handed to the Philip Bay Sheep Farming Company, a company also constituted specifically to gain control of a concession, in this case one awarded to Mauricio Braun. British capital in this company, according to Martinic, was probably on a par with Braun's own contribution.

The fourth concession was given to MacRae & Company, probably toward the end of the 1880s, and this led to the creation of the Porvenir sheep ranch. The two partners were the Scottish immigrant John MacRae and Rodolfo Stubenrauch.

The fifth concession—and the largest, and the most famous—was known as the Tierra del Fuego Exploitation Company, or simply the Sociedad Explotadora. In 1898, it covered an incredible 1,109,000 hectares! This computes to around eleven thousand square kilometers—almost the area covered by modern-day Yorkshire. When José Nogueira was given this large concession, he had to accept as a condition that this company be created. Following his death, his brother-in-law Mauricio Braun made good on the commitment, together with José Menéndez, whose families were linked by marriage. Many British interests were also involved, from the Duncan Fox Company, which held a controlling interest in the interwar years of the twentieth century, to a large number of English and Scottish farmers.

The history of most of the other concessions on continental Magallanes was different, and renting out the land stopped around 1901 or 1902. The concessionaries naturally wanted to own the properties in which they had invested so much. Martinic (2002) explains that vested interests, mainly speculators in Valparaíso and Santiago, helped persuade the Chilean Congress to pass an Act that offered in public auction the lands on the mainland. Accordingly, auctions were held in 1903 and 1906, and the great winners were the Sociedad Ganadera de Magallanes (expressly formed by Chilean investors for this purpose), the Sociedad Explotadora, and José Menéndez. The losers included many of the original British pioneers, although early names like Thomas Saunders and John Hamilton did survive, in their case forming the Patagonian Land & Estate Company, as did Henry Reynard.

In 1910, the hitherto business rivals, the Sociedad Explotadora and the Sociedad Ganadera merged, much to the surprise of regional public opinion, and the new company now commanded an area of three million hectares (including lands in Argentina) and over two million head of sheep! Martinic (2002) estimates that around 26 percent of the capital of the new Sociedad Exploratora was British, divided between Duncan Fox, British banks such as the Anglo-South American, and individual British investors resident in Chile, but from this year onwards the British share gradually dwindled.

Nevertheless, Aníbal Escobar in 1923 was able to report a British presence that was still strong in the region, with participation in the Gente Grande Farming Company—the manager in 1923 was Ernest Hobbs—and in Hamilton & Saunders Ltd., the Patagonian Sheep Farming Company, and the Estancia Fenton Station. There was also the import and export business of Townsend & Company. Frank Townsend had played a key role in the development of the region's freezer industry, founding the Puerto Sara *frigorífico* in 1908. Another freezer plant with British investment was the Frigorífico Rio Seco, run by the South American Export Syndicate Ltd., founded in 1903, and the first plant of its kind in Chile.

In a book written in 1936, *Bajo el cielo austral* (*Under the Southern Sky*), Claudio Chamorro estimated that in that year there were still around a thousand British residents in the Magallanes Territory of southern Chile. He added that people of British descent owned about one-fifth of the lands, including the *estancias* of Otway, Fenton, Punta Alta, Brazo Hoste, and Penitente, and one-fifth of the managers of the commercial, industrial, and banking ventures, together with around one-quarter of the farm managers, were also British.

Tragically, the growth of sheep farming brought the farmers into conflict with the indigenous peoples, who viewed the sheep ranging the pampa as they would their traditional game, the guanaco. This pitted Indian bows and arrows against the shepherds' guns. Elizabeth Dooley (1993) describes how the Salesian Fathers' Catholic order of priests moved Indians to mission stations, adding, with irony, that this conveniently left the land clear for the farmers. She quotes the manager of the *Explotadora*, who wrote in a letter in 1895, "I think it's the cheapest way to get rid of them, quicker than shooting them, which is more reprehensible" (Dooley 1993, 47).

Some of the farm workers were even contracted to hunt Indians. Dooley reports that a bounty of one pound sterling was set for a pair of ears. The American anthropologist Samuel Kirkland Lothrop, writing in 1928, goes further and says, "There soon sprang into being a class of professional head-hunters, recruited from the shepherds and miners, who received one pound sterling from the ranchers for each Indian head—man, woman, or child" (1928, 34). This "ethnic cleansing" started in 1894, but was not only the product of sheep farmers moving into the Indians' traditional lands; the gold rush of 1893 in Chilean Patagonia also contributed to the terrible confrontation.

These sanctioned murderers included Sam Hyslop, who called himself "the best Indian hunter in Patagonia" and was killed by Ona Indians in 1901, and John McRae, believed to have murdered sixty Indians. There was also "Mr. McInch"—Lucas Bridges' pseudonym for a failed farmer who took pride in persecuting and murdering Indians, who may well be the Scottish farm manager Alexander MacLennan, identified by Bruce Chatwin as the "Red Pig" (*In Patagonia* 1977, 111).

The authorities turned a blind eye for many years, and this was, ironically, at a time when British missionaries were making efforts in the south to save the lives of the indigenous people. After dedicating "three-quarters of a century to the eradication of the troublesome Indians," writes Kirkland Lothrop, "the Government decided to stop the scandals arising from head-hunting by turning the Indians over to the [Salesian] missions." In the 1890s, troops traveled over the countryside rounding up the Indians "and drove them like cattle to the mission stations. Families were mercilessly broken up. Strange foods caused sickness and implanted the belief that they were being poisoned. . . . Few indeed survived the 'civilizing' process" (Kirkland Lothrop 1928, 23).

By the 1920s, there was no further need for the missions.

A significant period of transformation for the region of Magallanes, from a miserable penal and military settlement into a growing colony, closed in 1890. This had started in 1868 with the arrival of native settlers, followed by successive waves of European immigrants in the 1870s. From the 1880s, the process of colonization had spread out from Punta Arenas and its immediate hinterland toward the north and northeast of Patagonia and Tierra del Fuego, in a process of expansion that would only be completed in the 1920s. However, the golden period of economic growth peaked around 1914, with the downturn in shipping resulting from the blockades of the Great War, and the opening of the Panama Canal.

Immigrants arrived from almost all the nations of pre-First World War Europe. Comparative census figures for 1885 and 1895 show that the greatest immigration came from Britain, surpassed by Croatia in the figure for 1906, and by both Croatia and Spain in the data for 1907, 1914, and 1920. Martinic estimates that around two thousand British immigrants arrived between 1891 and 1920, and at least half of these were from Scotland. Consular documents show that of those British subjects who were registered, 42 percent were from Scotland and 38 percent from England and Wales. In addition, around 10 percent were from the Falklands, and it is fair to assume that most of these were Scottish by descent.

With the growth of the British community came the need for clubs, a church, and newspapers in English. The British Association of Magallanes, known as the British Club, was founded in Punta Arenas in April 1899, by Frank Townsend. The club's aims were to promote social life among the British in Magallanes, help compatriots in need, and provide a meeting center for its members. The first premises were located on the upper floor of the Bank of Tarapacá and London, and the first president was the pioneer farmer, Henry Reynard. A later president was Leslie Greer, general manager of the Explotadora, who was sometimes referred to as the "King of Patagonia." Membership was limited to British males, although shepherds were frowned upon, and the premises were modeled on the style of a gentleman's club in London. Later, when the British presence in the region began to decline, the Club began to admit Chileans, as long as they could speak

English; and later still, those who could not speak English but were of British descent were accepted as members. In 1981, the building's owners, the Banco de Chile, closed the premises, and confiscated the contents as payment of rent arrears. There was also a British Club in Río Gallegos, from 1911.

For recreation, there was the British Sports Club and the Union Club, both founded before 1909, which merged in 1923 to form the British Athletic Club, offering facilities for soccer, tennis, and cricket. In 1924, the Magellan Dramatic Society was founded and lasted to around 1955. For communication, the Magallanes Telephone Company was created in 1898 by William Jones. Several newspapers in English circulated over time in the territory; the most famous were *The Punta Arenas Mail* (1900) and *The Magellan Times* (1914). For those down on their luck there was the British Benefit Society, started in 1898, which later became the British Benevolent Fund. During the First World War, the British Red Cross (1914) and the British Patriotic War Fund Committee (1914) were founded in Punta Arenas, and in 1915 the Anglican Society of Magellan was established with the purpose of acquiring and running the church and St. James School in Punta Arenas.

Another sizeable British community was established in the city of Concepción. An early British visitor, Captain Basil Hall of HMS *Conway*, noted in his *Extracts from a Journal* (1824, vol. 1, 228), "The district of Conception [*sic*], as far as natural advantages go, is much richer than any other part of Chili: it possesses also a hardy and intelligent population, a delightful climate, and a soil of the most fertile kind . . . Notwithstanding all these advantages, it is almost entirely depopulated, and the whole country allowed to run to waste."

One disadvantage not mentioned by Captain Hall was that Concepción was for many years difficult of access for travelers. The town is backed by Chile's biggest river, the Bío-Bío, with no bridge crossing until 1889. Visitors would come, like Charles Darwin and Robert FitzRoy, from the nearby port of Talcahuano, and increasingly from the bustling coal port of Coronel a little to the south.

The intrepid British traveler Annie Brassey described in 1878 what the journey from Coronel to Concepción was like.

> Half-way between Coronel and Concepcion, we met the return stage-coach, crowded with passengers, and looking as if it had just come out of the South Kensington Museum or Madame Tussaud's, or like the pictures of a coach of Queen Elizabeth's time. It was a long low vehicle, with unglazed windows all round it, painted bright scarlet decorated

with brilliant devices on every panel, and suspended, like our own, by means of innumerable leather straps, from huge C springs. The seats on either side held three passengers, and there was a stool in the middle, like the one in the Lord Mayor's coach, on which four people sat, back to back. (Annie Brassey 1878, 160)

William Russell arrived in Coronel in March 1889 and remarked on the port that he was not prepared for "the tokens of prosperity which the little town afforded us. Factory chimneys smoked; horsemen in ponchoes and sombreros, carts laden with sacks drawn by oxen or mules, toiled along the streets, enveloped in clouds of dust, and the names over the shops—German, Italian, Spanish, and English—indicated a cosmopolitan population" (1890, 34–35). He traveled on to look at Colonel North's railway bridge, then being built over the River Bío-Bío for his Arauco Railway. The bridge was not yet complete, but Concepción could be seen across the river on the other bank. Russell recalled, "The white houses and colored *miradores*, cupolas and spires of Concepción, looked so bright and graceful that it put one in mind of Venice. I am told that it was distance that lent enchantment to the view, for though the city is perhaps the best laid out and ordered in Chile, it has nothing of interest in churches or palaces to show" (Russell 1890, 38).

Censuses for the Province of Concepción trace how the British community grew and then fell in size over the years. In 1875, there were 335 British nationals living there, making up 27 percent of the foreigners, just behind the German colony. Twenty years later, this number had almost doubled, to 654, comprising nearly 22 percent of the foreign-born population in the Province of Concepción, second in importance only to the Spanish. This proved to be the high point for British settlement in the region, and numbers slowly dwindled to 574 (1907), 410 (1920), and 231 (1930).

There is a strong British link with the Plaza Independencia (Independence Square) in Concepción. The square began life as the Plaza de Armas in 1761, when the city was moved from Penco to Concepción after the earthquake of 1751, and its general outline was set out by Ambrose O'Higgins and John Garland. It was in this square that the Proclamation of Independence was made by Bernardo O'Higgins on January 1, 1818.

In the center of the square there is La Pila, consisting of a fountain and, on top of a tall column, the statue of Ceres—Roman goddess of agriculture. This column was manufactured at an ironworks in Liverpool, overseen by a Belgian artist named Augusto Bleuze, who followed the design of Pascual Binimelis Campos (whose initiative this was). The column was brought in sixteen large boxes by ship to Talcahuano, and construction work started in January 1856. The stone for the fountain came from San Rosendo and was crafted by an English stonemason, Alexander Strange. There is an interesting mistake in the fashioning of the *huemul* in the reproduction of the coat of arms on La Pila; it seems that the craftsmen in Liverpool did not recognize this Chilean deer and substituted it by a more European-looking version.

A publication to celebrate Concepción's importance in the national centenary year of 1910 lists several of the British companies present in that city: Williamson Balfour, Duncan Fox, Morrison, Allardice, MacKay, Weir Scott, Rogers & Company, and Franklin & Company. In addition, there were the stationers of Paton & Company and Wescott & Company, and the Tienda Inglesa (English Shop) of R. Meiklejohn.

In common with other large non-Catholic communities in Chile, a burial ground for "dissidents" was provided, from around the year 1878, within the main cemetery in Concepción, and was initially marked by an iron railing.

A memorable series of events involving the British took place in Concepción in 1939, the year of the great earthquake of January 24. HMS *Exeter* and HMS *Ajax* had called into the port of Talcahuano, and following a party at the English Club in Concepción in honor of the officers and crew, the two ships left for Valparaíso only to return when the earthquake struck. HMS *Ajax* took the first wave of injured to Valparaíso. British sailors helped to clear the streets of rubble, assembled a portable radio station on top of the Ritz Hotel, and gave away tinned soup and bully beef. Sailors from HMS *Exeter* also offered to blow up what remained of the cathedral towers, which were in a dangerous state, but this task was given to crewmen from the Chilean cruiser *Latorre*. The help given by these British sailors is commemorated in Concepción in the naming of a street as Calle Exeter.

Later that same year, the Second World War began, and both cruisers were involved, along with HMNZS *Achilles*, in the Battle of the River Plate. This Battle pitched the three cruisers against the German pocket battleship *Admiral Graf Spee*, named after the Admiral who had led the German squadron in the Battle of Coronel in the First World War. HMS *Exeter* was badly damaged in the battle and had to disengage from the scene. The *Graf Spee* put into the port of Montevideo and was scuttled by her crew on December 17, 1939.

Valparaíso, Punta Arenas, and Concepción were key centers of British community, but of course they were not the only ones in Chile.

Antofagasta had an English Club, founded 1914, which was the meeting place for British sporting societies. One lasting tribute to the British presence is the clock tower in the center of Plaza Colón, erected by the British community in 1912 in celebration of the Republic's centenary. The ceramic blocks for the tower were brought from England, and the surround of the clock is a replica of London's Big Ben, as is the ringing of the bell.

Iquique also had an English Club, founded in 1885, whose members had to be English speaking. The club housed also the Iquique Golf Club, Boating Club, and Lawn Tennis Club. A few British families established themselves in Arica, and they included the Hulse, Hill, Holmes, Jenkins, Seabrook, Stevenson, and Williams families.

So many British citizens resided in Chile that, naturally, Britain needed to provide consuls and ambassadors to represent their interests and intercede in times of need. Full recognition of Chile as an independent republic came in 1841, when Britain's consul general in Santiago, John Walpole, was given the additional title of chargé d'affaires (see Blakemore 1974). In 1872, the British representative was designated minister-resident and consul-general. The British Embassy (Chile) site quotes the diplomatic service list, which gives Sir Henry Getty Chilton as the first with the rank of British ambassador, in 1930, with the British Embassy established in 1932. (Appendix B provides a history of British diplomatic representation in Chile).

Relations between Chile and Britain are promoted today by the British Embassy in Santiago, the British Council, the Anglo-Chilean Society in London (founded in 1944), the Sociedad Anglo-Chilena in Santiago, and the Chilean-British Chamber of Commerce. Other groups with similar aims are the British Society of Valparaíso, the Royal British Legion, the St. Andrew's Society, the Chile Club, the British Commonwealth Society, and the British-Irish Business Group. Information on all these organizations can be found on the British Embassy's website.

Figure 7.2 Commemorative plaque on the Clock Tower, Antofagasta

Chapter 8

Commerce and Industry

> *The British merchants [were] of material use to the independent cause, by the large importations of arms and stores, both naval and military, which, in spite of every prohibition, they continued to furnish. It is true that sometimes they also supplied the royalists; but in general their cargoes of this nature were for the patriots.*
>
> —Maria Graham, Sketch of the History of Chile, *1824*

Throughout the period up to Chilean independence, Spain insisted on a monopoly of trade with her colonies in the New World, which, in the particular case of Britain, was stiffened by the state of belligerence that so often existed between the two nations.

There was one attempt in the late seventeenth century to establish a British colony for trading purposes in Latin America, at a place called Darien in what is today Panama. This rather bizarre and ultimately unsuccessful (and tragic) scheme was undertaken in 1695–1698 by a Scotsman named William Paterson, with the backing of the Scottish Parliament. Investors were sought in both England and Scotland, but King William and the English Parliament withdrew support, in part because this was a time when the English wanted to appease Spain. The expedition went ahead regardless, and around 1,200 Scots left Leith in July 1698 and landed at Darien, which they called New Caledonia. Thirteen hundred settlers followed in 1699. The venture quickly collapsed due to disease and an English trade boycott, and the settlement was abandoned in April 1700, at a cost of some two thousand dead and about one quarter of Scotland's liquid assets. This experience hastened the Act of Union between Scotland and England in 1707.

There was also one short period of very limited peaceful trade between Britain and the Spanish colonies in the eighteenth century, focused on an English company called the South Sea Company. This government-backed company sought a monopoly on trade with South America and has gone down in history as precipitating "the South Sea bubble." The company was founded in 1711 by the Lord Treasurer, Robert Harley, and was predicated on a successful conclusion to the War of the Spanish Succession. The intention was not so much to trade but to pay off British government debt by giving shares in the company to creditors. The war ended in 1713, with the Treaty of Utrecht (also known as the *Asiento* Treaty), which gave the company the right to send one trading ship, limited in tonnage and cargo, each year to the Spanish American possessions, including Chile.

The *asiento* referred to the additional exclusive right to import slaves into Spanish colonies, with the annual quota set at 4,800 African slaves. (Few slaves were actually brought to Chile, and slavery was abolished in two stages, in 1811, with the 'liberty of the womb' law, and in 1823, with full abolition—ten years before William Wilberforce saw the Abolition of Slavery Act passed in the British Parliament). The Company was permitted to take back its earnings in goods and money, although the King of Spain took a cut of one quarter of the profits. However, no trading voyage was made until 1717, and then in 1718 relations between Spain and Britain began to deteriorate. Oversubscribed speculation led to the bubble bursting on the stock market in September 1720.

Nevertheless, the South Sea Company continued to be involved in illicit trade with Spanish America well into the third decade of the eighteenth century. The English traders connived with the willing colonists to unload the one ship and then reload with cargo taken from other ships, or tenders, waiting at sea. Spain realized what was happening and that large amounts of contraband were also being smuggled, and at the conclusion of the Anglo-Spanish War in 1729, the Treaty of Seville committed the British not to trade at all with the Spanish colonies and gave the right to the Spanish to board British ships when in her territorial waters.

This led to the famous episode in 1731 when Captain Jenkins on the *Rebecca* alleged that a Spanish coastguard had cut off his ear after boarding his ship. This ear (pickled) was paraded in the House of Commons in 1738, and this precipitated the War of Jenkins' Ear in 1739. While this conflict focused on Spanish interests in the Caribbean, with an attack on the transshipment port of Puerto Bello (today called Portobello) on the coast of Panama, there were consequences for Chile. The Isthmus of Panama was the distribution hub for Central and South America—goods bound for Chile were shipped to Callao in Peru, and then loaded onto mules for the long journey down to Chile. Spain decided to diversify its trading practices, ending the tactic of gathering large fleets at a few key ports. Instead, they spread the risk by employing smaller fleets using more ports, and they began to travel around Cape Horn to carry on commerce on the Pacific coast.

The South Sea Company continued to trade, in times of peace, until 1748, when it ceased to be a trading company. Nevertheless, the company's exclusive commercial privileges in the South Seas lasted until 1807, when the British Parliament broke the monopoly by allowing British ships to enter the Pacific Ocean via Cape Horn as a means to challenge Spain's hegemony in South America. This followed the failure of Britain's military interventions in Rio de la Plata (Argentina and Uruguay) in 1806 and 1807.

One of the several British ships to take advantage of the new opportunities, albeit for contraband trade, was the frigate *Scorpion*, which visited Chile (for the second time) in March 1807 and precipitated a scandal that contributed directly to the recall of the Spanish Governor of Chile, and to the first calls for Chilean independence. The captain was Tristan Bunker, an Englishman (according to Barros Arana, vol. 7), or more likely a member of a Nantucket whaling family relocated to England as part of a government scheme in the 1790s to kick-start the industry in whale oil.

The *Scorpion* landed in Chile at Quilimarí, ostensibly as a whaler, but in reality carrying a contraband cargo of British cloth. Captain Bunker entered into negotiation with an American doctor named Henry Faulkner who was living in Quillota, just to the north of Valparaíso. Faulkner convinced Bunker to return to England and prepare another cargo of cloth, for a rendezvous in mid-1808 at an isolated coastal spot called Topocalma, in the district of Colchagua, south of Santiago. Faulkner provided the captain with a map of the area. Bunker raised eighty thousand pounds from investors in England, and decided to abandon the ship's disguise as a whaler. The ship was renovated, equipped with the necessary armaments to resist boarding, and arrived at Topocalma in July 1808.

Bunker met with José Fuenzalida Villela, the owner of a *hacienda* in Topocalma, who undertook to contact Faulkner but also informed a local Spanish authority named Francisco Antonio Carrera, the *subdelegado* of Colchagua. These three—Fuenzalida, Carrera and Faulkner—met together and hatched a plot to take over the ship and its valuable cargo on the pretext that it was illegal contraband. The aim was to then claim their share of the merchandise, in accordance with the laws of that time. Faulkner went on board, feigning interest in the cargo, and invited the captain and his crew to Fuenzalida's hacienda, where they were treated with great generosity. The plotters decided to postpone their plan, as they lacked sufficient men, and instead persuaded Bunker to return again in September, when they would have merchants with them ready to buy the contraband. Fuenzalida then traveled to Santiago and informed the Spanish Governor of Chile, Francisco Antonio García Carrasco Díaz, of their plan. Carrasco agreed to provide a group of *dragones* (police) in exchange for a share of the profits in the enterprise. Captain Bunker duly returned, and during a banquet at the hacienda was murdered, along with eight of his crew.

But there was a flaw in the conspirators' plan—Britain was at that time actually in a period of truce with Spain due to the war with France. This meant that the *Scorpion* was not an enemy ship and therefore its cargo was not forfeit. Governor Carrasco, however, decided to ignore this legal nicety and declared the merchandise impounded. Public opinion was roused against the plotters, who were insulted in public in Santiago and Valparaíso and very nearly lynched. These events destroyed the little prestige that Carrasco commanded and radicalized the Chileans' desire for independence. Spain decided to recall the governor, but by the time the royal order arrived, the governor had already been deposed by the independence movement. Compensation for the seizing of the cargo took many years to resolve, but in the 1830s, the English firm of Hullett successfully sued the King of Spain for the financial losses incurred.

Free trade between Chile and other countries came soon after the *Scorpion* incident and was announced by the young republican Junta de Gobierno in 1811. The Free Commerce Decree opened the ports of Valparaíso, Valdivia, Talcahuano, and Coquimbo to commerce with foreign nations, friends and allies of Spain, as well as neutrals. The governors of these ports were instructed to provide protection and assistance to the traders and ships' officers and crews who arrived.

Two English brothers—John and Joseph Crosbie—immediately fitted out a ship called the *Fly* on the Thames. They arrived in Valparaíso the same year, laden with such products as iron tools and textiles and with instructions to bring back hemp and copper. "The well-assorted cargo of the *Fly* in 1811 was quite a novelty, almost a marvel for the Chilians of that period" (Mackenna 1884, 20).

On board this ship was John James Barnard, who was so impressed with the profits that had been made that he prepared a new voyage of his own, on the *Emily*, mainly carrying firearms, which he expected to sell now that there was a war going on in Chile against Spanish colonial rule. The *Emily* arrived in Valparaíso in August 1813, in the midst of the battles for independence. Maria Graham (1824) reports that when the royalist government ruled again, following the restoration of Ferdinand

VII in Spain in 1814, strangers were not allowed to enter the ports of Chile, even to trade in copper. To justify this ruling, they alleged that "Don Juan Diego Bernard [*sic*]" had provided the patriots with ninety-eight pairs of pistols. Perhaps for this reason, Barnard became known as Patriot Barnard and was designated chairman of the English Committee of Santiago; in principle, the first representative of Britain in Chile, until 1823, when the first British consul, Christopher Nugent, was appointed.

Independence was effectively achieved at the Battle of Maipú in April 1818, and the patriot government craved recognition from foreign governments, especially from Britain. This focus on the British had several roots. First of all, Supreme Director Bernardo O'Higgins was predisposed to the British and their liberal ideas, and Bernardo had lived and studied in England. Secondly, O'Higgins saw how useful the Chilean navy under Admiral Cochrane had been in securing victories against the Spanish, and he was anxious that Britain's Pacific fleet should at least remain neutral, if not friendly. Access to the capital market in London was also important to the new nation. All of this gave the British traders in Chile a certain leverage, and a British traders' association was set up in Valparaíso in 1819, with Barnard as the first secretary.

British government policy in the region during the various wars of independence in Spanish America was also critical. Michelle Prain (2007) reports that O'Higgins' Minister for Foreign Relations, Antonio José de Irisarri, met the British Foreign Secretary (Castlereagh) in 1819. Irisarri's mission was to request the commercial support of Britain. This was a tricky issue, but Castlereagh decided in 1822 on a policy of de facto commercial recognition by extending the Navigation Acts to permit Latin American ships to call into British ports. In October 1822, Maria Graham was writing in Valparaíso about "exorbitant duties . . . announced [in Chile] on various English goods" and how much she wished that the British government "would acknowledge the independence of the states of South America at once; and send proper consuls or agents to guard our trade, and take from it the disgrace of being little else than smuggling on a larger scale" (Graham, October 2, 1822).

As we have seen, George Canning decided to continue with Castlereagh's policy of cautious recognition. At the same time, unemployment following the close of the campaign in Europe against Napoleon in 1815 led to several British citizens trying their luck in Chile, including merchants whose businesses had been disturbed by the blockade in Europe. Alexander Caldcleugh, the British traveler and trader, and attached to the British Mission in Brazil, visited Chile in 1821 and looked at commercial opportunities now that independence was being consolidated. He commented on the contemporary state of trade: "The direct commerce between England and Chile consists of cargoes of every description of manufactured goods; and in return gold, silver, copper, tallow and hides, are the usual remittances" (Caldcleugh 1825, vol. 1, 357).

More officially, the British government sent HMS *Conway* to Chile to check what was going on. The ship stayed in Chilean and Peruvian waters from December 1820 to February 1822. In November 1821, Captain Basil Hall was instructed to leave Valparaíso and journey toward Lima, calling in at all the ports in between. According to Hall (1824, vol. 2, 1), the aims were "to inquire into British interests at those places; to assist and protect any of his Majesty's trading subjects; and, in a general way, to ascertain the commercial resources of the coast." Clearly, Britain was readying herself for the prospects of increased trade with an independent Chile.

These prospects did not impress an early British mining engineer named John Miers, whose opinions cast a long shadow. He was in Chile in 1823 and gave this sour judgment on the commercial panorama: "I should regret exceedingly that any foreign artizan or manufacturer should think of settling in Chile for many years to come. I should lament to hear that any British capitalist, however flattering the offers made to him, should invest his capital in any enterprize upon the soil of Chile: having myself failed in such an attempt" (John Miers 1826, vol. 2, 276).

At around the same time, Robert Proctor was in Chile and also formed a poor impression—not of Chile and the Chileans, but of the first British traders who had arrived. He published his *Narrative* in 1825 and commented, "The town is full of English, many of them of the lowest description, and of the worst characters; they act as brokers, smugglers &c., and pounce on the poor stranger arriving with a consignment of goods, and generally leave him to repent his credulity" (1825, 109). This poor reputation of British businessmen seems to have remained for a few years. Rory Miller (1993, 83) quotes the opinion of an angry Chilean who remonstrated in 1828: "These merchants' only rule of conduct is to consider legitimate anything which will not peremptorily and inevitably take them to the gallows."

By 1819, there were six important British traders established in Valparaíso, concentrating at first on importing manufactured goods and then on organizing the export trade that paid for them. This number grew rapidly to thirty-one wholesale businesses in the 1820s, and over the following decades British interests covered a wide spectrum of commerce, from import and export, brokering, and wholesale to representation for national and foreign firms—mostly British.

Juan Ricardo Couyoumdjian (2000) points out that the growth of commerce in Valparaíso was linked at first to the trading importance of

Callao—Lima's port in Peru. This was second nature, since in colonial times trade in Chile was subservient to the Spanish monopoly centered on the viceroy in Peru. In the eighteenth century, Valparaíso was "the poor and forced market of Callao, which had made of Valparaíso a simple *bodega* [warehouse] and counting-house of Lima" (Mackenna 1884, 35). But it was significant that between the two ports lay the increasingly important nitrates region. The fact that Chile won the War of the Pacific, and with this the Tarapacá and Antofagasta nitrate-bearing provinces, meant that the center of gravity swung firmly southwards in favor of Valparaíso toward the end of the nineteenth century. Not that this was entirely new for the port—in 1842, Valparaíso was already the business center for the infant nitrates industry, and by the beginning of the 1870s, three-quarters of nitrates transactions were carried out in Valparaíso.

A key development was that, probably more than elsewhere in Latin America, the big merchant houses dominated business in Chile well into the twentieth century, and in many cases they were British owned and run. They tended to be well financed and well managed, with directors who had accumulated both experience and reputation, and this helped them survive through periods of difficulty, when smaller local businesses frequently collapsed. Several of these businesses lasted for over one hundred years, and many became household names in Chile.

Another peculiarity was that the main partners in these businesses often lived abroad, typically in London or Liverpool in the case of the British firms, and the lower level partners and managers tended to be foreigners who, generally speaking, did not put down roots in Chile. Curiously, this was not true of the first generation of British traders to settle in Chile, who mostly were immigrants in the truest sense. These men often fell in love with and married Chileans and settled down in their adopted country; unlike the later generations who arrived, who tended to marry within their national community and spent their days of retirement "back home" in Britain.

This does not mean to say that Chileans were excluded from these ventures. John Mayo's important study (1981) of the relationship between Britain and Chile in the years 1851 to 1886 makes the point that British merchants and Chilean investors joined forces in a mutually rewarding collaboration that balanced export with import— Chile's natural resources for products and services from Britain.

There was another interesting phenomenon, which was true of Latin America as a whole, and especially of the Pacific coast of the Americas. Rory Miller (1998) describes how, prior to 1914, British investment focused on a galaxy of autonomous businesses listed separately on the stock exchange. The fact that these companies were largely free-standing made them different from the multinational companies of more modern times. They tended not to be the branching out from a home base of existing companies wanting to have access to supplies or to markets, and they had very little connection with the British economy, except the financial center of London and the engineering companies where they placed orders. They were free-standing but registered in Britain and therefore subject to British laws, and this gave confidence to the investors.

Rory Miller (1998) describes how, by 1913, there were two categories of independent free-standing companies on the west coast of South America. First, there were those that had evolved out of investment groups. Examples include the Anglo-South American Bank and the Antofagasta (Chili) and Bolivia Railway Company. There were also the several free-standing companies formed in Britain by Colonel North to exploit the nitrate deposits after Chile's victory in the War of the Pacific. These enterprises also included the companies that were essential components in the nitrate industry—the railways, waterworks, finance, and shipping. These businesses were managerially independent of other companies.

Secondly, there were those that were controlled by investment groups, mainly the merchant houses. In Chile, the British merchant houses were active in commodity trades, and by the early twentieth century they had spawned groups of free-standing companies that were based around them. This was true of trade in wheat and the production and processing of nitrate. Two British companies in Chile were clear examples of this—Gibbs & Company and Williamson, Balfour & Company.

British-run businesses of both kinds took root in Chile in phases that can be delineated during the nineteenth century. The first wave arrived after independence, taking something of a risk in the still-turbulent years that prevailed until the 1830s.

Huth & Company was one of the first British companies to establish itself in Chile, in Valparaíso (1824). The company actually started with the name Frederick, Huth, Grüning & Company until the name change in 1878. The business focused on banking but was also involved in exporting minerals and importing a variety of products into Chile. Branches were established in Santiago, Concepción, and Coquimbo. Later on, Huth & Company specialized in electrical installations as representatives of the General Electric Company in Britain.

Perhaps the most famous, and certainly among the most enduring British companies, was Gibbs & Company, founded in London in 1808 as Antony Gibbs & Sons. The founder, Antony Gibbs, focused at first on trading in Spain, with his two sons, William and George, taken later into the partnership. Following Antony's death, the sons concentrated initially on trade in guano from the former Spanish colonies, taking advantage of the new republics' freedom to engage in commerce. The company opened a branch in Lima in 1822 and then in Chile opened first in Valparaíso in 1822 and in Santiago in 1826. Later in the century, in 1880, a Chilean subsidiary was opened in Valparaíso and called Gibbs & Company. This subsidiary and Antony Gibbs & Sons (London) became known collectively as the House of Gibbs, as merchants and bankers, in a partnership where the London firm was the senior partner.

Gibbs was not at first a significant company until the Lima branch negotiated an exclusive contract with the Peruvian government to trade in guano in 1842, which was sold in England as fertilizer and produced huge profits. Derrick-Jehu (1965, 165) quotes the following rhyme which circulated in London:

> Gibbs
> first made their dibs
> out of the turds
> of foreign birds.

The income from this trade was so great that William Gibbs became one of the richest men in England. In 1843, William purchased a Gothic Revival house called Tyntes Place as the country home for the family, and in 1863, he started the renovation work that produced the estate called Tyntesfield, which some regard as the greatest surviving Victorian house in Britain. The estate lies seven miles from Bristol and was acquired by the National Trust in 2002.

When the Peruvian monopoly in guano trade was taken away from Gibbs in 1861, the firm sought to diversify by investing in railways and nitrates. For example, they invested in the Tarapacá Nitrate Company from 1865, in what was then a province in southern Peru, and became in 1869 the largest shareholder in a company exploiting nitrates in the then-Bolivian province of Antofagasta to the south of Tarapacá. Following Peru's decision to nationalize the nitrate industries, Gibbs administered the state nitrate company for Peru in the period 1875 to 1878. An office was opened in Iquique in 1881, following Chile's first victories in the War of the Pacific, where the firm specialized in imports, especially of machinery for the nitrate industry, and the export of nitrates. In the 1880s, Gibbs was second only to Colonel North in promoting nitrate companies, including the Alianza, Tamarugal, Salar del Carmen, and Pan de Azucar firms. Branches were opened in other nitrate region towns, Antofagasta and Mejillones, as well as in towns in the south—Concepción, Talcahuano, and Temuco.

The firm's export business focused on nitrates, and they had a monopoly for many years on the production and sale of iodine, a byproduct of the nitrates industry. The company diversified as time went on and came to export wheat and other agricultural products, including fruit, and to import coal, iron, steel, agricultural machinery, cars, and general merchandise. Gibbs also acted as agents and bankers to the Chilean and British nitrate companies and represented British insurance firms and a wide spectrum of other services and products. Gibbs lost a great deal in the collapse of the nitrate prices in Chile following the global depression, and in 1934 Gibbs merged its trading operations with Balfour Williamson to form the jointly owned Gibbs, Williamson & Company Ltd.

The second phase for foreign investment in Chile started in 1830, when, following the Battle of Lircay, a period of Conservative rule was ushered in under Diego Portales. A new constitution was passed in 1833 that introduced a Congress of Deputies and Senators, and for much of the remainder of the century Chile enjoyed the reputation internationally of possessing a stable government. This was naturally attractive to investors from abroad, especially from Britain, which had the products of the Industrial Revolution and the money to spend.

An example from this second period is Graham Rowe & Company. The roots of this company go back to a partnership set up in Lima in 1822. They opened in Valparaíso with Charles Rowe as manager in 1842, the same year that Chile renegotiated its postindependence debts, which spurred the resumption of investment in the country. This led to a key presence in both these South American countries, with the company bringing sugar from Peru for its refinery in Viña del Mar. The firm was also the general agency in Valparaíso for the Anglo-Chilian Nitrate Railway Company of Tocopilla, both for the provision of tools and machinery and for financial matters. The company went into liquidation in 1931.

Attracted by Chile's growing reputation as one of the most stable Latin American countries, many companies established themselves in the 1850s and 1860s, beginning the third period of foreign investment in Chile. By the 1870s, British commercial interests in Chile were considerable. Simon Collier (1993) notes that throughout that decade, Britain accounted for at least one-third of Chile's exports and imports, and when the War of the Pacific broke out in 1879, opening up the northern mineral-rich provinces, this led to an exponential growth of British business interests. Blakemore (1974) reports that between 1844 and 1898 the total value of imports into Chile from Britain exceeded the combined total of imports from the United States, France, and Germany.

Williamson, Balfour & Company set up in Chile in the early 1850s and is a notable instance of British commercial interest in this period. Founded by three Scotsmen, Stephen Williamson, Alexander Balfour, and David Duncan, the company started in 1851 in Liverpool as "Stephen Williamson & Co." with the intention of exporting goods from Europe to the Pacific coast of South America. The Chilean partnership was established in Valparaíso in 1852, and later, in 1863, when the partnership was renegotiated and David Duncan withdrew, the decision was taken to distinguish between the Liverpool trading company, Balfour Williamson, and the Chilean company, which was named Williamson Balfour.

The firm specialized in the export from Chile of copper and nitrates, as well as wheat. At the end of the nineteenth century, Williamson Balfour was, along with Gibbs and Duncan Fox, a major exporter of wheat from Chile. This led the company to establish a mill in Concepción—the largest of its kind in Chile at that time. Branches were opened in Iquique in 1882 to better focus on the nitrates trade, where they came to own nitrate firms in Agua Santa and Taltal, and in Concepción in 1890, to cover the south for trade in agricultural products, with subbranches in Chillán, Yungay, Talcahuano, Mulchén, Traiguén, Valdivia, and Osorno.

Figure 8.1 Steam engine in southern Chile, imported by Williamson Balfour

An intriguing feature of the story of Williamson Balfour concerns the early history of Easter Island after its annexation by Chile in 1888. The government leased the Island to Enrique Merlet, a Valparaíso businessman, who turned the island into a large sheep ranch and dealt badly with the natives, the Rapa Nui. The islanders were obliged to build a stone wall around their village of Hangaroa, and it is said that, except for work, permission was needed to leave this area, even to bring water, and that those who transgressed were exiled to continental Chile. Merlet later sold his control to Williamson Balfour, who then created a subsidiary in 1903 called the Compañia Explotadora de la Isla de Pascua (The Easter Island Exploitation Company), which ran Easter Island as a sheep farm until 1953, when the Chilean government refused to renew the lease.

During the company's stay on the island, they ran it virtually as a fiefdom, controlling every element of life from employment to food supply. The entrepreneurs involved were of Scottish descent, and perhaps it is no coincidence that the island was transformed by a similar process to that which had so radically altered Scotland in the late eighteenth century, complete with the "absentee laird," the resident manager, and the Polynesians as "crofters." Reports began to emerge of the pitiful conditions lived by the islanders, and these were verified by Bishop Rafael Edwards on his visit to Easter Island in 1916, although few improvements resulted from his observations. Sadly, when the government took away the company's hegemony and gave control over to the Chilean Navy as overseers, the islanders continued to be confined to the one village, and the new rule proved to be even harsher than that imposed previously by the sheep ranchers. Incidentally, Easter Islanders gained full Chilean citizenship in 1966 when the Island was awarded the status of a civil department with a municipal constitution.

Another major British business interest in Chile was Duncan, Fox & Company. When David Duncan left the Stephen Williamson & Company partnership in 1863, he joined with Henry Frederick Fox to found this famous company in Liverpool in 1864. Henry Fox had been a partner in the firm of Ravenscroft Brothers, which had been in Valparaíso since 1843. The new company appeared in Valparaíso as Sawers, Duncan & Company and in 1876 became Duncan, Fox & Company. Branches were opened in Lima (1876) and in Manchester (1879), the latter so as to acquire cloth. The company specialized in import and export, for which it employed its own ships, and acted as an agency for insurance, steam ships, and the purchase of minerals, leather and wool.

David Duncan never came to Chile, but Henry Fox lived in Valparaíso for several years before returning to Liverpool. Branches were opened in Concepción (1878), Santiago (1900), and Antofagasta (1906), from where subbranches were opened in La Paz and Oruro in Bolivia. In the interwar period Duncan Fox controlled three affiliates in Chile—a sugar refinery, a flour-milling company, and the Patagonian sheep farm Sociedad Explotadora de Tierra del Fuego.

Buchanan, Jones & Company also dates from 1876 in Chile and started to operate under the name H. B. James & Company in Iquique and Pisagua in the nitrates business. According to Estrada (1987), this firm was responsible at the beginning of the twentieth century for the exploitation and management of approximately 10 percent of the nitrate fields in Chile, which belonged to the New Tamarugal Nitrate Company and the London Nitrate Company. The head office was established in Valparaíso. Toward the end of the 1920s, Buchanan, Jones & Company had a capital of three hundred thousand pounds, and around six thousand people were working in the nitrate *oficinas* under their administration. Two other important British companies in Chile were Weir Scott & Company, founded in 1856, which established branches in Santiago, Antofagasta and Concepción, and Geo C. Kenrick & Company, founded in 1910 in Valparaíso, initially to import coal and coke and general merchandise.

There was a concentration of British business in Valparaíso, where they were strong in various retail and service businesses. General stores included Riddel & Company (founded 1870), which was succeeded by Alexander J. Latto & Company; W. L. Donaldson (1907); and Robson, Kay & Company (1919). There were several bookshops: R. W. Bailey & Company; Wescott & Company; R. Magowan (1885); Curphey & Company (1900); The Souvenir House of Alan Phillips (1910); and Hardy & Company (1903). The latter had opened in 1876 as a stationers run by three Scots, David Steward, Ramsey Gordon, and Andrew Henderson. They were joined in 1903 by John William Hardy, who had arrived in Chile in 1879.

Other British commercial businesses in Valparaíso included Fraser & Southward's chemical laboratories (1866); Whyte & Sons' bread and cake shop; Price South America Ltd.'s candle factory; and the butchers of George Goodwin and H. Humphrey. Inevitably, there were tearooms, restaurants, and hotels such as the English Tea Room, Robyns' English Bar, George Daniels' Albion, and Campbell & Maggs' English Hotel. Of particular interest is the commercial house of Wallace & Company, a pioneer in national radio in Chile when "Radio Wallace" began to broadcast in 1926.

The British were also heavily involved in developing key services in Chile—electricity, water, telephone, roads, railways, trams, and so on. For example, there was the Chili Telephone Company (Compañia Inglesa de Teléfonos) in Valparaíso from 1924, and the Chilian Electric Tramway & Light Company (Compañia de Tranvías y Alumbrado Eléctrico) in Santiago, which was founded in London in 1898. Other service companies include the Valparaíso Drainage Company; the Chilean Mills Company; the Tarapacá Waterworks Company; the Arauco Company (railway and coalmine); and the Magallanes Telephone Company (started by the British engineer William Jones in 1898).

Toward the end of the nineteenth century, and especially after the War of the Pacific, Chile began a process of industrialization, and the British played an important role in this development. The initial focus was naturally on Valparaíso, given its status as the main port, its concentration of business and financial services, its experience in providing industrial materials for the nitrates business, and the presence of so many foreigners who were inclined toward modernization. These early industries manufactured machinery and parts for the railways and for the port, and were very dependent on foreign expertise—principally British—and foreign technicians, and on the import of primary material. British companies involved in this development included Morrison; Balfour, Lyon; Brower & Hardie; J. Reynolds; A. Oswald; Cameron & Young; T. Rider; Mouat & Borrowman; Henderson-Finch; R. J. Grove; Carley & Campbell; Lucker & Rider; Lever & Murphy; and Brown & Darley.

Morrison & Company was founded by the Scottish engineer John Morrison, who arrived from Edinburgh to Chile in 1846 contracted by the Chilean government for service in the navy, specifically to look at port works and inspect naval boat machinery. Morrison left this service after a few years and joined a partnership, Cuthill, Croxier & Company, of which he later became the sole owner. John Morrison brought in his son J. J. Morrison in 1891, and later his other sons, William and Frank, in 1902, to enlarge the company. When a fire destroyed his workshops in 1904, Morrison rebuilt them, only to have everything lost again in the fire resulting from the earthquake of 1906. From this point on, the firm specialized in importing machinery for mining, industrial, and agricultural use from Britain and North America. In 1923, the head office was established in Santiago. Morrison & Company became exclusive agents of the Armstrong Withworth ship-builders in Newcastle-upon-Tyne and negotiated the construction of two super Dreadnaughts for the Chilean navy, the *Almirante Latorre* and the *Almirante Cochrane*. However, at the outset of the First World War, the British government appropriated these two battleships, paying an indemnity to Chile.

Balfour, Lyon & Company (founded 1859) is an interesting example of a company with industrial links, having started in Valparaíso as the Fundición Victoria (Victoria Ironworks) in 1849. In the late nineteenth century, the firm produced coaches, wagons, boilers, and even locomotives for the State Railways.

As a coda to this chapter on the British presence in commerce and industry, there is the parallel and intertwined story of British shipping interests in Chile. The British merchant Joshua Waddington founded in 1827 (in Valparaíso) the first shipping firm to be registered on the Pacific cost. The greatest name, however, is the Pacific Steam Navigation Company (PSNC). While it was the initiative of an American, William Wheelwright, the company he founded in 1835 was British. The enterprise started as the Compañía de Vapores del Pacífico (Pacific Steamship Company), and the PSNC (known also as the Compañía Inglesa de Vapores) as such was formed in London in 1838 and incorporated by Royal Charter in 1840.

The first PSNC steamships arrived from England in 1840 with the names *Chile* and *Peru*. These paddle steamers were built by Curling & Young in London, and they entered the bay of Valparaíso together on October 15, 1840 in a triumphant and long-remembered display of the wonders of the modern steam age. In 1846, the PSNC launched Chile's first international postal service, and in 1868 a direct steamer service between Valparaíso and Liverpool was inaugurated. One later PSNC steamer, the *Tacna* (built at Birkenhead in 1873 for the Chilean coastal trade), was the focus of a diplomatic incident when, in 1874, she sank on leaving Valparaíso with the loss of nineteen lives. Captain Hyde was sent to prison by the Chilean authorities but later released after the British lodged an official protest (see Centner 1942).

William Russell took a Chilean ship in 1889—the *Chiloé*—along the coast from Coronel to Valparaíso. He commented that there were two companies of coastal steamers, the PSNC and the Chilean company, working between the southern ports of Chile and Panama in what he described as "rather needless competition." He added, "The ships are built and engined in England, commanded and officered by Englishmen, though they sail under different flags" (Russell 1890, 59). In 1905, the Royal Mail Steam Packet Company took over the PSNC's route from London to Sydney and then in 1910 acquired the entire company, although the ships continued to sail under separate flags. The opening of the Panama Canal in 1914 was a blow to the PSNC, given the sudden increase in competition, and Chile's decision in 1922 to reserve the coastal trade to national carriers was also a key reversal for the company's fortunes.

Nevertheless, writing in 1923, Aníbal Escobar glowingly describes the "modern cargo boats" traveling to ports in Britain, France, Belgium, Holland, and Germany, with the PSNC ships *Lobos*, *La Paz*, *Losada*, *Kenuta*, *Junín*, *Duendes*, *Huanchaco*, *Magellan*, *Potosí*, *Bogotá*, and *Ballena*. He also mentions the PSNC steamers that carried mail, passengers, and cargo to Cuba, the United States, and Europe—the *Oropesa*, *Oroya*, *Orcoma*, *Orita*, *Oriana*, *Ortega*, *Ebro*, and *Essequibo*. The latter two were traveling monthly from Valparaíso to New York via the Panama Canal. The PSNC ran a joint service, called "combinations," with the Royal Mail Steam Packet Company using the steamships *Orduña*, *Orca*, *Orbita*, and *Ohio*, with services between New York and Cherbourg, Southampton, and Hamburg. In this same year, the PSNC accounted for two-thirds of the ships that arrived in Britain from the South American Pacific coast.

The Royal Mail Steam Packet group collapsed in 1931, during the world recession, but resurfaced in 1932 as the Royal Mail Lines Ltd., which assumed the assets of the Steam Packet and PSNC lines. In 1965, Furness Withy & Company gained control of these lines, which in turn were acquired (together with the PSNC brand) by a Hong Kong ship owner, and then sold to the German Hamburg Süd shipping group in 1990.

A number of the names so famously associated with the history of British commercial interests in Chile still exist today. As a subsidiary of Inchcape, Williamson Balfour had a bottling plant in Concepción until 2000 and now owns the BMW franchise in Chile as Williamson Balfour Motors. Gibbs & Company sells verification services to the insurance industry. Also in insurance, there is the Royal & Sun Alliance Seguros (Chile) S.A., whose history in Chile can be traced back to 1905, when they acquired the La República insurance company. There is also the accountancy firm of PriceWaterhouseCooper, which started business in Chile as Price Waterhouse nearly a century ago. These are exemplary of the trend over recent decades of Britain's move from a manufacturing to a service economy, given the United Kingdom's excellence in consultancy, finance, insurance, accountancy, and the provision of legal advice. Another trend is that of globalization, and Britain is still present in Chile as a key partner in multinational companies such as BHP Billiton, Rio Tinto, Anglo American, Xstrata in the copper industry, Shell, Unilever, British-American Tobacco, GlaxoSmithKline, and HSBC.

Chapter 9

Mining

> *The state of the mines, the condition of the miners, the want of means for mining purposes, and the nature of the country show most plainly that English projects for mining on a large scale, with great capitals, cannot be accomplished. Any attempt to mine there by Englishmen, or under English management, must fail.*
>
> —*John Miers,* Travels in Chile and La Plata, *1826*

John Miers was shown to be terribly wrong in this assessment. Later that same century, British companies came to dominate and profit greatly from the rich deposits of nitrates in the north, and many British engineers and managers were involved in the mining of coal south of the River Bío-Bío.

There were also a number of copper industries and mines that were British owned, such as the Copiapó Mining Company (founded in 1836), later known as the Copper Mines of Copiapó. The British merchant-trader Joshua Waddington was involved in copper mining in the early 1840s in Chañaral Alto, north of Copiapó. British investors owned copper mines, such as Edward Abbott's mines in the area of Caldera and the valuable mines belonging to a Mr. Waters in the Chañaral district. An English company called the Panucillo Copper Company mined copper in Coquimbo. Charles Centner (1942) notes that British mining engineers in the 1850s were mainly responsible for the development of the important Carrizalillo mine in the Chañaral district as well as the Limbo mine of Salado and the Mondaca mine of Carrizal.

Many of these mining engineers came from Cornwall. In August 1834, Charles Darwin visited copper mines in the Andes, at a place called Jajuel, and noted in his diary, "These copper mines are superintended by a shrewd but ignorant Cornish miner; he has married a

Spanish woman & does not mean to return, yet his admiration for Cornwall was unbounded; he never ceased to descant upon the wonders of the mines" (Beagle *Diary*, August 21, 1834).

By 1864, British investments in copper were greater than any other foreign country, but from this date they decreased in importance with French and especially American capital correspondingly increasing, so that by end of the First World War, British capital represented less than 2 percent of the total invested.

Much more important in terms of the British presence in Chilean mining was the capital investment in the extraction, processing and export of nitrates in the north, and the fascinating story of British involvement in Chile's coal mining industry in the south, in a connection which started much earlier.

The first mention of coal deposits in Chile occurs in 1557. According to the Jesuit priest Diego de Rosales in his *General History of the Kingdom of Chile* (1674), soldiers of Don García Hurtado de Mendoza found small quantities of coal in that year on Quiriquina Island, in the Bay of Concepción, and used it to heat their food and to keep warm. However, little advantage was taken of the coal deposits, since wood was so plentiful. Later that century there is another mention of coal, in the account entitled *Reyno de Chile* (1595), where Pedro Mariño de Lovera noted that the Mapuche Indians in the south used coal in the preparation of their food.

However, it was only in the nineteenth century that investors began to consider the commercial potential of the coal seams. British interest in mining in Chile (not just coal) can be said to have started in 1818 with the visit of an English mineralogist named David Barry. He looked at the coal deposits in southern Chile, and his subsequent report was positive. Two years later, the captain of HMS *Conway*, Basil Hall, also came away with a constructive opinion when he looked at coal excavations near Penco and concluded that "The seam is thick and apparently extensive, and might, probably, with due care and skill, be wrought to any extent" (1824, vol. 1, 224).

Alexander Caldcleugh visited Chile in 1821 and was also able to comment favorably on the quality of the coal, writing, "It is of excellent quality, and will, before many years have passed away, be looked on as one of the chief sources of wealth in the country" (1825, vol. 1, 355). However, it was expensive to produce, and Maria Graham commented in her *Journal* that in 1822 "the coal of Conception [*sic*], though abundant and good, and worked within 300 miles, is dearer in Valparaiso than that brought from England" (July 7, 1822). Maria Graham blamed the lack of coasting ships in Chile and the excessive taxes charged on such trade. Another factor, however, may be that coal came out from Britain as ballast in the hulls of ships, which lowered freight costs.

This was a promising start for the commercial prospects of extracting coal in Chile, but doubters soon began to prevail, focusing on the quality of the deposits. In a paper read to the Royal Geographical Society of London (published 1855, 172–75), William Bollaert commented on the "various opinions" that had been expressed on the quality of coal in Chile, and gave his own observations, formed while living in Peru from 1825 to 1827. He found that the coal brought from Talcahuano in Chile to be used in a forge was "so inferior that it was thrown aside." In 1828 he visited Talcahuano, as well as Quiriquina Island (in Concepción Bay), and found evidence of lignite, "a very imperfect coal, and it did not appear to us that by following the seam, an article of much better quality would be obtained."

Charles Darwin and Robert FitzRoy did not help in this respect. They visited the Bay of Concepción in 1835, calling there just after the great earthquake of that year. FitzRoy was aware of the controversy surrounding the quality of the coal deposits in the region and commented in his *Narrative* (1838, 423), "Not far from Old Penco is the stratum of coal about which there has lately been much discussion . . . It is said to be bituminous—that it burns too quickly to ashes to answer well for smith's work, because it does not give heat enough—and that it is liable to spontaneous combustion." Charles Darwin was also curious, and he crossed the bay to Lirquén to look at "the best coal-mine of Concepción" where he judged that the deposits "as all the rest which I have seen, [are] rather Lignite than Coal." He added, "The mine is not worked, for the coal when placed in a heap has the singular property of spontaneously igniting, it is certain that several vessels have been set on fire" (Beagle *Diary*, March 5, 1835).

So, Chilean coal did not enjoy a good reputation in these early days. Nevertheless, opinions began slowly to change, for the better, and crucial to this transition were the efforts made by an American, William Wheelwright, on behalf of the British Pacific Steam Navigation Company (PSNC). In 1843, the PSNC steamship *Chile* took on Chilean coal, but after just a few hours at sea the ship stopped because of lack of pressure. It is said that Wheelwright personally went down to the ship's boilers to make the necessary adjustments until the right pressure was reached and that he spent all night doing this. This act convinced PSNC Captain Peacock that Chilean coal could be used to build up steam.

Never one to miss an investment opportunity, it seems that Wheelwright actually engaged in looking for coal in Talcahuano, in partnership with Captain Peacock, using the crew from his ships while they were docked in port. Cowling Taylor (1848) says that they also hired workers and that forty tons of coal were sent on to Valparaíso to be tried out on the other early PSNC steamer, the *Peru*, and that the consumption they observed of sixteen tons of Chilean coal to thirteen tons of British coal was considered a satisfactory result. In his study of the British presence in the southern coal-fields, Leonardo Mazzei de Grazia (1924) adds that it was soon obvious that a more serious and consistent approach was needed, and three British families were brought over and settled in Talcahuano—Nisbet, Sonett, and Shopter (or more likely, Shapter). The names may have been corrupted, as is common in early sources found in Chile.

Nevertheless, Chilean coal was always recognized as inferior to coal imported from Britain, but it stood the test of time, in part because it was shown that mixing imported and local coal was ideal for smelting operations. In 1843, Thomas Smith opened small coal mines to supply a copper smelting plant established in Lirquén by his brother-in-law Joaquín Edwards. The following year, Dr. John Mackay found coal in Las Vegas de Talcahuano on the banks of the River Andalién, near Concepción. He may in fact have started to exploit this coal deposit earlier, perhaps in 1841, and it is possible that he sold some coal to the PSNC in 1842. John Mackay is considered the main British pioneer of the early days of coal mining. He was born in Inverness, Scotland, in 1819, and he arrived in Chile in 1839, apparently coming from New South Wales for supplies, but, on arriving, he decided to stay. In 1841, he was appointed as a doctor in the Concepción Hospital, but his real vocation was in industry and business.

Mackay suspended the Talcahuano workings in 1847, and he was instrumental in moving attention away from the Bay of Concepción to the Province of Arauco further south, when he began searching around the port of Coronel in the company of an Englishman named William Cunningham, brother of the British Vice Consul. By 1852, there were a dozen mine-owners extracting coal near Coronel, including Mackay, and by 1855 there were twenty-three mines, including one owned by Mackay and four others of British origin. Mackay's mine in Coronel was called El Cuatro (The Four), and in time it sold coal to the Compañía de Lota, which belonged to the true "father of Chilean coal," Matías Cousiño. In 1855, Cousiño purchased Mackay's mine, but Mackay remained as Administrator of this mine in Coronel and was also appointed Administrator of Cousiño's mine in Lota.

Mackay now turned his attention further south, to the area around Lebu, where he prospected with William Cunningham in 1854. Finding coal, Mackay obtained funding from two owners of copper smelters in the north of Chile, Tomás Urmeneta and Maximiano Errázuriz, and founded a coal mining company with the name of Juan Mackay & Company in partnership with these northern investors. After six years, Mackay sold his share of the firm to Maximiano Errázuriz.

Another British mine-owner in the region of Coronel in these early years was Henderson Smith, an Englishman who acquired three small mines at Puchoco Point, and rented two of them to the partners William Southerland and Ralph Pearson, and to Henry Shapter and Manuel Cordero, respectively. It is possible that the British Vice Consul in Concepción, Robert Cunningham, invested in this enterprise, since Smith was committed by contract to providing Cunningham with five thousand tons of coal. There is a document that carries his signature as "Roberto Cunningham," dated 1853, where he seeks permission to operate an exclusive steamboat service on the River Bío-Bío for a period of ten years. It seems that Cunningham did manage to take a steamboat one hundred kilometers upriver from Concepción to Nacimiento and that he kept up a steamboat service in that region for many years.

In 1852, Matías Cousiño appeared on the scene. This was the year that he bought the Hacienda Colcura from Juan Alemparte and a man named Arteaga. The Alemparte brothers, Juan and José Antonio, had bought land in Lota in 1837 from an Indian chief named Carbullanca for 150 "pesos de plata sellada," and by 1844 had started to mine the coal on this land. The work was hard, and they considered throwing in the towel, when it occurred to them that Matías Cousiño might be interested. He had the reputation of being an entrepreneur and for not giving up, and he had the capital that was needed. Cousiño had made money already in silver and copper in the north of Chile.

Matías Cousiño organized his company in 1852 with a British businessman named Thomas Bland Garland as a partner, along with Arteaga and Alemparte. They called this company the Compañía de Lota. Later, Arteaga and Alemparte sold their shares to Cousiño and Garland. Later still, Garland withdrew from the company; his contribution was essentially to seek loans from the merchant houses of Valparaíso. The early years were difficult for Cousiño, whose business suffered from the poor reputation of Chilean coal. He died young in 1863, three years after visiting Britain to familiarize himself with the coal mining industry there. The company continued under his only son Luis Cousiño Squella, who died prematurely in Peru in 1873. Luis's wife, Isidora Goyenechea, took over the running of the company from this moment until 1881, handing over to her son Carlos. From 1870, the company operated under the name Compañía Explotadora de Lota y Coronel. In 1905, this company was reorganized as Compañía de Lota y Coronel, and then renamed the Compañía Minera e Industrial de Chile in 1921.

Many of the engineers and technicians were British. Mark Beresford Whyte was the first chief mining engineer in charge of operations at the Compañía de Lota, and supervised the digging of the first pits. He also contributed a great deal to early development by introducing English methods of mining, including the first use of steam driven machinery, which was installed under his direction in 1852. Many others figure in this story, and include such names as John and Joseph Simpson, William Stephenson (engaged by Matías Cousiño in 1857 to survey the coal deposits around Lota), Mr. Johnson (a mining engineer who worked in Lota in the mid 1850s), and Matthew Wilson (who held administrative posts in the Compañía de Lota between 1854 and 1870).

Other key names are William Perry, his brother Henry Perry (who administrated the Lota mines in two periods, 1889–1892 and 1900–1902, and also became mayor of Lota), Thomas Dodds, and John Bull. There were also William Raby and Gregory Raby (chief mining engineer from 1902 to his death in 1917); William Condon (administrator of Lota mine in 1903–1914); Robert Price (general administrator of the Lota mines in 1914–1921); and Henry Stevens (chief engineer in 1917–1922).

Hugh Gardiner, a Scottish mining engineer, arrived in 1894 to the post of Chief Engineer in the Arauco Mining Company and stayed on until this company was sold in 1919. There was also John Grahame, who designed a new and audacious mine at Puchoco that bored under the sea and over the inundated workings of a previous attempt to excavate coal away from the land. Thompson Matthews arrived in Chile in 1855, and, together with his brother William, he managed the industrial area for the Lota Company and the firebrick plant that adjoined the mine.

Several of these technicians and managers settled in the region and had sons who contributed further to the development of the coal mining industry. Significant examples are John Mackay's sons Roberto (who studied mining engineering in Scotland) and Bronlow (who qualified as a mining engineer in England). William Raby's son Gregorio was chief engineer in Lota from 1912 to 1917. Thompson Matthews' two sons followed him in the coal business: Henry was the Administrator of Lota mine from 1893 to 1899, and Thompson Jr. was the Administrator of the Lota and Coronel Mines from 1899 to 1914 and became President of the Board in Lota in 1915. In the 1880s, the English "long wall" method of coal extraction was introduced, and several British engineers were contracted to put this into practice, Hunter, Malome, Mottram, Cox, Nesbit, and Bulman.

Another name with strong British connections is Frederick William Schwäger. Although he was born in Zerbst, Anhalt, Germany, he arrived in Valparaíso around 1830 on a boat carrying British immigrants to Chile, which suggests that he may have spent some time previously in Britain. At first, he worked in Valparaíso in insurance and shipping and acted as an agent for the sale of coal. But he made his fortune when he moved south and started in the coal mining business in Puchoco, near Coronel. Schwäger & Son (his son was also named Frederick Schwäger), set up the Compañía Minera de Puchoco in 1859 in partnership with Guillermo Délano & Company. Later Schwäger bought out Délano's share and formed the Compañía Carbonífera y de Fundición Schwäger.

Frederick Schwäger (son) paid for the construction in 1881 of a tower in Coronel to celebrate the Naval Battle of Iquique in the War of the Pacific and donated the clock, which was specially imported from England. Intended to be known as the "Heroes Tower" it was, and still is, called the Torre de los Ingleses, and the square around the tower is referred to locally as the Plaza de los Ingleses. At the age of sixty-eight, Schwäger became very ill and decided to go to England but died in 1892 on board a British ship off Pernambuco in Brazil.

An American journalist, Theodore Child, visited the coal mining region in 1891 as part of a tour round South America, and in an article for *Harper's Weekly* commented that, with only one exception, "the heads of the various departments at Lota are all English; several of them, it is true, born in Chili, but still English in language, habits and genius" (February 14, 1891, 118). The British were so numerous in the coal mining region that, not surprisingly, they introduced their pastimes and sports. Mazzei de Grazia (1924) notes that by 1887 there were cricket clubs established in Lota, Coronel, and Concepción and that they popularized football (soccer), rowing, and boxing in the communities where they lived. The Anglican faith arrived too—a chaplaincy was established in Lota in the early 1860s, and there was a temperance club called the "Blue Ribbon."

Later in the nineteenth century came Britain's first important investment in coal mining, with the founding in London (1886) of The Arauco Coal and Railway Company by the Nitrate King, John Thomas North. This was the only British company established to exploit coal in Chile. Colonel North's company owned the railway and the bridge over the River Bío-Bío and also operated several of the coal mines south of Concepción. The general manager for the company from 1894 to 1909 was a Scotsman named David Thomas (see Mair 1989; Couyoumdjian 2003). In 1915, the Arauco Company accounted for 11 percent of the coal produced in Chile. It remained British until 1919, when it was sold to the Compañia Los Ríos de Curanilahue, which in turn passed control, in 1920, to the Compañia Carbonífera e Industrial de Lota y Coronel, the largest coal company in Chile at that time.

The Chilean workmen worked hard, and the norm was a working day of "sun to sun." This was sometimes literally so. Henry Jolley, who arrived in Lota in 1911, recalled seeing a section head named Llewellen Stephan, who would wait at the mine exit with an enormous pocket watch in his hand, waiting for the sun to touch the horizon, upon which he would turn around and go home, with the workers trailing behind him.

British engineers were still involved at the outbreak of the Second World War, when the Schwäger Company decided to open a coal seam one kilometer down—the first time this had been attempted in Chile—and the project architects were company employees Henry Cahill (administrator), William Ward (chief engineer), and Robert Smith (maintenance engineer). Later still, in the mid 1980s, the operations manager in Lota was a Scotsman named Peter Crorkan.

British names, then, are intimately linked to the history of coal mining in Chile, but British capital played only a small role in its development, and in fact much more significant to the economic development of Chile as a whole were the imports of coal from Britain. This coal was imported in large quantities until domestic production started to make a difference. In 1862 (see Centner 1942), a big import of British coal to the mining regions of northern Chile caused work almost to be suspended in the coal mines of Lota and Coronel, and even as late as 1913 nearly one million tons were imported from Britain.

The Lota Company, which Matías Cousiño organized in 1852 in partnership with Thomas Bland Garland, was an enormous gamble, given the poor reputation of Chilean coal, the competition from better quality coal imported from Britain, and the absence of mining expertise in Chile at that time. But they had a stroke of amazing good fortune the following year with the chance arrival of experienced miners from Scotland.

According to an item published in the Santiago newspaper *El Mercurio* on September 17, 1853, a ship called the *Colinda* had arrived in Chile that month en route from Britain to Vancouver Island in Canada via the Magellan Strait. The newspaper reported that the majority of the 260 passengers had disembarked in Corral, the port of Valdivia in the south of Chile and had taken up employment in the coal mines of Lota. Several of these passengers were in fact miners traveling with their wives and children, and they were under contract to the Hudson's Bay Company to work at the coal mines on Vancouver Island.

It turns out that the voyage had not been a happy one, and an explanatory message sent on March 10, 1854, by David Cameron in San Francisco to Archibald Barclay, secretary of the Hudson's Bay Company in London, started with bad news: "I am sorry to say that within the past few days I have received very unpleasant news of the *Colinda*" (HBC Archives A.11/75 fo. 85d). In a postscript added on March 15 he wrote that "most of the Emigrants had left the *Colinda*, that they had been wandering about the streets in a destitute state and declared that they would not go in the ship with Captain Mills but that they were quite willing to go to Vancouvers Island with any other Captain."

Sources differ as to whether the passengers actually disembarked in Valparaíso, as in Cameron's report, while others suggest that Thomas Garland happened to be in Valdivia when the *Colinda* called in at the port of Corral and that he took immediate advantage of the situation. One important, but not always reliable book, *Old Timers, British and American, in Chile* (1900) by "Quién sabe" (a pseudonym for Charles Fletcher Hillman) calls the boat the *Celinda* and says that the passengers obliged the captain to put in at Corral in August 1853. Fletcher adds that forty-five of the families left from Corral with Thomas Garland to work in the emerging coalmines of Lota.

Judith Hudson Beattie's research (2007) suggests strongly that there is some truth in both versions. The *Colinda* did call in at Corral, but "the passengers were not allowed off the ship except to wash their clothes (although some swam from the ship or got in boats to get drunk on the shore). After they had spent about five weeks there, they were taken to Valparaíso where they were submitted to a trial where they were accused, with the crew, of mutiny, but the charges were dismissed. They were wandering the port, destitute and refusing to go back on the ship, when Thomas Bland Garland hired them for the mines in Lota" (correspondence with the author).

Whether coming from Valparaíso or Corral, many of the miners from the *Colinda* certainly did arrive in Lota, and an official report prepared by Rafael Sotomayor, the provincial intendant of Concepción, published in the *El Diario* newspaper of that city on February 6, 1854, gives important details. The report states that there arrived in Lota "156 Scots" contracted by "the House of Garland and Cousiño," consisting of fifty-one men and thirty-six married women, with seventy-four children of fifteen years and below.

Mary Stathers (1987) provides the background to the voyage before it left Scotland. David Landale, The Hudson's Bay Company's agent in Scotland, had been commissioned in early 1853 to recruit miners and their families from Ayrshire to emigrate to Vancouver Island. Despite local opposition to the idea of losing experienced miners, by the middle of June, David Landale had lists of miners recruited at Kilmarnock and Crosshouse, and advances were paid to get them kitted out for the voyage. Once on board the *Colinda*, these Ayrshire colliers and their families, and forty Norwegian laborers, soon found that a nightmare voyage had begun: "It was soon clear that all was not well aboard the Colinda, for disagreements grew between the Master, Captain John Powell Mills, and his surgeon, Dr. Henry William Alexander Coleman, and all the others . . . Captain Mills challenged his surgeon to a duel with pistols across the table, terrorized the passengers and laid charges of Mutiny and Piratical Acts against the passengers and crew" (Stathers 1987, 326).

There is a document in the Hudson's Bay Archives (A. 6/30 fos. 118–118d) which lists the "Labourers engaged for Vancouver's Island by Mr. D. Landale," dated June 17, 1853. This is a list of thirty-five families, mostly with clearly Scottish names, each meticulously given the corresponding "Dargs" (or days' work for the family) and details of the age of each family member. For example, there is John Kerr, allocated "3½ Dargs," on account of himself (aged forty-three), two boys of twenty and sixteen, and a third boy of fourteen (presumably the half Darg).

Another of the miners in this list is Alexander Campbell Watt of Kilmarnock, aged twenty-three, with a wife of twenty-one and one son aged two years. A tombstone in Lota Cemetery shows that Alexander died aged sixty-three, and his wife Mary Ann aged eighty-four. Newspaper accounts in Lota show that Alexander was in fact murdered. The same tombstone and the one next to it bear witness to three children born in Lota, John Watt Graham (who became the administrator of the Schwäger Mines in Coronel), John William Hamilton, and Albert Llewelyn Steven, but none corresponds in age to the two-year-old boy who left Scotland on the *Colinda*.

While the Watts did stay on in Chile, and so did a number of the miners' families, such as Millar, Wilson and Hunter, it seems that many of these Scottish miners and their families left within a few years of arriving. The 1865 census gives evidence of only four Scottish males and one woman in the *departamento* of Lautaro, where Lota and Coronel were located, and another two in Arauco. Nevertheless, their chance arrival when the coal business was in its infancy was undoubtedly crucial to the early development of the industry.

One very special aspect of the coal mining region in the south is Lota Park or Parque Isidora Cousiño. The park is clearly modeled on the Victorian urban park, and it is therefore not surprising that there are strong British connections in its history. The park is laid out on a peninsula at the edge of Lota Bay and can still be visited today. It was the initiative of Luis Cousiño who, when his father died, had the idea of landscaping the park, building the Cousiño family residence there, and calling it after his wife Isidora Goyenechea de Cousiño. Much of the work on this urban park was undertaken in the years 1862 to 1872. The design of the park was undertaken by an English landscape gardener, Mr. Bartlet, and later administered by an Irishman, William O'Reilly, in the period 1873 to 1898, following the death of Luis Cousiño, when his wife Isidora Cousiño continued with the work of building up the park. Walter Baster was head gardener in the 1870s. William Perry helped with the design of the gardens, artificial lakes, and bridges, and he arranged for several species of tree to be brought over from Europe.

Visitors to the park came away with different opinions, generally flattering, but not always. An early visitor was Annie Brassey who visited Chile in the SS *Sunbeam* and came to Lota in October 1876. She left the ship to visit the park, and her impressions are worth quoting:

> Tended by over a hundred men, whose efforts are directed by highly paid and thoroughly experienced Scotch gardeners, these grounds contain a collection of plants from all the four quarters of the globe, and from New Zealand, Polynesia, and Australia. Amid them were scattered all kinds of fantastic grottoes, fountains, statues, and ferneries; flights of steps, leading downwards to the beach, and upwards to sylvan nooks; arcades, arched over with bamboos, and containing trellis-work from Derbyshire, and Minton tiles from Staffordshire; seats of all sorts and shapes, under trees, in trees, and over trees; besides summer-houses and pagodas, at every corner where there was a pretty view over land or sea. (Brassey 1878, 156)

Thirteen years later, in 1889, William Russell described his own visit to the park in less-than-glowing terms. "[It is] an extensive and well-arranged park and gardens, laid out with pleasure-grounds and hothouses, marvellous tropical vegetation, amid which hummingbirds were flitting"; but all of this beauty "seemed out of place in surroundings where one came upon sham stalactite caves, with glass balls swinging from the roof, giving the impression that the place was a Cockney tea-garden"! Russell concluded that "provided that the beautiful park was spared, the rockeries, the statuary, and the grottoes might, even if the house went with them, be most advantageously removed by one of the tidal waves" (Russell 1890, 41).

There is another "Lota Park," in the center of Fishguard, Pembrokeshire, Wales. The land for this park was donated in 1923 by Walter Williams, the son of a local sea captain named William Williams. Walter became a solicitor and coroner in Fishguard but was born in Lota. His father William had moved to Chile in 1863, where he spent several years trading on the west coast.

While the British presence in Chile's coal mining industry is all but forgotten these days, this is not the case with the nitrates industry. British capital and British names are still closely associated with the activity that they rose to dominate in the late nineteenth century. The watershed for this remarkable connection was the War of the Pacific of 1879–1883. Prior to this war, Chilean exports had focused largely on copper and silver, where the British had a relatively small stake, but afterwards and for the next forty years the Chilean economy was primarily tied to nitrates.

The story of large-scale British investments in nitrates dates back to the early 1880s, shortly before the end of the War of the Pacific. On the eve of the War, in 1879, the British share in total nitrate output was just over 13 percent of the total, with all production in provinces that were then Peruvian and Bolivian but would shortly become Chilean. By 1890, there were twenty-five British companies operating in these northern nitrate fields (now annexed by Chile), with a total paid-in capital of at least twelve million pounds, and a peak was reached in 1895, when the British share in overall production amounted to 60 percent. This share then began to decline, down to 55 percent in 1901, and then to 35 percent in 1921, by which year Chilean-owned industry accounted for just over half of the production.

The immediate origins of the War of the Pacific go back to the 1860s, and the early extraction of nitrates. Two Chilean businessmen (José Santos Ossa and Francisco Puelma) started processing nitrates in the Antofagasta region, which then belonged to Bolivia. The product was soon in great demand overseas as a fertilizer. Ossa and Puelma opened a nitrate processing factory, but this failed, and they were compelled to return to Valparaíso to seek additional financing. This funding came from a partnership of Chilean and British investors called Melbourne Clark and Company. The other British partner was William Gibbs, and the Chilean partners were Francisco Puelma and Agustín Edwards, a Chilean banker of British descent. Melbourne Clark appointed George Hicks to run the operation in Antofagasta. At the time that war broke out in 1879, the network of nitrate extracting firms was mainly run by Chilean and British interests, in both Peruvian Tarapacá and Bolivian Antofagasta. In fact, the majority of the people living on the coast in these two provinces were Chilean.

The War of the Pacific pitted Chile against both Peru and Bolivia, and the reasons behind the conflict with each of these countries were both different and at the same time intertwined. The early history of the frontier in the north between Chile and Bolivia is of relevance. In 1825, the new Republic of Bolivia decided to declare the bay of Cobija the official port (*puerto mayor*) in their territory of Atacama, which belonged at that time to the Bolivian *departamento* of Potosí. Simón Bolívar had asked Peru to cede Arica as the main port for Bolivia, but they refused, and so he commissioned an Irish Colonel, Francis Burdett O'Connor, to find an alternative along the Pacific coast. O'Connor surveyed the region and came up with Cobija, called at that time Lamar, which from the start faced many difficulties. Access across the desert was problematic, and the rival port of Arica was favored by Bolivian (and Peruvian) commerce. This rivalry actually led to Peru sending two warships on an unsuccessful mission to destroy the port at Cobija. The port was virtually wiped from the map in the earthquake of 1865 and a tsunami in 1877, and today the site is in ruins.

In 1842, the Chilean government gave tacit agreement to a border at 23 degrees south, known as the "Mejillones Parallel," but Bolivia complained and insisted on a border further south. In 1866, faced by a common danger (that of Spain), Chile and Bolivia signed a treaty agreeing to 24 degrees south as the border between their countries. They also agreed to share the profits from the mineral wealth found between the twenty-third and twenty-fifth parallels, and Bolivia undertook to charge no export tax on Chilean guano. This agreement was regarded as rather vague, and it did not reduce the sense of distrust that existed between these countries. In 1874, Chile set out to settle once and for all the long-standing dispute over where the frontier lay and agreed to having this border fixed at 24 degrees south in return for a promise from Bolivia that there would be no further taxation of Chilean nitrate businesses in the Antofagasta region during the following twenty-five years.

The Bolivian government had given generous concessions in the Atacama region to the Antofagasta Nitrate & Railway Company, which was a very powerful Chilean-British corporation. In 1878, Bolivia suddenly introduced an additional export tax, arguing that this move did not offend the treaty because this was a British and not a Chilean company. The Company refused to pay, and the Bolivian government threatened confiscation. Then the war broke out. In February 1879, a small Chilean military force took over the port of Antofagasta and then assumed control of the coastal settlements. This action triggered an escalation of the dispute, and Peru was brought into the conflict on account of a secret treaty of mutual alliance with Bolivia.

Peru had its own reasons to enter the dispute. Rory Miller (1993) argues that the depletion of guano resources and poor management of the economy in Peru had provoked a crisis. This had caused Peru to default on its external debt in 1876, a measure that particularly hurt British and French bondholders. This came on top of the partial nationalization of the nitrates industry in the Tarapacá region (belonging to Peru) in 1875. In that year, the Peruvian government decided to procure a loan of seven million pounds, of which four million pounds was earmarked to purchase privately owned *oficinas* (nitrate producing plants). State certificates were given to the owners as compensation, and many of them were British, but Peru never received the loan and defaulted again on its external debt in 1877. Significantly, the certificates were never cancelled, and they were made payable to bearer.

In April 1879, Chile declared war on both countries. Lima fell to Chilean troops in early 1881, which effectively brought military operations to a close. The war with Peru formally ended in October 1883 with the Treaty of Ancon, which ceded Peru's Tarapacá province to Chile. Peace with Bolivia was arrived at separately with the Treaty of Valparaíso in April 1884, by which Bolivia ceded control of its entire coastline of Antofagasta to Chile until a full peace agreement could be negotiated, which happened only in 1904. Chile increased her territory by more than one third.

The British name most associated with British activity in these two northern provinces is the larger-than-life, legend-in-his-time figure of John Thomas North, the Nitrate King. North was born at Holbeck near Leeds in 1842, the son of a prosperous coal merchant, and he trained for eight years as a mechanical engineer before joining John Fowler & Company of Leeds at their steam plough works. His firm sent him to Chile to maintain steam locomotives in the copper-mining region on the Carrizal Bajo railway near Caldera. This was probably in 1869 (sources differ on the actual year). In 1871, North decided to leave his British employer and follow his fortune, first in Iquique, where he worked in a Peruvian nitrate *oficina*, becoming chief engineer at the Peruvian Santa Rita nitrate-producing plant.

The nitrates were found mainly in the Province of Tarapacá and were worked in deposits known as *salitreras*. Tarapacá is an immense desert region, and there was no water. North saw his chance in 1875 and bought a tanker, the *Marañon*, to hold water, and then in 1878 he rented for two years the facilities of the Compañia de Aguas de Tarapacá (Tarapacá Water Company). The War of the Pacific started in the following year, and the company founders—all Englishmen— left Iquique. The Chilean army arrived in the port, and the authorities decided to recognize North as the owner of the company. Most of the company's tankers survived the conflict, and on this basis North came to have a monopoly for the provision of water to the port. Then he began to invest heavily in the nitrate industry. In April 1881, North entered into a partnership in Iquique with Maurice Jewell (British Consul from June 1889), to import machinery and tools for the nitrate plants, and to act as agents for steamship companies that were beginning to call more often at the port.

It is commonly believed that Colonel North instigated the war in some way, but these claims have been refuted by modern historians, especially Harold Blakemore (1974). However, it is probable that North had access to key information and to investment funds through two well-placed friends. At the outbreak of the war, his associate Robert Harvey held the post of Inspector General of Nitrates for the Peruvian Government and was the source of insider knowledge for North about the nitrate industry. The funds came through his acquaintance with John Dawson, who at different times had been the manager of the London Bank of Mexico and South America in Lima and Valparaíso, but in 1879 was manager of the Chilean Bank of Valparaíso in Iquique. Dawson remained a banker all his life and never became a director of a nitrate company.

Robert Harvey, on the other hand, had a similar career to Thomas North, and the two became intertwined in commerce. Harvey was born in 1847 in Truro, Cornwall, and after finishing school he worked at a foundry. This firm sent Harvey to the port of Tocopilla in Chile to set up machinery for the Carmelita mine, where he worked for a number of years. In 1875, hearing of the boom in nitrates, Harvey decided to try his luck further north, in the then Peruvian port of Iquique. He worked for a time in an *oficina*, and then, when the Peruvian government decided in 1875 to nationalize the nitrate fields and needed comprehensive information about the industry, Harvey was appointed Inspector General of Nitrates.

He was also made an honorary colonel in the Peruvian army. When the war started, the Chilean army advanced quickly into the Province of Tarapacá, and Harvey found himself a prisoner of the Chilean forces and was taken to Iquique. Admiral Patricio Lynch interviewed him, and Harvey's defense was that quite naturally he had supported Peru at that stage, since they were his employers. The Chilean view was that they were in Tarapacá for the long term and that Harvey's expertise was valuable to them. So they made an offer that he could hardly turn down, and Harvey became again Inspector-General of Nitrates from February 1880, this time working for the Chilean government.

In June 1881, with Chilean forces in control of the northern provinces, but before the War was in fact finished, the Chilean government was subjected to pressure from Peru's creditors, which included British bondholders, in particular Antony Gibbs and the London Bank of Mexico and South America. These creditors threatened Chile's credit in Europe if their claims were not met. So, Chile issued a decree in 1881 (reinforced in 1882)—while the war was still in progress—by which it committed itself to returning the nitrate industry to private ownership. The Chilean government wanted to revive nitrate exports as soon as possible in order to help pay off the costs of the war and also to establish its sovereignty and control over the newly won territory. For these reasons, the government undertook to honor the rights of those who held nitrate certificates, as long as they held certificates equal to three-quarters of the value of a *salitrera* and could deposit the remainder in cash. It is possible that Robert Harvey knew that this was the intention of the Chilean government, since he had remained as Inspector General of Nitrates, but this has not been substantiated.

North and Harvey went to Lima in 1881 to purchase nitrates certificates at rock-bottom prices. Much of the funding came through the Iquique branch of the Bank of Valparaíso, managed by North's friend, John Dawson. The next move for North and his associates was to launch joint-stock companies in London to exploit the concessions that they had acquired, and to sell the nitrate industries to these companies.

In 1882, North went back to Britain, and with further financing there he formed the Liverpool Nitrate Company Ltd. (1883) with himself as chairman and Harvey as one of the directors. It was this company that confirmed North as the Nitrate King. This was no exaggeration; North and his associates dominated what was a near global monopoly, since the only substantial deposits of *salitre* (sodium nitrate) in the world are found in the Atacama Desert. Chilean nitrates were used as fertilizer, underpinning the huge expansion of agriculture in the world toward the end of the nineteenth century, and as an ingredient in the manufacture of explosives until the start of the First World War.

North's activities set off a nitrate boom on the London Stock Exchange. Although the flotations were initially slow to start, by 1886 there were three companies that had established themselves, all of them organized by North: the Liverpool Nitrate Company, the Colorado Nitrate Company (1885), and the Primitiva Nitrate Company (1886). Following this, North and his group bought a major interest in the Nitrate Railways Company, which had the sole concession for railways in the nitrate fields. Another railway followed—the Arauco Railway Company— giving North access to the coal deposits in Lota, needed for the gas plants he had installed in the nitrates fields. In 1888, North took control of the Tarapacá Waterworks Company, which supplied Iquique's water needs from spring waters at Pica, and in 1889 he created the Nitrates Provisions Supply Company, with Robert Harvey as Chairman of the Board. He also had a substantial stake in the Nitrate Producers' Steamship Company, from 1895. With so much business under North's control, a bank was needed, and this led to the founding of the Bank of Tarapacá and London, launched at the end of 1888.

North's sudden, spectacular, and widely reported rise to prosperity and social prominence spawned defenders and detractors. Among his detractors was *The Financial News*, which in June 1888 published a sarcastic comment—"the latest good story about our friend Colonel North":

> He was heard lamenting there were not more elements in nature than air, earth and water, as they were such nice things to finance. In Tarapacá he has made himself master of all the existing elements. With his Nitrate Companies and Nitrate Railways he controls all the saleable earth in the province. With his sea-water condensers, his water barrels and his Pica concession he monopolises the drinking materials. It is generally understood that [recently] he was elaborating a scheme for placing the atmosphere of Tarapacá under the care of a limited liability company, with an airy capital of several millions sterling. (Quoted in Blakemore 1974, 68)

Other British companies included the Alianza Nitrate Company (1895) and the Rosario Nitrate Company (1889), but North was the undisputed Nitrate King. This had not gone unnoticed by the Chilean government, and there was increasing apprehension about the power and influence that had accumulated in his hands.

North left London for Chile in early 1889, having been away since 1882. He was worried about recent announcements by Chilean President Balmaceda regarding foreign investment in the nitrates industry that threatened his business interests. He was also concerned about his investments in the Nitrate Railways Company, having become chairman of the firm in the same year. This all led to the famous confrontation between Colonel North and President Balmaceda.

However, before leaving London, North gave an extravagant farewell ball for over a thousand guests at the London Hotel Métropole, which had been decorated with shields bearing the letter "N." In attendance was the volunteer regiment of the 2nd. Tower Hamlets (East London) Royal Engineers, of which North was their honorary

Colonel from March 1885. North at this time had become very fat, and he came to the ball as Henry VIII.

North resolved to gain further publicity by taking with him to Chile Melton Prior, an artist from the *Illustrated London News* (who was also a director in the Nitrates Railways Company) and two journalists—Montague Vizetelly of *The Financial Times* and the veteran *Times* correspondent William Howard Russell. Russell went to Chile with his wife as the result of "an accidental meeting and a few minutes' conversation with Colonel North at a luncheon party" (1890, 1). This led to an invitation to "see and report what had been done and what was being done, and to examine the works which had transformed the desert of Tarapacá—wastes without a sign of life or vegetation—into a centre of commercial enterprise" (1890, 2).

North and his entourage sailed on the SS *Galicia* of the Pacific Steamship Navigation Company and arrived at the port of Coronel in Chile in March 1889. North then learned that President Balmaceda had recently been touring northern Chile and making troublesome pronouncements, especially at Iquique, "which indicated the possibility of important changes, affecting materially the great interests of the strangers within her gates" (Russell 1890, 42), especially the mining and railway interests. North resolved to leave for Santiago immediately, to catch the President in Valparaíso, and he was ferried across the River Bío-Bío to catch the train going north from Concepción.

In Viña del Mar, North had the first of three meetings with President Balmaceda, who had just returned from a tour of the Province of Tarapacá. In Iquique, on this journey, Balmaceda had announced his views on the future of the nitrate industry, which included bringing the nitrate fields and railways under state ownership. He also later undertook to reserve these government holdings in nitrates only for Chileans. But perhaps his bark was worse than his bite. William Russell attended the first meeting, in Viña del Mar, and "the gist of the interview was that he had not the smallest intention of making war on vested interests" (Russell 1890, 82). Oddly enough, Russell reported that the President "was especially full of praise for the Nitrate Railway . . . and he said he considered it a complete model of good management and organization" (1890, 82).

Nevertheless, after these meetings, notwithstanding the pleasantries in Viña del Mar, President Balmaceda continued to move against North's railway monopoly and utilized other British business interests, which also had a stake in breaking his stranglehold on transport. The main British opposition came from Gibbs & Company, who rather resented North as an ostentatious Johnny-come-lately to the nitrates business and for enjoying the railway monopoly that seriously affected their own nitrates output and profits.

North traveled to Iquique by ship, presented a new fire engine to the municipality, visited several *oficinas* by train, and then returned to England in June 1889. During North's short absence from Britain, nitrate prices had dropped significantly, due to high production, and a crisis loomed for the Nitrate King, showing just how much his own personality and style was behind the boom in investment. His return served to restrain the worst losses, but only for a while, and by late 1889 the fundamental weaknesses of world trade in nitrates could no longer be papered over.

There followed a year of political and constitutional crisis in Chile, with President Balmaceda opposed by many deputies in Congress. The cancellation of the Nitrate Railways concession (and therefore its monopoly) by Balmaceda's administrative decree, and the denial of the right of appeal to the Chilean judiciary, was an affront to the rights of Congress, according to the mounting opposition, and a clear example of the President's abuse of executive power. It was during yet another debate in Congress on the Nitrate Railways Company in January 1890 that Balmaceda closed Congress and started to choose a new ministry without consulting the political parties. This triggered off a year of political crisis in Chile, during which the Nitrate Railways issue remained before the Chilean courts.

The matter had started as an economic question but quickly became embroiled in the country's constitutional crisis and then entered the international arena. In an exceptional example of Britain's Foreign Office interfering diplomatically on the side of British commercial interests in Chile, the British government and the minister-resident in Santiago showed their disquiet with how the Nitrate Railways Company was being dealt with and registered an official protest in February 1890. Naturally, the company of Gibbs & Company had a different opinion, and in March 1890 they protested to the British government that Colonel North's company's monopoly was actually detrimental to British capital invested in the same region. The Foreign Office was deeply embarrassed to discover that there was another side to the story.

Civil war broke out in January 1891 when the tensions between President Balmaceda and Congress could no longer be contained. The President accused North of instigating and even funding the revolution, using the Bank of Tarapacá and London to send funds to the rebels; others alleged that he was in collusion with Chilean bankers. The insurgents did seize nitrate fields, and they operated from that region, and North's nitrate companies did pay taxes to the rebels, but there is no irrefutable evidence pointing to North's complicity in setting off the conflict, nor in the involvement of his bank. Nevertheless, shareholders in the bank were told that the conclusion of the civil war was "very satisfactory," with the insurgents winning, although time would show that the new government would follow a policy very similar to that of Balmaceda's, if not actually more rigorously set against monopoly.

The British minister-resident, Sir J. G. Kennedy, had to deny a report published in *The Times* on May 22, 1891, that British and Chilean business interests had instigated the rebellion against President Balmaceda. He insisted that the British community in Chile had remained formally neutral during the Civil War. This was not quite true. The same diplomat admitted after the Civil War that the British community in Chile had given material assistance to the revolutionary forces, and it is clear that North's sympathies lay with the opposition. But the question of British commercial involvement in actually instigating the Civil War is another matter, and evidence of such complicity is sparse (see Blakemore 1974).

Now back in Britain in the 1890s, Colonel North embarked on several schemes, unsuccessfully running for Parliament in 1895 and replacing much of his dependence on nitrates by investing in industries in France and Belgium, coal in Wales, gold-mines in Australia, plantations in the Congo, and even in tramways in Egypt. He quietly divested himself of thousands of shares in nitrates industries and in the Nitrate Railways Company, and he was wise to do so, since there was a glut of nitrates in the world market and the price plummeted, and so of course did the dividends paid to shareholders.

The empire he had built up came to a sudden end when North collapsed and died in May 1896 while chairing a meeting of his Buena Ventura Company in London, a few days after entertaining four hundred guests at his palatial Avery Hill home. He was just fifty-four years old. In an interesting contrast, Balmaceda has, over time, enjoyed rehabilitation in Chile, while John Thomas North has largely been forgotten. There is no memorial to Colonel North, the Nitrate King, in Chile, and there are few remembrances in Britain. However, a Yorkshire Society Plaque was resited and unveiled in 2008 in the Visitors' Center of Kirkstall Abbey, which North purchased and donated in 1889 to the city of Leeds, and his grave can be visited in the Eltham Parish Church cemetery in London.

Sadly for the historical record, as Rory Miller (1993) points out, the nitrate companies were terrible employers. There was little effort made to invest in hospitals and in education for the workers. While the money earned tended to be higher than the wages paid in central Chile, this difference was lost when the cost of living was taken into consideration. Many British nitrate companies continued to pay with *fichas* (tokens), although ruled illegal from 1852. These companies also ran their own stores, called *pulperías*, where the *fichas* were redeemed and much of their wage bill was recovered.

In 1920, the Sociedad de Fomento Fabril (the agency for industrial development) in Chile conducted a survey of the nitrate *oficinas* and found that of the 125 producers just over half were Chilean, while British ownership still accounted for 32 percent (forty-three *oficinas*) and American owners had only two *oficinas*. Nevertheless, this was the last act of British involvement, and during the 1920s competition from synthetic nitrates in Europe and the devastating effect of the Great Depression on Chile brought the nitrates industry to its knees, so that by 1933 most of the industry had collapsed. This was despite the introduction of the Guggenheim process to improve nitrate extraction, for example at the Oficina Maria Elena, inaugurated in 1926 with roads and buildings laid out in the pattern of the Union Jack.

Going against the grain, it was in 1933 that operations actually expanded in one of the most famous nitrates *oficinas*, the La Palma. This works was started by the Peruvian Nitrate Company in 1872, and its history spans the entire period of nitrates extraction, reaching even into modern times. Until 1889, La Palma was one of the largest nitrates mines in the Tarapacá province and probably comprised a population of around three thousand. This *oficina* closed during the worst period of recession in nitrates production but actually reopened in 1933 as a COSACH (Chilean Nitrates Company) investment, owned by the Compañía Salitrera de Tarapacá y Antofagasta.

There was a change of name; the works became known as the Santiago Humberstone *oficina*, in homage to James Humberstone, a British chemical engineer who had doubled the efficiency of the nitrates processing plants by introducing the Shanks process in around 1875. In the period up to 1940, following investment in modernizing the works, this *oficina* reached a population of 3,700 inhabitants, but the company entered into crisis in 1958, leading to the closure of the plant. By 1960, the site was completely abandoned.

Near the Humberstone works is the Santa Laura *oficina*, which also started up in 1872 but was always much smaller than the La Palma. There were around five hundred inhabitants in 1920. It is probable that this *oficina* worked only intermittently, since it did not meet expectations in terms of productivity. The New Tamarugal Nitrate Company took over ownership in around 1901, but work stopped in 1913, when the new Shanks system was introduced in an effort to improve efficiency. Production started again in 1921, but, as with Humberstone, the plant closed down in 1959, and both sites were then auctioned off in 1962.

The same private investor bought both properties for their scrap value, but then the two *oficinas* were declared national monuments in Chile and later nominated as a UNESCO World Heritage Site. Sadly, this legal protection has not prevented the dismantling of machinery and looting of construction materials, although enough remains to give a good impression of life and work in a nitrates industry community. The two works complement each other, since the Santa Laura site exemplifies many of the nitrate treatment processes and Humberstone shows how people lived and entertained themselves, and both are well worth visiting. In Humberstone, for example, there is a theater, which has recently been restored, a general store, a swimming pool—constructed of bolted sheets of iron—a hotel, chapel, school, hospital, and an administration building with canteen built in 1883.

The 2005 citation recommending inscription as a UNESCO World Heritage Site draws attention to the following justification: "The two saltpeter works nominated are clearly of outstanding universal value as the sole remaining vestiges of an industry that transformed the lives of a large proportion of the population of Chile, brought great wealth to the country, and indirectly supported the agricultural revolution of the late nineteenth century in many parts of the world."

Figure 9.1 Swimming pool at the Oficina Humberstone

Chapter 10

Banking

> *[British immigrants] came from a country in which improved farming and stock breeding were already widely practised, where commerce was an old and respected avocation, and merchants were long familiar with trade to distant lands. [Moreover,] a developed stock market and a vigorous, if unstable, banking system were further proofs of its economic maturity.*
>
> —David Joslin, 1963

In the period when Latin American countries in the early 1800s were struggling for independence from Spain and Portugal, British Foreign Secretary Castlereagh realized that Britain's real interests were bound up not with acquiring territory in the region but in trade with, and investment in, independent republics. Canning and Palmerston followed the same policy of promoting these nations' independence and avoiding any intervention by European powers in the conflicts that broke out.

British investments in Latin America were of two kinds. First of all, there were loans to governments, which paid the most interest, given that there was a considerable element of risk. Most countries in fact defaulted on the loans in time, but Chile was among the small number of countries in the region that struggled to fulfill its repayment obligations and, generally speaking, actually used the money for sensible ends.

The second type of investment was the setting up of joint-stock companies, especially during the periods that also coincided with the issuing of loans to the government, in 1862 to 1865, and from 1868 to 1873. These companies were behind the construction and running of railways, as well as cable-laying and the telegraph, city drainage, gas street lighting, trams, and the trading houses responsible for import-export. Imports to Chile included coal, iron, steel, machinery, and textiles. Exports to Britain encompassed nitrates, silver, and, later, copper and wool.

Much of this capital investment was in British hands, in the banking sector, and was especially heavy in the late nineteenth and early twentieth centuries. However, British involvement in banking in Chile, and Latin America in general, dates from earlier times and is linked not so much with banks in the modern sense but to trading companies and their merchant owners.

In Chile, British merchant houses such as Gibbs and Williamson Balfour added banking functions to their commercial business, especially in the 1850s and 1860s. Referring to Latin America as a whole, Geoffrey Jones (2000) explains that this was a natural business extension for the merchant houses that already extended credit to their customers and suppliers, and dealt in foreign currency.

John Mayo's study (1981) of the British-Chilean relationship in the second half of the nineteenth century identifies the start of British involvement in banking in Chile with a law passed by Congress in 1854. This law set down the rules for limited liability companies and effectively opened the way for joint-stock banks. The first bank that resulted was the Banco de Valparaíso, established in 1855. John Mayo shows that there was British influence in this bank, as shown in the names of several of the bank's directors published in 1894, when the bank merged with others to form the Banco de Chile. This strong presence on the Board was due not so much to investment in the bank's shares but to the fact that the British had valuable experience in how to run a bank. The trend in Chile until the founding in 1888 of the first British bank in Chile—the Bank of Tarapacá and London—was to bring British banking expertise onto the boards and into day-to-day management.

By 1870, there were branches open in Latin America belonging to four British banks—the London and Brazilian Bank, the London and River Plate Bank, the English Bank of Rio de Janeiro, and the London Bank of Mexico and South America—although none at this time had offices in Chile.

The London and Brazilian Bank was founded in 1862 and was the first British bank to be incorporated in South America. The London and River Plate Bank was also founded in 1862, as the London, Buenos Ayres and River Plate Bank (the name was shortened later). Started in January 1863, this was the first British joint-stock bank to open branches in South America. The London Bank of Mexico and South America resulted from the merger in 1864 of the London and South American Bank with the Mexican Bank and opened its first branch in Lima.

The first bank with British connections to operate in Chile started (and finished) as a Chilean bank—the Banco de A. Edwards, founded around 1866 (sources differ on the actual year). This was Chile's first domestic privately owned bank and was set up by Agustín Edwards Ossandón, the most financially successful of the eight children of George Edwards, an English physician immigrant to Chile. The Banco A. Edwards was very profitable and was closely linked to both the nitrate and copper booms, and, while accounting for only 8 percent of Chile's banking market in the period 1870–1885, this bank enjoyed 30 percent of the profits. Agustín Edwards Ossandón's son, Agustín Edwards Ross, established partnerships between his family's holdings in railways and nitrates and major British companies. In 1920 the family sold a 60 percent share of the bank to the Anglo-South American Bank but later, in the 1930s and 1940s, regained control of the bank. Another Chilean bank with British connections through descent was the Banco José Bunster, which opened in the south of Chile in 1882, following the "pacification" of Araucanía. José Bunster was a Chilean born of Welsh (or Cornish) descent and was sometimes called the Wheat King.

The first British bank with pretensions to open in Chile was the London and South American Bank, founded in 1863, according to the bank's prospectus, "for the purpose of affording banking facilities to Peru, Chile and the Western Coast of South America," but it seems that no branches were actually opened in Chile. The pioneer was the London Bank of Mexico and South America, which opened a branch in Iquique in 1872 (then in Peru), in order to participate actively in the growing importance of nitrate exports from the Province of Tarapacá. A branch in Valparaíso soon followed, but when the bank's business faltered as the guano boom faded during this decade, this branch was closed down. The War of the Pacific naturally affected this bank, since its head office was in Lima, and the Tarapacá nitrate fields now came into Chilean ownership. When Chilean forces first blockaded and then overran Lima in December 1880, the bank's manager felt compelled to take the bank's silver deposits and securities aboard HMS *Shannon* in the bay for safety. At the end of the war, this was the only bank still open in Lima. Foreign banking interest now moved south to Chile, given its recent gain of the valuable nitrate fields, and Chile became the preferred target of British capital investment in the 1880s. In this decade, two new British banks focused on Latin America were established: the English Bank of the River Plate (founded 1881), and the Anglo-Argentine Bank (1889).

In his published reminiscences of fifty-two years spent in Chile, William Russell Young (1933) recalled that in Valparaíso in the 1880s there existed five banks: Banco de Valparaíso, Banco Nacional, Banco Agrícola, Banco Mobiliario, and Banco A. Edwards. He remembered too that discontented shareholders in the Banco Nacional started up the Banco Internacional, but this was liquidated, as were the Banco Comercial de Chile, the Banco de Santiago, the Banco Mobiliario, and the Banco de Valparaíso. Russell Young also called to mind a branch in Valparaíso of the most famous and enduring of them all, the Bank of Tarapacá and London, which was founded in 1888 and opened to business in June 1889.

This was the bank that successfully launched British banking into Chile, and in the 1890s a network of branches was established in Chile. The bank was set up at the height of the "nitrate boom" orchestrated by the Nitrate King, John Thomas North. The initiative followed the annexation by Chile of the Antofagasta and Tarapacá Provinces during the War of the Pacific and consequently of the nitrate fields that were being exploited there. North soon had a great deal of business under his control, including nitrates, railways, coal, and water, and a bank was badly needed. This led to the founding of the Bank of Tarapacá and London in 1888. North became the bank's deputy chairman and he engaged actively in the bank's affairs in the early years, riding out the threats to his business interests represented by the policies of the Chilean President Balmaceda, although it was his associate John Dawson who played the main role in the bank's beginnings and organization.

Two branches were opened in the principal ports for nitrates, Iquique and Pisagua. Later, there were differences between Dawson and the bank over his remuneration, and he left the bank, only to be reappointed in 1892. The bank experienced difficulties in its early years of operations because it was too heavily dependent on North and on the state of the nitrates industry. For example, North's companies received large loans and advances from 1890 to 1895, and worse, North used his influence in the bank to compel other clients to conform to the rules of the Permanent Nitrate Committee, which he controlled, or else lose their access to overdraft facilities. However, this influence began to wane, and when North died suddenly in London in 1896, an applicant for a vacancy on the bank board was told, "The lamented death of Colonel North did not appreciably affect their labours, he having rarely attended meetings" (Joslin 1963, 185).

Branches of the Bank of Tarapacá and London were opened in Santiago (1895), Punta Arenas (1895), Concepción (1897), and Antofagasta (1897), together with smaller branches in the copper region in Calama, Copiapó, Coquimbo, and La Serena, in a period when this bank was practically alone in Chile in foreign banking. In 1900, the bank had to decide where it wanted to go; it had reduced its dependence on the nitrate industry but was now beset by strong competition from German banks. The immediate answer was to merge with the Anglo-Argentine Bank, a small British bank with offices in Buenos Aires and Montevideo. The new bank now changed its name to the Bank of Tarapacá and Argentina and in 1906 became the Anglo-South American Bank. In the same year, the London and River Plate Bank decided to open a branch in Valparaíso. Unfortunately, this coincided with the great earthquake of that year. The first branch manager arrived to a city that had been largely destroyed, and perhaps this contributed to the bank's enduring reputation as very conservative.

By 1910, there were five British banks with branches in Latin America: the London and River Plate Bank, the London and Brazilian Bank, the British Bank of South America, the Anglo-South American Bank, and the Cortés Commercial and Banking Company. In Chile, there were branches of two of these banks—the Anglo-South American Bank (in Iquique, Antofagasta, La Serena, Coquimbo, Valparaíso, Santiago, Chillán, Concepción, and Punta Arenas) and the London and River Plate Bank in Valparaíso. There were no British banks present in Peru in that year.

By 1914, British banks in Chile accounted for over one quarter of all deposits, and three-quarters of the deposits held in foreign banks. Britain was still the largest exporter to Chile and the other southern nations of Argentina, Brazil, and Uruguay, but Germany was a strong competitor. In fact, German exports to Chile had grown faster from 1900 than British exports, and British shipments to Chile were lower in 1913 than they had been in 1907. In terms of exports from Chile, by 1914 the main market for Chilean copper was the United States, and its nitrates were mainly sold on the continent of Europe.

At the close of the First World War in 1918, Lloyds Bank bought the London and River Plate Bank, although it continued to operate as a separate entity. In another significant move, the Anglo-South American Bank purchased in 1920 a controlling 60 percent interest in the Banco A. Edwards y Cía., by then a well-established private banking company. On his retirement from the Chilean Embassy in London, Don Agustín Edwards, great-grandson of the immigrant physician, became a director of the Anglo-South American Bank.

In October 1923, the Bank of London and South America (BOLSA) was formed by Lloyds Bank as a merger of the London and Brazilian Bank and the London and River Plate Bank. This amalgamation was engineered to prevent the two banks from competing, since they had the same kind of business and had many branches in the same cities. Lloyds was the major shareholder and retained control over this new bank.

By 1924, there were just two existing British banks in South America, both of which had branches in Chile—BOLSA and the Anglo-South American Bank. The Wall Street crash of 1929 and the ensuing depression badly affected both banks' operations, especially in Chile and Colombia, and the Board of BOLSA actually debated whether to close in both countries in February 1930, deciding in the end to continue in Chile but on a reduced scale.

In the late 1920s, the Anglo-South American Bank faced the problems of still managing the accounts of the traditional nitrate *oficinas*, which had received financing greater than the total of the bank's capital and reserves, when the competition from synthetic nitrates was inexorably undercutting the value of nitrates from Chile. The bank decided on a fateful decision, to make further loans to the industry. This was in the hope that with the industry's reorganization as the Compañía Salitrera Chilena (COSACH), during the government of Ibáñez, and the adoption of the new "Guggenheim" process for purifying nitrate, it would recover. But the situation worsened when Ibáñez was overthrown in a revolution, followed by the collapse of the nitrate industry in the years 1930 to 1932. The Bank of England had to launch an expensive rescue operation to save the Anglo-South American. In 1936, BOLSA took over the Anglo-South American Bank, which had itself absorbed the British Bank of South America, the Commercial Bank of Spanish America, and the London Bank of Mexico & South America.

In 1971, the Chairman of Lloyds, Eric Faulkner, wanted to develop an international banking group, and he merged the Bank of London and South America with Lloyds Bank Europe to create the Lloyds and BOLSA International Bank, in which Lloyds had a 51 percent interest. Three years later, Lloyds Bank acquired almost all the stock of the Lloyds and BOLSA International Bank, making it a wholly owned subsidiary with the name Lloyds Bank International. In 1986, Lloyds Bank International was merged into Lloyds Bank, and in 1995, Lloyds Bank Group merged with TSB Group to form Lloyds TSB Group plc. In 2002, the Banco de Chile merged with the Banco A. Edwards to form a newly constituted Banco de Chile. The history of both these modern banks involves a British bank founded by the Nitrate King with the unusual and now forgotten name of Bank of Tarapacá and London. In the case of Lloyds, this is a direct lineage; and in the case of the Banco de Chile, the link derives from the majority share in Banco A. Edwards being purchased by the Anglo-South American Bank for a time in the 1920s.

Chapter 11

Railways

> *The following morning we started gaily, and passed the Biobio [railway] bridge with interest, for it measures 1864 metres, and is, I believe, the longest bridge in the world except those over the Tay and the Forth, and a wooden bridge over the Oxus built by General Onnenkoff.*
>
> —Theodore Child, Harper's Weekly, *1891*

The construction in Chile of the second railway to be built in South America, after a line in British Guyana, was started in 1849, on a fifty-mile track linking silver and copper mines inland of Copiapó with the port of Caldera. On December 25, 1851, a train traveled the entire route for the first time. The original initiative was taken in 1845 by Juan Mouart, who may have been British (probably Scottish)—*John Mouart* (see Santa Cruz 1968; Thomson 1999). This concession was purchased by William Wheelwright, the American engineer who had made his name by founding the British PSNC company, and the Copiapó Railway Company was established in October 1849. Initially, most of the shareholders were Chilean, and the company remained Chilean throughout its history. However, by the early 1880s, following the War of the Pacific, the majority of shares were in British hands. One of the first engineers to work on the line was Charles Wood, the Englishman famous for designing the Chilean coat of arms. This line closed in 1978, after almost 130 years of operation.

The first important phase of railway development in Chile began in 1852 with the building of the Santiago and Valparaíso Railway. Prior to the construction of this railway there had been a weekly stagecoach service between the two cities, starting as a concession for passenger transport given in 1821 to Charles Neville and Joseph Moss, who were probably British (see Thomson 2001).

The first stretch of this second railway to be built in Chile was inaugurated in 1855. This was between Valparaíso and Viña del Mar and was largely built by the British engineer William Lloyd. William Wheelwright had conceived the idea of joining the port of Valparaíso with the capital Santiago as early as 1842, and he left Chile to look for investors in Europe, mainly in England. In 1845, a Liverpool businessman, Frederick Boardman, traveled to Chile to represent Wheelwright, and he asked the government for exclusive rights in the construction of this railway, plus a guarantee of 5 percent interest earned on the capital invested, and a ninety year monopoly on the railway. The government later reduced the exclusive rights to thirty years, and Congress passed a law in 1851 authorizing the construction.

The first head engineer was Allan Campbell, an American who had worked on the Copiapó–Caldera railway. He was replaced in 1853 by the British engineer George Maughan, who died of typhus soon after arriving. His deputy, William Robertson, took over but fell very ill. The company contracted William Lloyd, who arrived from England in May 1854, to find that only five miles had been laid on the way to Viña del Mar. Lloyd changed the route considerably, and this involved the construction of the first railway tunnel in South America, which later was destroyed to make way for the road that today links Valparaíso with Viña del Mar.

The railway had started as a mixed venture, whereby the government contributed about half the capital. Matías Cousiño and Joshua Waddington were among the principal private investors, but the consortium was not able to raise the capital needed, and in 1857 a British loan of seven million pesos made it possible for the government to continue with the railway, from Quillota to Santiago. In 1858, the state bought out most of the private investors. There were many further difficulties, and a new law in 1861 led to the famous American railway engineer, Henry Meiggs, being commissioned to finish the job. The entire line was inaugurated in 1863, and throughout its history as an independent railway, until 1884, there was a marked preference for British-built locomotives. Thereafter, British engines continued to run on the line until electrification in the period 1922 to 1924.

The third railway on which construction started in Chile, in 1855, was the mostly one-meter gauge Longitudinal Railway, which eventually ran for three thousand kilometers from Iquique in the north to Puerto Montt in the south. This venture also started with mixed capital, state and private, but the government of President Errázuriz assumed full control in 1873. The railway reached Puerto Montt in 1913. Since 1884, both these key railways have always been operated by the Chilean government enterprise, the Empresa de Ferrocarriles del Estado (EFE).

Participation by British firms in railway construction and their actual operation started when some of the existing short-distance railways in the 1850s and 1860s were purchased, and shares offered on the London Stock Exchange. These railways included the Arica and Tacna Railway (then in Peru), the Caldera–Copiapó and Coquimbo–La Serena lines in Chile, and the Nitrates and Railroad Company of Antofagasta (then in Bolivia), all of which were British owned by the end of the 1870s.

The Arica and Tacna Railway Company was formed in London in 1853, and the line was entirely in Peru when it opened in 1856, but it came into Chilean territory as a consequence of the War of the Pacific and remained so until 1929, when Chile returned the *departamento* of Tacna to Peru. British engineers also worked on the Ferrocarril de Carrizal, a mining railway near Caldera which operated from 1860 with horse power and from 1866 with steam locomotives on the Carrizal Bajo section. The president of this railway from 1864 was David Thomas, an Englishman who owned his own bank, the Bank of David Thomas. A Scotsman named John King became the engineer-manager of the Carrizal Railway in 1866; he had arrived in Chile accompanying a group of railway men from Glasgow in 1862. The future Nitrate King, John Thomas North, arrived (probably in 1869) on a contract with John Fowler & Company of Leeds to help look after the steam locomotives on this line. British engineers were also employed between 1868 and 1875 on the construction of the link between Iquique and Pisagua, the railway line belonging to the Nitrate Railways Company, which the journalist William Howard Russell traveled on in 1889, when it then lay within Chilean territory.

The 1880s saw huge British investments during and after the War of the Pacific in Chile's new nitrates-rich provinces of Tarapacá and Antofagasta, which were taken from Peru and Bolivia. This started in the northern sector with the Nitrate Railways Company, founded in 1882 (when the war was still in progress), but on the back of a railway that had existed when Tarapacá was Peruvian. The history of this railway goes back to 1868 and 1869 when the Peruvian government approved concessions to the company of Ramón Montero and Brothers for the construction of railways linking the port of Iquique with the nitrate deposits of La Noria and, separately, the port of Pisagua with the nitrate fields of Zapiga in Tarapacá. These lines were finished by 1875. A third concession was for a railway from La Noria to the Bolivian border, but this was never started.

The Montero Brothers transferred most of their rights in 1874 to the National Nitrate Railways Company of Peru but retained a large number of shares for themselves. This company was set up in 1874 and had directors in London but was a Peruvian company. The transfer did not include the concession for the line to the Bolivian frontier. The Peruvian government's approval for the transaction took a long time to come through; this happened only in February 1879, the same year that the War of the Pacific broke out. In the middle of the war, in 1881, the lines were returned to the National Nitrates Railways Company, but this company was not able to meet its obligations. This led to the formation of a new company, the Nitrate Railways Company (sometimes referred to as the English Company), which was registered in London in 1882 with the aim of acquiring the National Nitrate Railways. This company soon held a monopoly over railway transport in the Province of Tarapacá, centered on the port of Iquique. Colonel North became involved later by purchasing many shares from the Monteros in 1887, then as a director and deputy chairman in 1888, and as chairman of the board in the following year. (See Russell 1890, Appendix, 355–59, for a detailed early history).

Challenging the monopoly in this northern sector, the narrow gauge Junín Railway (Compañia de Salitres y Ferrocarril de Junín) opened a line to nitrate workings in 1894, in a concession which gave the Chilean government the right to acquire the railway whenever it wished. The origins of this initiative are far from clear. Some sources say the contract for building the line was given to Brooking, Child & Company, who transferred the contract to the *compañia*, while others, citing the original concession of 1890, point out that the spelling and other details do not coincide exactly. Nevertheless, it is very probable that the railway was built by a British construction company and that, while the actual shareholders in the initial company are difficult to identify, the line was later operated by Gibbs & Company from Iquique, from at least 1927.

The network connected several nitrates *oficinas* in the Province of Tarapacá, such as San Antonio, Santa Rita, California, and Asturias, to the port of Junín, covering the hinterland just to the south of Pisagua—a waterless plateau. Operating costs were high on account of the need to condense sea water to supply thirsty coal-driven locomotives, the line's isolation from other networks, and the need to install an aerial ropeway—replaced in 1924 by a cable-worked incline railway 1,250 meters long—to take the nitrate down 674 meters from the plateau to the beach at Junín.

The railway line changed from coal to petrol in the late 1920s, but this also proved to be expensive, and the decision was made to switch to cheaper diesel. This was a risky decision, since diesel locomotive power was still in its infancy. Nevertheless, in March 1929, the company placed an order with Hudswell Clarke & Company in Leeds for the world's first commercially built diesel locomotive, which arrived in Iquique via the Panama Canal in May 1930. The locomotive was named *Junín*, and, although the locomotive lived up to expectations, with overall running costs around one third those of a steam engine, it turned out to be a poor investment. The manufacture had cost £5,625, including the services of an engineer to put the locomotive into operation, but not including the freight to Chile. Then the Great Depression started, causing many of the *oficinas* served by the railway to close down. When nitrate production picked up later, much of the production went to the competing Nitrate Railways Company, and the Junín Railway ceased to function in 1934. The railway was acquired by the Rica Aventura *oficina* and continued to function rather precariously until 1956.

The central zone of the northern provinces was dominated by the Antofagasta (Chili) and Railway Company (1888), along with the Anglo-Chilian Nitrate Railway Company (1888). The southern zone of the nitrates area was home to the Taltal Railway Co, founded in Britain in 1881.

In 1900, there were 2,317 kilometers of privately owned railway track, compared to 1,664 kilometers which were state owned (Marín Vicuña 1900). The eighteen private railways existing in that year included the Nitrate Railways Company and several other railways in the nitrates region, together with the Transandine Railway and railways in the coal mining area south of Concepción. The latter included the Arauco Coal & Railway Company and two lines that joined Laraquete on the coast to the coal seams that had been acquired in 1890 by the Huena Piden (Chile) Colliery & Railway Company. The Chilean State Railways (EFE) had been established in 1884, but in 1900 there were just four state-owned railways: the Chañaral (which had been started as a concession given to George Stephenson in 1865 but was taken over by the State in 1888); the Huasco; and the Coquimbo—all in the north of Chile. The fourth railway was the Red Central—the Central Network connecting Valparaíso with Santiago and Temuco along with the accompanying branch lines.

Later came the state-owned railway from Arica to La Paz, constructed by Chile in part-fulfillment of the 1904 Peace and Friendship Treaty with Bolivia, which ended the truce that had existed between the two countries after the War of the Pacific. Its history, however, dates from the early 1870s, when the Arica and Tacna Railway Company, at that time in Peruvian territory, considered the possibility of extending its line to La Paz. Nothing was achieved until, following the War of the Pacific and the acquisition of the *departamento* of Tacna by Chile, the company commissioned another feasibility study. Nevertheless, it was only in 1903 that a New Zealand–born engineer named Josiah Harding was contracted by the Chilean government to recommend a route from Arica to La Paz.

The government issued a tender in August 1905. One of the four proposals came from the Chile & Bolivia Railway Construction Company, represented by Matthew Clark, whose Transandine Railway had started building a line over the Andes in 1887. This was not successful, and the winning proposal in 1906 came from the Sindicato de Obras Públicas de Chile (Public Works Syndicate of Chile), but little work was done, and the government cancelled the contract in August 1907. Work continued under a Chilean engineer, Benjamín Vivanco, until the government issued a second tender, which was won by the Deutsche Bank of Berlin. This too was cancelled, when the parties could not agree on the form of payment. A third, and successful, tender was awarded in 1909 to the British Sir John Jackson (Chile) Partnership, one of whose members was the Anglo-South American Bank.

The agreement stipulated that Bolivia would own the Bolivian section after fifteen years. The inauguration took place in May 1913, and at a cost of £2,750,000 the line finally opened to traffic in 1914. In this same year, Chile had 8,638 kilometers of railway track—more than doubling the total length since 1900. Over 60 percent of the network was now state owned, a reversal of the situation at the turn of the previous century. This was a different experience from other countries in the region in that throughout the development of railways in Chile, British companies coexisted with a quite extensive state-controlled network, whereas in the rest of South America state participation in railways was much less pronounced.

Nevertheless, British investment in Chilean railways grew quickly, so that by 1909 (see Centner 1942) of all the British capital invested in Chile listed on the London Stock Exchange, roughly fifteen million pounds was tied up in railways, substantially more than the nine million pounds related to nitrates and other miscellaneous investments.

Perhaps the most famous of the British railways in Chile was the Nitrate Railways Company, created in London in August 1882, before the War of the Pacific had in fact finished. After the War was over, toward the end of this decade, the Chilean government decided to end the company's monopoly in the region, and there was a court case that had the immediate effect of driving the unprofitable company toward bankruptcy. Colonel North bought a controlling interest in the railway in 1887, becoming President of the Board in 1889, but this was assuming quite a risk on his part. If the Chilean court ruled in favor of the government's position, he would lose heavily. However, North tried to ensure that this was not properly resolved by engaging expensive lawyers and lobbying Congress. Colonel North visited Chile in 1889, and in September that year, following his return to England, the Council of State in Chile ruled by decree against the company's interests by annulling the concessions on which it was based.

In the same month, the British firm of Campbell Outram & Company requested from the Chilean government a concession to build a railway from the *oficina* of Agua Santa to the port of Caleta Buena, and the Nitrate Railways' monopoly was finally under attack. (The Agua Santa concession awarded to Campbell Outram was handed within days to Chilean investors who transferred it to the Compañía de Salitres y Ferrocarril de Agua Santa, until the State acquired the company in 1915). Antony Gibbs & Company weighed in with protests to the British government in March 1890 that the Nitrate Railways Company was a monopoly and prejudicial to Britain's wider commercial interests in Tarapacá. Gibbs argued that the monopoly was "weighing unmercifully on the British capital invested in the Nitrate works" (quoted in Binns 2007, 37). Gibbs wanted to construct a railway line in the south of this province connecting the company's nitrate fields of Pan de Azúcar and Alianza to Chucumata on the coast—fields that they had not worked on account of the monopoly and the consequent high freight charges.

This became an issue in the political crisis of 1890 and the Civil War of 1891. President Balmaceda lost the civil war, but his successors turned out to be just as determined to end the Nitrate Railways' monopoly by giving concessions for competing lines. The Agua Santa Nitrate & Railway Company was the key means to establishing this policy, and eventually the Nitrate Railways Company had to come to terms with competition from newly formed railway companies in the Province, and the monopoly was effectively broken from late 1893 onwards. By the time of his death in 1896, North had sold off most of his shares in the company, and by 1913, it had become an autonomous free-standing company.

In an advertisement published in 1925, the Nitrate Railways Company (Ferrocarriles Saliteros de Tarapacá) describes itself as "the oldest nitrate carrying railway in Chile," serving seventy nitrate *oficinas* through the ports of Iquique and Pisagua. From 1928 onwards, the company had to compete in a much-reduced market with the state-owned Iquique to Pintados Railway, which was specially formed to break the monopoly hold of the Nitrate Railways Company in the center and south of the Province of Tarapacá. The company survived this and the crash of the nitrate industry following the world depression in the early 1930s, and it lasted until 1940 as an independent company.

The Antofagasta (Chili) and Bolivia Railway Company survived even longer as a British company—in the case of the portion of the line in Chile, a majority share was acquired by Chilean industrial interests only in 1980. The railway was first built to a narrow gauge of 2 feet 6 inches and later converted to one-meter gauge. It is still in operation today. The line climbs from sea level at Antofagasta to over 4,500 meters (15,000 feet). Several branches were built to serve mines, and the Collahuasi branch actually reached 4,815 meters (15,795 feet); this was considered the highest railway in the world at the time of its construction.

The history of this railway begins in 1872, at a time when the Province of Antofagasta was Bolivian. The Bolivian government granted a concession to Melbourne Clark & Company to build a railway from Antofagasta to this company's nitrate field at Pampa Alta, and a company, called the Antofagasta Nitrate & Railway Company, was formed in Valparaíso in 1872. Construction began in 1873, supervised by Josiah Harding, and the first section was operating later that year, although this was with mule power. Agustín Edwards Ossandón became the most important partner in this company. Steam locomotives were introduced in 1876, and the railway had reached some 150 kilometers back into the interior by 1879, the year that the War of the Pacific broke out.

Control of the railway passed to the Compañia Huanchaca in Bolivia in 1887, and this company then floated the railway on the London Stock Exchange the following year as the Antofagasta (Chili) and Bolivia Railway Company/Ferrocarril de Antofagasta a Bolivia [FCAB], with the right reserved to the Huanchaca Mining Company to work the line for a fifteen-year period. The funds raised by this flotation were used to complete the construction of the railway.

The engineering required to build the railway was one of the great triumphs of the age. Away from the mountains, on the Chilean side, a viaduct had to be built over the River Loa, and a steel and iron girder bridge was specially constructed in England. This was considered at that time one of the most daring technological challenges to be faced by engineers on account of the height of over one hundred meters above the river. This bridge stills stands and is known as the

Puente Conchi. Built in 1890, sixty-eight kilometers from Calama on the route from Antofagasta to Bolivia, it stands 105 meters above the river and is 244 meters long.

In 1892, the railway reached Oruro in Bolivia. British business interests regained control of the entire existing network in Chile and Bolivia in 1903. The Bolivian government supported the construction of the line from Oruro to La Paz in the period 1908 to 1913 and leased this line to the FCAB. This line was constructed to one-meter gauge, and there was now effectively a two-gauge system. The FCAB decided to start conversion to an all-one-meter gauge network in 1916, but the First World War intervened, and most of the work was not completed until 1928. The Bolivian assets of the FCAB were nationalized in 1964, but the British company survived in Chile until 1982, when Chilean business interests assumed control of the company and the head office moved from London to Chile. The railway is now a division of Antofagasta plc, which also has mining interests.

The railway runs through a desert—the Atacama Desert is one of the world's driest regions. Water was first obtained in Antofagasta by a process of distillation. Later, the company found spring water high in Andes mountains and then built reservoirs and pipes that brought water for their locomotives and the nitrate mines; in 1888 they obtained the concession to supply the town of Antofagasta with its water.

The first steam locomotives purchased by the company were British, made by Robert Stephenson & Company of Newcastle-Upon-Tyne. When control passed to the Compañia Huanchaca in 1887, the preference switched to American locomotives, but when control reverted to British interests in 1903, British machines were again seen on the railway—a preference that continued until the introduction of diesel locomotives in 1958, and beyond.

The Antofagasta (Chili) and Bolivia Railway Company (FCAB), was not always confined to the route between the two countries; the company took over the operation of the Northern Longitudinal Railway in 1919 on behalf of the Chilian Northern Railway Company. The Chilean Longitudinal Railway Construction Company had won a tender in 1909 to build a one-meter gauge railway from Pueblo Hundido, in the Atacama region south of Antofagasta, to the Lagunas station of the Nitrate Railways network. In 1910, the Chilian Railway Finance Company was integrated as a partner, and the contract was transferred to the Chilian Northern Railway Company. The construction was undertaken by MacDonald, Gibbs & MacGougall, and the northern destination moved from Lagunas to Pintados, with Baquedano at the junction with the FCAB railway. The railway opened in

January 1914 and was run by the FCAB from 1919 until the Chilean State Railways (EFE) assumed control in 1957.

Another British railway company linked to the nitrates industry was the Anglo-Chilian Nitrate and Railway Company. Founded in 1888 and based on a concession given at the conclusion of the War of the Pacific to a British investor named Edward Squire, the network eventually served the nitrate fields in the central zone around the towns of El Toco, María Elena, and Pedro de Valdivia, inland of the port of Tocopilla. This company constructed a 3-foot 6-inch gauge railway in 1890, later known as the Ferrocarril de Tocopilla al Toco, which subsequently belonged to the Nitrate Railways Company. The 115-kilometer line from Tocopilla through María Elena to Pedro de Valdivia was electrified in 1927, but the original line to El Toco was not electrified, and this branch closed in 1957.

Along with Iquique and Pisagua, Taltal was one of the great nitrate exporting ports. The Taltal Railway Company, founded in Britain in 1881, with an initial capital of five hundred thousand pounds, ran in the southern zone of the nitrates area. Construction started in earnest on the line in 1882, and by 1889 the railway had reached its destination at Cachinal de la Sierra, 149 kilometers from Taltal, and over time, branch lines were built to all the nitrate *oficinas* in the region. The company also built the port facilities, including several piers whose structures were manufactured in England, one of which still stands today.

Further south in Chile, in the coal mining region, the Arauco Coal and Railway Company was also a British initiative. A railway line was built from Concepción to Curanilahue, linking the port of Coronel, the town of Lota, and the coal fields of Puchoco and Lota, in the region of Arauco. The main reason for the undertaking was to connect the company's coalmines with the state railway at Concepción. This railway had started south from Santiago in 1857 and had reached Concepción in 1872. The decade of the 1880s was the time of the nitrates boom, and coal was urgently needed to fuel gas plants in the northern deserts, as well as for the growing cities of Santiago and Concepción.

This was not the first railway line in the region; there were short lines linking the extraction of coal with the ports—from the Maquehua mines to Laraquete, and from Raimenco to Triana and Trauco. Also, in 1910, the British-owned Chilian Eastern Central Railway Company obtained from Gervasio Alarcón the concession to run a line from Lebu, on the coast, to Los Sauces. The company went bankrupt in 1915, and the railway was taken over by the Compañia Carbonífera de Lebu for the sum of £222,000. Branch lines from Lebu to Peleco and from Los Sauces to Purén were completed by 1923.

There had also been at least one previous attempt to link Concepción with Coronel by rail—an authorization in 1873 to Guillermo Délano supported by John Marks and John Murphy, which came to nothing.

However, there was a problem; the River Bío-Bío is just south of Concepción and is Chile's widest river. It had to be crossed to reach the coal mining region of Arauco, and so the company was faced by "the delightful difficulty of constructing one of the greatest bridges in the world" and embarked on "one of the finest engineering works of the kind in the world." This was William Howard Russell's description (1890, 39) when he saw for himself the closing stages of the construction of the railway bridge across the River Bío-Bío on his visit to Chile in 1889. Colonel North was chairman and the major shareholder in the Arauco Coal and Railway Company. The iron bridge was finished in 1889, soon after Russell's visit—the same year that the great Forth Bridge and the Eiffel Tower were also completed.

Prior to the construction of this railway, coal had been sent inefficiently to the north by ship or had crossed the River Bío-Bío in small boats and on rafts. The bridge and the ninety-five kilometer railway now effectively linked the important coal mining region of Arauco to the rest of the country. The railway bridge over the River Bío-Bío enjoys the fame of having as many meters in length as the number of the year of its opening to traffic—1,889 meters from bank to bank—and this was William Russell's opinion. However, at least one photograph gives the distance as 1,864 meters, while other sources give 1,865 meters.

The construction of this bridge was truly one of the engineering triumphs of the age. The cost was £75,000, a fortune at that time. For the sake of comparison, the government-guaranteed cost of the railway line was £4,500 per kilometer. The technological expertise that was needed was available only in Britain, and in fact the contractor, Abbott & Company, all the engineers, as well as the machinery and ironwork, all came from Britain. An English engineer, Edward Manby, was responsible for designing the bridge and had to deal with the thorny problem of how to find footholds in the shifting river sands for the piers of the massive bridge. George Hicks was the General Manager; Mr. Bidder was the chief railway engineer in 1889 as well as manager of the company's colliery operations; and Edward Edmondson was the first owner of the company before Colonel North took it over in 1886.

The wrought-iron superstructure of lattice girders had a total weight of around 2,500 tons and was manufactured by John Butler & Company of Stanningley, near Leeds. The piers were made up of bundles of six cast-iron columns that added up to about 1,800 tons and were supplied by Fawcett, Preston & Company of Liverpool. The solution to the problem of the river sand is attributed by William Russell to Sir James Brunless. The pillars were hollow, and the sand was blown away by driving water from a pump down the tube at great force, allowing the pillars to settle into place thirty feet beneath the river bed. It is an impressive tribute to these engineers that the bridge still stands, and that it weathered the great earthquake of 1960—one of the most violent tremors ever recorded in the world—that cracked the nearby road bridge (opened only in 1943) and rendered the railway the only means of land communication north and south of the river for several weeks. Cargo trains still cross the bridge.

The need for a bridge was the major obstacle to the construction of the railway, but it was not the only difficulty. One short stretch of the line, between Lota and Laraquete, required 1,800 workers to bore and construct nine tunnels measuring in all 1,600 meters, as well as fourteen deep cuttings and two bridges. The rock was extremely hard, and despite the use of compressed air drills and explosives, sometimes progress was made at only ten inches per eight-hour shift. In fact, it took nearly five years to construct the railway line, and the official inauguration of the last stretch of track and the bridge took place only in February 1890.

The first locomotives in use on the railway were British and manufactured by Fowler & Company of Leeds, Robert Stephenson & Company of Newcastle, and Manning Wardle & Company of Leeds. The Lancaster Wagon Company provided the first cars, although they were modeled on an American design. The railway passed through Coronel, which at the end of the nineteenth century, before the opening of the Panama Canal, was one of the most important ports on the Pacific seaboard. The once elegant railway station in Coronel still exists, although the second floor, which housed the administrative quarters, was destroyed in the 1960 earthquake.

The Transandine Railway (Ferrocarril Transandino) was a combined rack and adhesion railway that operated between Mendoza in Argentina, across the Andes mountain range via the Uspallata Pass, to Santa Rosa de Los Andes in Chile, a distance of 248 kilometers. The idea of building a transandine railway was first promoted by William Wheelwright in 1852, when he suggested to the Argentinean government that Buenos Aires could capture in this way some of Chile's growing export trade. The project was taken up by John and Matthew Clark, Chilean brothers of British descent, who were successful entrepreneurs in Valparaíso. In 1871, they built the first telegraph service across the Andes, between Mendoza in Argentina and Santiago in Chile, and in 1872 they submitted their plan to construct a line crossing the mountains via the Uspallata Pass to both governments. Concessions were granted by Argentina in 1873 and by Chile in 1874.

Due to financial problems their company, Ferrocarril Transandino Clark, did not begin work until 1887, starting on the Argentinean side, and then the work proved so expensive that in 1892 they ran out of capital. Construction continued in fits and starts, and finally in 1896 a London-based company—the Transandine Construction Company— obtained a concession from the Chilean government and undertook to complete the work. When the entire line was opened to traffic in 1910, the company had been taken over by another British-owned firm, the Argentine Transandine Railway.

The line followed roughly the ancient route taken by travelers and mule trains crossing the Andes between Chile and Argentina and connected the railway networks of the two countries, rising to an altitude of 12,000 feet at Las Cuevas, where the track entered the Cumbre tunnel on the international border. The railway was very important in that it made possible the first rail link in South America between the Atlantic and Pacific Oceans—a 1,408 kilometer railway between Buenos Aires in Argentina and the port of Valparaíso in Chile. However, for several years the journey entailed traveling by train from Buenos Aires to Mendoza on the Buenos Aires & Pacific Railway (completed in 1888), then from Mendoza to Villa Mercedes by the Argentine Great Western Company (opened in 1886), followed by the narrow gauge Argentine Transandine Railway to a railhead in the mountains, and then by mule over the Andes at an altitude of 14,500 feet to the Chilean side. In 1909, the three-kilometer Cumbre tunnel was opened, and this finally completed the rail link. By 1925, the Chilian Transandine Railway Company was able to announce that the railway (jointly administered with the Argentine Transandine Railway Company) made possible a journey from Santiago to Buenos Aires in thirty-six hours. This railway has been out of service since 1984.

There was limited British investment too in Chile in street railways and streetcars. Santiago boasted one of the first street railways in South America (1858), but this was horse drawn. The second street railway in Chile opened in 1863 in Valparaíso as the Ferrocarril Urbano de Valparaíso, in a venture led by the English banker David Thomas. The streetcar company in Temuco (1881) was British owned. The Chilian Electric Tramway & Light Company (Compañia de Tranvías y Alumbrado Eléctrico) existed in Santiago and was founded by British and German investors in London in 1898. Morrison (1992) notes that financial control of the streetcar systems in

Santiago and Valparaíso passed to British companies in the early 1920s until they were acquired by an American consortium in 1929. However, much of the investment in such ventures, and consequently the rolling stock, was American and German, and unlike its experience in other countries in the region, Britain played only a minor role in the development and running of street railways and tramways in Chile.

The British stamp on Chile's railway history can today be appreciated by visiting the railway museums and displays of steam locomotives. These include the railway station at Baquedano (a National Monument) where the Northern Longitudinal Railway crosses the Antofagasta-to-Bolivia line. Nearby is the Baquedano Railway Museum, an open-air roundhouse with many locomotives, which served in early 2008 as a location for the filming of the James Bond film *Quantum of Solace*.

Visitors to the Taltal Nitrate Railway complex (Recinto del Ferrocarril Salitrero de Taltal, declared a national monument in 1983) can take in the workshops, train depot, administration buildings, guesthouse, and pier of the industrial area, all dating from around 1885. There is a renovated British-built 3-foot 6-inch gauge Kitson Meyer articulated steam locomotive on display, together with two carriages, which are also a designated national monument. The design was an initiative of Robert Stirling, locomotive superintendent of the Anglo-Chilian Nitrate & Railway Company, who suggested to Kitson & Company of Leeds that this articulated version would better serve the needs of the nitrate railways. The company developed the idea further and in 1894 manufactured the first locomotive of this type. This particular engine was constructed around 1907 and is the only survivor of the simpler model of the famous Kitson Meyer articulated steam locomotive. It had the inglorious task of leading the train that dismantled the Taltal line when it was closed down.

Another Kitson Meyer locomotive survives at the open-air Santiago Railway Museum at Quinta Normal. This is Number 3349, of one-meter gauge, one of only two that survive today in Chile—the other is at Los Andes. These locomotives were in use on the Transandine Railway between 1911 and 1971. Another British-built locomotive on display is a North British Locomotive Company engine, Number 631, which worked in Chile from 1908 to 1984, based in the city of Concepción. The North British locomotives were the largest fleet of steam locomotives to work in the country.

The Chilean railway heritage association (Asociación Chilena de Conservación del Patrimonio Ferroviario) plans to establish a museum in Los Andes dedicated to preserving the memory of the

Transandino. The displays are expected to include the second meter-gauge Kitson Meyer locomotive (Number 3348, manufactured 1908), and a first-class passenger coach manufactured in England by Gloucester Wagons in 1905.

Further south, in Temuco, there is the Pablo Neruda National Railway Museum, based in a locomotive depot, which was declared a national monument in 1989 and submitted in 1998 as a candidate for UNESCO World Heritage Center status. Fourteen steam locomotives and eight carriages are on display. There are thirty-four tracks in the roundhouse, surrounding a twenty-seven meter radius turntable capable of turning a locomotive with tender weighing over 160 tons. The locomotives include No. 532, built by the North British Locomotives Company in Glasgow in 1908, and No. 429, built in Chile in 1913 to a North British design. There is also a British-built steam crane on display.

There are heritage steam-railway excursions in Chile that have British connections, but details of operations need to be checked before any visit. A Chilean-built (to a North British design) locomotive, No. 602, dating from around 1913, was taken from Temuco to Valdivia, and this engine has apparently pulled a steam excursion from Valdivia to Antilhué during the summer holiday month of February since 2002. Chile's best known heritage line is the Colchagua Tren del Vino (Wine Train) starting from San Fernando, just to the south of Santiago, which runs every Saturday with No. 607, another Chilean-built (North British design) steam locomotive constructed in 1913.

Arguably the most famous British locomotive linked to Chile to have survived until today is (controversially) no longer to be found in Chile. This is the world's first commercially built diesel railway engine, which arrived in Chile in 1930 to work on the Junín Railway just as nitrate production began to fall, and the engine traveled a mere ten thousand kilometers in its working lifetime. Known today as the *Junín*, it was categorized in Chile as a historic monument in 1989 in an attempt by the Chilean railway heritage association [ACCPF] to keep the machine in Chile. However, it seems that a company was set up in Chile by British interests with the express purpose of acquiring and then exporting the locomotive to England (illegally, according to sources in Chile) in 1990.

Sources in Britain tell the story of an English railway enthusiast who found the locomotive in 1978, abandoned and derelict, at the Oficina Prosperidad, near the Oficina Rica Aventura, north of Antofagasta. Since the Atacama region has the driest desert in the world, the locomotive was in good condition, with no rusting, and plans were made to ship it back to Leeds. The immediate problem was that the owner was a scrap merchant who fantasized that he was sitting on a virtual gold mine and demanded a fortune to take it off his hands, from both the ACCPF and the English side. The two bidders had to sit and wait and, according to Redman (1992), this was a long wait, because the owner was at the time serving a prison sentence. Once the purchase was made, the *Junín* was shipped in 1990 to Liverpool, then on to a Civic Hall reception in Leeds, and finally to display in the Armley Mills Industrial Center.

Chapter 12

Education

> [Mr. Thomson] spent some time in Santiago, where, under the patronage of the supreme director, he has established a school of mutual instruction on the plan of Lancaster. He has been in Valparaiso some time superintending the formation of a similar school, to the maintenance of which part of the revenue of a suppressed monastery has been appropriated.
>
> —Maria Graham, Journal of a Residence in Chile, *June 19, 1822*

British educators arrived in Chile during the closing stages of the War of Independence. Bernardo O'Higgins contracted James Thomson, a Scottish missionary and educator, who arrived in Chile from Argentina in 1821. His commission was to start up a school first in Santiago and then another in Valparaíso. A British visitor to Santiago in 1822, Gilbert Mathison, visited "a school for mutual instruction according to the Lancasterian plan, and patronized by the Society in London" (1825, 187), which he reports as being run by Mr. Thomson and supported by Bernardo O'Higgins. The approach was pioneered by Joseph Lancaster and essentially involved one teacher teaching the brighter children who, in turn, as monitors, taught the younger and less able pupils. These schools were apparently successful, and perhaps five schools were established by James Thomson in Chile before he went to Peru in 1822 at General San Martín's invitation.

In a second phase, British merchants in Valparaíso began to contract tutors from Britain for their children. Examples include Thomas Kendall, who arrived around 1837 as the private tutor to the children of the British vice consul, Henry William Rouse. In the same year, John Rowlandson arrived as a tutor to the children of a businessman named Richard Price. The merchant Joshua Waddington set up a room in the attic of his house on Calle Santa Victoria (today this is Calle Lautaro Rosas) for John Rowlandson to direct a small private school.

Later in the nineteenth century, more English-medium schools were established in Chile, accompanying the growth of the British communities in the larger towns. Aníbal Escobar (1923) provides an interesting snapshot of the schools functioning that year in Valparaíso and nearby Viña del Mar. He mentions several schools for boys: the Mackay School (boarding and day school); St. Peter's School in Villa Alemana, directed by Rev. Mac-Donald Hobley; the Open Air School, which functioned in the grounds of the Mackay boarding school in Cerro Alegre; and St. Paul's School, in Viña del Mar. The schools for girls were the Giffen School for Girls, in Miramar (probably from 1922, when Mrs. Giffen closed her school in Punta Arenas); the English Nuns' School, in Playa Ancha; and the High School for Girls, in Cerro Alegre.

The Mackay School has an interesting history. It started as the Valparaíso Artizans' School (1857–1877), whose mission was to provide education to the children of British and American families, and especially for those of Scottish craftsmen who worked in the railway workshops of Valparaíso. Derrick-Jehu (1965) says that the school was founded by the Scotsman Alexander Balfour, of the Williamson Balfour trading company, and that it was he who engaged Peter Mackay from Glasgow as the headmaster. By 1866, there was an average enrollment of 140 pupils, all English speaking, but in 1871 a course was opened for the children of Chilean families who did not speak English. Thomas Somerscales was contracted as a teacher of drawing and painting, as well as English, arithmetic, and geography. George Sutherland arrived from Edinburgh as an assistant to Peter Mackay.

There were disagreements with the British community over religious matters. The school had started as a nondenominational and generally lay school for boys who came from homes that had different religions. However, the Lord's Prayer was said on starting classes, and there was half an hour set aside for reading from the Bible and singing hymns. But in the 1870s, under the influence of the American missionary David Trumbull and the Scottish businessmen Stephen Williamson and Alexander Balfour, the school took on a confessional character. Somerscales was agnostic, and apparently he refused to pray in front of the pupils, which led to his dismissal and the resignation of Peter Mackay and George Sutherland.

They all left to start a new school, the Mackay and Sutherland School (1877–1905). The original Artizans' School changed its name to the English Board School. When Mackay died in 1905, the name was changed to the Mackay School in his memory. Sixty-five former pupils of the school fought in the First World War, of whom fifteen died. George Robertson succeeded Peter Mackay and managed the school until 1928, when he returned to Scotland. A group of ex-pupils met together in 1939 and founded the Mackay School Old Boys Association, which, in 1946, bought land on Avenida Los Castaños in Viña del Mar to start the school again. The Mackay School still exists today in Viña del Mar, along with St. Peter's School (founded 1918), St. Margaret's British School for Girls (founded 1941), and St. Paul's School (founded 1940).

Other schools in Valparaíso and Viña del Mar that existed, but have not survived, include Mr. Watkins' Seminario Inglés (from 1839 in Valparaíso), Mr. Lackington's Colegio Comercial Inglés (from 1850), Mr. Knight's School (from 1850), Mr. Doll's School (from 1869, in Valparaíso), Mr. Wheelwright's English and Classical Seminary (1850), and Mr Radford's English School (from 1883 in Valparaíso, later transferred to Santiago). Michelle Prain (2007) mentions the Colegio Inglés-Alemán (founded in 1855), the English School for Young Ladies (Cerro Concepción), and the English College—all in Valparaíso.

Aníbal Escobar gives a list of the directors of schools for girls who existed in the nineteenth century: Miss Catharine Swett (1839, Valparaíso), Mr. Helsby (1841, Valparaíso), Mrs. Mitchel (1848, Valparaíso), Mr. Lackington (1850), Mr. Wheelwright (1850), and Miss Mackeney (1860). In 1923, there existed the Bell View School for Girls, in Villa Alemana, run by Mrs. Oswald Evans, and Miss Hysop's School, in Viña del Mar.

Sources mention two schools in Santiago in the nineteenth century, J. B. Persy's Instituto Sud-Americano, from 1840 (which may not have been English medium), and a school run from 1852 by Miss Whitelock. In 1923, there was the English Academy in Providencia, Santiago, "the only English school for boys that there is in the capital," (Escobar 1923, 22), as well as the Cambridge High School, directed by F. Finn and M. Heasman; the Colegio Universitario Inglés, run by Elizabeth Weber; the English Catholic College in Providencia; and the Miramar School and Kindergarten for Boys, "run by the Misses Merington."

The British schools that exist today in Santiago were all established in the twentieth century. John Jackson, a Chilean born in Valparaíso and grandson of John Stewart Jackson who arrived in Chile in 1854 and started Jackson & Company, founded the Grange School in 1928. The school started in a private house which, one story goes, resembled a *granja* or grange or country farmhouse. John Jackson was the first headmaster until his death in 1958. Dunalastair School was founded by Ada Crew in 1937 as a bilingual school offering a British type of education. The name comes from the burial grounds of the chiefs of the Clan Donnachaidh in Perthshire, Scotland. Craighouse School was founded in 1959 by Charles Darling and his wife Joan Gibson Craig-Carmichael. Redland School was founded in 1965 by Richard Collingwood-Selby and his Chilean wife, Julia Ojeda

There is mention of a school in Concepción that started around 1852 and was run by Miss Michael. However, the two British schools that exist today were founded in the twentieth century. St. John's English School began as a small school founded by John Hemans in 1935. This was later taken over and managed by Georgina Sadlier. In 1942, during the Second World War, the British Council took control and amalgamated the school with a small private school owned by Nora Grimsditch, whose students were of British descent. The setting up of the Sociedad Anónima Colegio Inglés was formalized at a meeting in the English Club of Concepción in October 1945. The director has to be of British nationality. Secondary education was introduced in 1976. A second British school exists in Concepción, the Wessex School, founded in 1989.

There is also an Escuela Gran Bretaña (Great Britain School) in Concepción, which is a state school—the Escuela de Hombres No. 29. This school was renamed after the earthquake of May 1960, when the premises were rebuilt with financial help from the Anglo-Chilean Society in London and the Rotary Club. The foundation stone was laid by the British ambassador to Chile, David Scott-Fox, on November 20, 1962. The Rotary Club provided fifty thousand pounds for the reconstruction of the school on the site where the school had stood before the devastating earthquake.

In nearby Lota, there was an English School headed by J. B. Smith, serving the large British community in this coal mining town. Further south, the Chilean government encouraged settlement in the 1880s by European colonists in Araucanía—Mapuche Indian territory. Many German, Swiss, Spanish, French, Italian, and British settlers came. The majority of them were Protestants, and they were naturally keen to establish their own non-Catholic schools. It is estimated that nearly seven thousand European immigrants arrived in this region between 1883 and 1890 and set up at least nineteen schools in the period to 1915, mostly with a German orientation. However, according to Zavala Cepeda (2008), two primary schools were established in Temuco from around 1910, one for boys and the other for girls, focused on the children of British immigrants and Chileans. This was an initiative of the British South American Missionary Society, which contracted a British couple, George Chaytor and Ethel Shilcock, to run the boys school. They arrived in Temuco in late 1914, and in the following year the Colegio Inglés de Temuco was founded. This school was later purchased by the couple and is today called the Colegio Inglés George Chaytor. For his dedication to education, George Chaytor was awarded the Libertador Bernardo O'Higgins Merit Medal in 1967, as was his wife in 1980. Following George Chaytor's death, Ethel Shilcock continued to run the school until 1984, when control was invested in the Sociedad Inmobilaria Nueva Escocia, and from 1990 coeducation and secondary education were introduced.

Several schools with a British orientation were set up in Punta Arenas, and one, the British School of Punta Arenas, still functions today. Its history goes back to 1896, when Rev. John Williams arrived and opened the English Church School. In 1904, St. James College was established on the same site as the current Confessional Anglican British School, managed by a committee appointed by the Anglican Society of Punta Arenas. In 1938, St. James College closed, but reopened during the Second World War in 1943 as the British School. The idea was for a school run under the auspices of the British Council and the Anglican Society, but the latter changed its mind. The school resumed life, but as an initiative of the British community with the support of the British Council, with a subsidy that lasted until 1974, and only in the 1980s did the school have close links once again with the Anglican Church.

Other schools that existed in Punta Arenas include the Giffen School, founded by Mrs. Giffen in 1914 (which continued to around 1922); the San Julián Colegio Inglés (from 1920); Mr. Stephens' School (from 1922); Miss Goudie's English School for Girls (from 1923); the Magellan English College, founded by Rev. John Williams (from around 1925 to 1936); and Miss Sharp's School, founded by Miss Mildred Sharp (1937 to 1993).

In the northern provinces, the Antofagasta British School was founded as the English School in Antofagasta in 1918 on the grounds of the FCAB/Antofagasta (Chili) and Railway Company. In La Serena, there was Mr. Simon Kingfit's School, which functioned for at least twenty five years. In Iquique, the Iquique English College was founded in 1885 and still functions today.

Today there is an Association of British Schools of Chile, with eighteen members: Bradford School, Craighouse, Dunalastair School, Redland School, Santiago College, St. Gabriel's School, Wenlock School, the Mayflower School, the Grange School (all in Santiago); Caernarfon College (in the Valley of Casablanca); St. John's School, Wessex School (in Concepción); St. Margaret's School, St. Paul's

School, St. Peter's School, the Mackay School (in Viña del Mar); the Antofagasta British School in Antofagasta; and the British School in Punta Arenas. As an interesting comparison, in Brazil there are today jjust two British Schools. Finally, there is an Escuela Gran Bretaña (Great Britain School) in Valparaíso, which is for handicapped children and is supported by the British community in that city.

There are four Chilean British Cultural Institutes in Chile. The first to be founded was the Instituto Chileno Británico de Cultura (ICBC) in Santiago in 1938. There are now six branches: Santiago Center, Providencia, Las Condes, Ñuñoa, La Florida, and Maipú. The institute became a Teacher Training College in 1982, with degrees recognized by the Chilean Ministry of Education, and a university was established in 2006. The ICBC in Concepción dates back to 1940. Several directors were recruited and salaried by the British Council, including John Mehan, Jeremy Jacobson, Nigel McEwen and Eddie Edmundson. The ICBC in Viña del Mar was established in 1941. The Institute in Arica was set up in 1975 by Joseph and Gladys Hulse as a non-profit-making body under the auspices of the British Council and was granted recognition as a member of the Comisión Chilena de Cooperación Intelectual of the Universidad de Chile. This followed the founding, also by the Hulses, of the Arica English School in 1962. The Arica ICBC was destroyed by an earthquake in 1987 and moved premises to the center of the city.

Britain's official international organization for educational and cultural affairs, the British Council, has been present in Chile since 1934. A cultural convention was signed in 1972 between the two governments that recognizes the British Council as the implementation body for cultural relations work on behalf of the British government and as the cultural section of the British Embassy in Chile. The British Council director has diplomatic status and is the cultural attaché of the British Embassy.

Chapter 13

Religion

> We plans to take 'em back to Cape Horn in a couple of years, to teach the savages an' cannibals Christian ways, an' to lead up their heathen people to the light, an' to teach 'em English manners.
>
> —*Robert FitzRoy's coxswain James Bennett*

Much of the story of British involvement in Chile for reasons of religion relates to contact with the indigenous peoples on Tierra del Fuego. There were four native cultures in the archipelago, two of those called Canoe Indians by Europeans and two called Foot Indians.

The Yahgan inhabited southern Tierra del Fuego in an area that surrounded Beagle Channel. They were marine nomads, living most of their lives on canoes. The missionary Thomas Bridges estimated that before contact with Europeans there were probably around three thousand Yahgan Indians. They actually called themselves Yámana, meaning "the people," or simply "living, alive." When he started his study of this people, Bridges chose the Murray Narrows, lying roughly in the center of their territory, and the Indians called this geographical feature Yahgashaga ("Mountain Valley Channel"), and the inhabitants the Yahgashagalumoala, which Bridges shortened to Yahgan. Thomas Bridges' son Lucas describes them as "fearless cragsmen and splendid sailors [who] seldom ventured far inland" (Bridges 1951, 62).

The Alacaluf or "Alacaloof," in Lucas Bridges' spelling, called themselves Kawéskar, and were also marine nomads. They inhabited the western islands facing the open Pacific, encompassing the western reaches of the Magellan Strait and reaching inland as far as present-day Punta Arenas. Magellan had seen the signal fires of the Alacaluf; this event gave rise to the name of "Land of Fire." Lucas Bridges reports that intermarriage between these two canoe Indian groups occurred from time to time.

The Ona were so called by the Yahgan, who feared them. These foot Indians inhabited the eastern lands facing the Atlantic south from the mouth of the Magellan Strait to the Beagle Channel. They in fact called themselves Selk`nam. The Haush (or "Aush," in Lucas Bridges' spelling) were sometimes called the Eastern Ona. Also foot Indians, they feared the Ona even more than the Yahgan did and occupied a small territory at the extreme eastern tip of Tierra del Fuego.

On his first circumnavigation, James Cook found himself in the Bay of Good Success, Tierra del Fuego, in January 1769, where he met with a group of indigenous people and did not "discover any appearance of religion among them" (Wharton 1893). Early in the following century, James Weddell also met with Fuegian Indians and described his impressions of their religious beliefs in his *Voyage towards the South Pole Performed in the Years 1822–24*:

> I was anxious to discover if they had any object of divine worship, and accordingly called them together about me, and read a chapter in the Bible; not that they were expected to understand what was read, but it was proper to show them the Bible, and to read it, in connection with making signs of death, resurrection, and supplication to heaven. They manifested no understanding of my meaning, but as I read and made signs, they imitated me, following me with a gabble when reading, raising and lowering their voices as I did . . . One of them held his ear down to the book, believing that it spoke. (Weddell 1825, 166–67)

Weddell concluded that: "I have only now to recommend these people . . . to the philanthropic part of the world, as presenting an untouched field for their exertions to ameliorate the condition of their fellow men" (1825, 191).

Philanthropy appeared in the person of Robert FitzRoy on the two voyages he commanded on the *Beagle*. He arrived back in England from the first voyage in October 1830 with four Fuegians on board: York Minster, Fuegia Basket, Jemmy Button, and Boat Memory (who soon died from smallpox). FitzRoy's Fuegian experiment was helped by the Church Missionary Society, which focused at the time on a single diocese—the British colonies of New South Wales and New Zealand. FitzRoy's decision fitted well in the ethos of the time, of a Britain flexing its imperial muscles, with the practice of bringing human curiosities to England to be put on display, and the growing zeal for missionary work to bring "civilization" to the four corners of the earth. Through the society, FitzRoy met with Rev. William Wilson of Walthamstow, a village close to London, where the three Fuegians were sent to be educated. FitzRoy's coxswain James Bennett stayed with the Fuegians during this time.

Following an incident where it seems that York Minster attempted to have sex with Fuegia Basket, FitzRoy decided that they would all return on a merchant vessel named the *John of London*, which he chartered, and he would take a year's leave of absence from the Royal Navy. Plans changed suddenly in the summer of 1831, when the Admiralty ordered FitzRoy and the *Beagle* back to Patagonia, and on hearing this, nine months after the Fuegians had come to Walthamstow, Rev. Wilson asked FitzRoy to allow him to send two missionaries to the region. In the end, there was room for only one missionary, Richard Matthews, and a young naturalist named Charles Darwin.

Darwin first saw Fuegian Indians in December 1832, when the *Beagle* came into Good Success Bay in Tierra del Fuego, and described the scene in his diary: "It was without exception the most curious & interesting spectacle I ever beheld" (Beagle *Diary*, December 18, 1832). Darwin did not think much of the indigenous peoples and, sadly, his observations were influential on opinion over many years to come. The same diary entry continues: "I would not have believed how entire the difference between savage & civilized man is. It is greater than between a wild & domesticated animal, in as much as in man there is greater power of improvement." Darwin contributed too to the long-lingering myth that the Indians were cannibals.

FitzRoy's impression of the missionary Matthews was that he was "rather too young, and less experienced than might have been wished" (1838, 16). Nevertheless, in January 1833, after the customary battering from a fierce storm, Matthews went ashore with FitzRoy and Darwin and the Fuegians near Cape York Minster in the country of Jemmy Button's tribe, the Woollya. They unloaded the cargo of necessities sent over by members of the Church Missionary Society, which included crockery, marmalade, and warm mufflers! Three constructions were prepared—for Matthews, for Jemmy Button, and for York Minster together with Fuegia Basket. The goods sent by the missionary society were buried in a kind of cellar under Matthews and hidden above him in a loft. A garden was dug by the sailors and sowed with potatoes, carrots, peas, onions, and other vegetables, to teach the fishing and hunting Indians the benefits of diversifying their diet.

Matthews' first impression was that the Indians were no worse than he had supposed them to be. FitzRoy left the missionary for one night, to see if he was really safe, and then decided to spend a longer period away, exploring the western arm of the Beagle Channel. When they returned, they found Matthews had been badly mistreated, with some of his stores stolen and the garden trampled on. The remaining stores were unearthed, and, together with Matthews, were taken back to the *Beagle*. Jemmy Button's opinion was that "My people very bad, great fool, know nothing at all, very great fool" (FitzRoy 1838, 222).

Thirteen months later, in March 1834, FitzRoy returned to the settlement in the Murray Narrows. Canoes appeared, and in one they identified Jemmy Button, but he was so altered. Darwin described the scene: "Soon a canoe, with a little flag flying, was seen approaching, with one of the men in it washing the paint off his face. This man was poor Jemmy, now a thin haggard savage, with long disordered hair, and naked, except for a bit of a blanket round his waist. We did not recognise him till he was close to us; for he was ashamed of himself, and turned his back to the ship. We had left him plump, fat, clean, and well dressed; I never saw so complete and grievous a change" (*Journal of Researches* 1845, 228).

Jemmy told of how York Minster had completed a large canoe and invited him and his mother to accompany York and Fuegia to the territory of the Alacaluf. All their joint belongings had been loaded onto two canoes, and York had made off with everything while Jemmy was sleeping. He and his family had moved to the island FitzRoy had named after him, Jemmy Button Island.

Jemmy advised against sending Matthews back to the shore. FitzRoy confided in his journal: "Perhaps a ship-wrecked seaman may hereafter receive help and kind treatment from Jemmy Button's children; prompted, as they can hardly fail to be, by the traditions they will have heard of men of other lands, and by the idea however faint, of their duty to God as well as their neighbour" (*Narrative* 1838, 327). Sadly, as far as Jemmy is concerned, this turned out not to be true. In 1859, eight British missionaries were massacred on shore in an attack that it seems Jemmy orchestrated.

York Minster was never seen again, but forty years later Fuegia turned up in the eastern part of the Beagle Channel and met with Thomas Bridges. Bridges estimated her age at around fifty-five, and he had a conversation with Fuegia in the Yahgan language. She remembered little, except for FitzRoy and the *Beagle;* nothing of religion, something of London, and how kind the people in Walthamstow had been to her. She told of how she had two sons by York and how he was murdered in an act of revenge by the family of a man he had killed. Thomas Bridges actually met her once again in 1883, ten years later, when she was close to death, surrounded by her sons and relatives.

The next visitor to comment on the Fuegians' religion, or apparent lack of it, was James Clark Ross, on the scientific expedition with the ships *Erebus* and *Terror*. He stayed for a month in 1842 in Wigwam Cove, just to the north of Cape Horn. The naturalist Dr. McCormick and his assistant Joseph Hooker were on board, and they met with Yahgan Indians. Joseph Hooker dismissed them as "degraded savages," while Ross hoped they could somehow receive "the blessings of civilization and the joyful tidings of the Gospel" (*A Voyage of Discovery and Research* 1847, 307).

Soon afterwards, the British version of Christianity was carried to Tierra del Fuego by Captain Allen Gardiner, R.N., with generally dire results, for both sides, in this clash of cultures. Gardiner heard the call of God at around the time FitzRoy was finishing his work in Tierra del Fuego. He had spent some time in Chile earlier in his career, when, during the War of 1812, the U.S. frigate *Essex* had been captured by a British squadron off Valparaíso. He was then a midshipman on HMS *Phoebe* and was detailed to help sail the *Essex* to England. He had also seen Yahgan Indians while rounding Cape Horn.

After the death of his wife in 1834, he resigned from the Navy. Gardiner was then involved in a number of attempted conversions— all failures. The first was with the Zulu in South Africa, just as war broke out between the Zulu and the Boers. He was then in Bolivia, which he found in revolution, and, in any case, unsympathetic to non-Catholic proselytizers. His next attempt was in New Guinea, which the Dutch colonists did not take kindly to. He then returned to South America, this time to the Araucanian Indians, who were fighting the Argentineans on the road that was to lead to their genocide. His 1838 journey from Buenos Aires to Chile was written up as *A Visit to the Indians on the Frontiers of Chili*, published in 1861.

The Patagonian Missionary Society was founded in 1844, and Gardiner became acting secretary. Four years later, at the age of fifty-four, he and four others sailed on a ship called the *Clymene*, bound from England for Lima with coal. They landed on Picton Island, near the Atlantic entrance of the Beagle Channel. The Yaghan menaced and compelled the party to leave. Gardiner returned to England, convinced that he needed a proper missionary ship, and raised the cash through a campaign. He returned in 1850 with six companions in the *Ocean Queen*; he landed again at Picton Island with two very unsuitable ship's boats called the *Pioneer* and the *Speedwell*. The mission got off to a bad start. As soon as the *Ocean Queen* had departed, they discovered that they had left their ammunition on board.

They started by constructing a mission building and planting vegetables on a small island in front of Banner Cove, so called by Gardiner from a line in the Bible: "Thou has given a banner to them that fear thee, that it might be displayed because of the truth" (Psalm 60). They called the island Garden Island on account of the planting. Unfortunately, the Yaghan were even more hostile than before, and Gardiner decided to withdraw overland to "Spaniard Harbour" (now known as Bahía Aguirre), near the eastern mouth of the Beagle Channel, where they slowly starved for six weeks.

Realizing that no-one would look for them in that position, Gardiner and a few of the fitter men set off back to Banner Cove, where he painted in white on a bare rock the letters "DIG BELOW. GO TO SPANIARD HARBOUR. MARCH 1851" (this is Lucas Bridges' version of the text) and buried a bottle containing messages. Returning to "Spaniard Harbour," they all died one by one of starvation, Gardiner last, sometime after September 3, 1851, when we know from his journal that the last of their food had run out. Gardiner faced the certainty of death with stoicism: "Yet a little while, and through grace we may join that blessed throng to sing the praises of Christ throughout eternity. I neither hunger nor thirst, though five days without food!" (see Marsh and Stirling 1867, 81).

A relief schooner, the *John E. Davidson*, captained by William Smyley, was sent from Montevideo. Smyley followed their trail, and on October 21 found their bodies and Gardiner's journal. This caused a great impact in England and revived the moribund Missionary Society. Funds were raised to build a schooner called the *Allen Gardiner*, but with a different strategy, that of carrying on outreach work with the Yaghan from the safer Falklands/Malvinas, where a missionary station was established on Keppel Island in West Falkland. The *Allen Gardiner* left Bristol in October 1854, captained by Parker Snow, an experienced sailor whose account was written up as *A Two Years' Cruise off Tierra del Fuego, the Falkland Islands, Patagonia, and the River Plate: A Narrative of Life in the Southern Seas*, published in 1857. The hope was that Jemmy Button would become the nucleus of the project, assuring Yahgans that if they left of their own accord, they would be well treated at the mission station, and, amazingly, they did find him, somewhere near Wulaia. However, Jemmy refused to stay with the boat and go to the Falklands.

Rev. George Pakenham Despard had been appointed honorary secretary of the Patagonian Missionary Society by Gardiner, and he heard of Jemmy's refusal, or rather (it seemed to him), Snow's inability to persuade Jemmy to accompany him. Despard chartered a boat called the *Hydaspes* and sailed in 1856 with his wife, his six children, and building materials for the Falklands. Among these children was a thirteen-year-old who was adopted—Thomas Bridges. Dallas Murphy (2004) retells the story of an infant being found in a basket under a bridge and taken to Despard's church. The baby was wearing a tunic with the letter 'T' embroidered on the chest, and so he became Thomas Bridges, and Despard adopted Thomas into his family.

After seeing to new constructions on Keppel Island, Despard sent the *Allen Gardiner* to Wulaia to locate Jemmy Button, and, somewhat surprisingly, he was not only found again but readily agreed to accompany the ship back to the Falklands, taking his wife and a child with him. Unfortunately for the enterprise, Jemmy was not happy on Keppel Island, and Despard reluctantly let him return home, but only after Jemmy promised to encourage other Yahgans to consider joining the mission. Despard looked for a site for a more permanent mission on Tierra del Fuego, and, like Robert FitzRoy, he chose Wulaia, inside modern-day Chile. Jemmy duly provided nine Yahgans, including one of his sons, Billy Button, who all embarked for Keppel Island, where, during their ten-month stay, Thomas Bridges became fluent in their language.

From Despard's point of view, things were going extremely well, and in 1859 he decided to send the group back to Wulaia under the leadership of Captain Fell and Garland Phillips, a catechist, with the objective of starting up a permanent mission there. The Yahgans on board included one named Schwaiamugunjiz, whose name the English sailors corrupted to "Squire Muggins." This voyage started badly; the Yahgans were discovered with personal possessions of the mission staff hidden in their bundles and ended ominously as Jemmy Button came on board to find that there were no presents for him. "Squire Muggins" attacked Captain Fell, and the Indians left the boat in a blind rage. Nevertheless, Fell set about building a small chapel, and the group marched unarmed to hold a Sunday service there on November 6, 1859. They were set upon and massacred. The only survivor was the cook, Robert Coles, who had stayed alone on the *Allen Gardiner*.

When the *Allen Gardiner* failed to return to the Falklands, Despard hired Captain Smyley to carry out a search on the *Nancy*. The ship was found at Wulaia, three months after the massacre, entirely stripped of everything portable. When they went ashore, a man in a dreadful physical state ran screaming out of the trees. This naked, starving man was Robert Coles, the cook. Suddenly, a canoe appeared by the ship, and soon Jemmy Button was on board. Smyley ordered the ship to make sail and return to the Falklands, with Jemmy on board. Lucas Bridges has a different version; he says that Jemmy asked to be taken to Keppel Island.

Once they had arrived at Port Stanley, Governor Thomas Moore convened a panel to take declarations from the witnesses, and Jemmy denied any wrongdoing. Lucas Bridges comments, "It was subsequently established beyond all reasonable doubt that Jemmy Button had been the chief instigator of the Massacre" (1951, 46). Moore summoned Despard to Port Stanley, but he refused to go. In the end, the Governor's board decided that in fact most of the blame for what had happened lay with the Patagonian Missionary Society, and this precipitated the end of Despard's missionary career. The *Allen Gardiner* was refitted, and Despard packed to return to England, but only after asking if Thomas Bridges—then nineteen years old—would like to remain. Thomas said he would stay and run the mission until a new mission head arrived, and in the meantime concentrate on perfecting the Yahgan language. As for Jemmy Button, he died in an epidemic in 1864, after a bizarre career of contact with British culture that started in 1829 on board the *Beagle*.

Rev. Waite Hocking Stirling was the most recent honorary secretary of the Society, and he became the new mission head. He was designated the first Bishop of an Anglican diocese based on the Falklands, which was the largest in the world at that time, covering all of South America. Stirling journeyed through the Beagle Channel in late 1863, along with Thomas Bridges, on what he termed the "Trip of Pardon" (for the massacre at Wulaia), thinking to take Yahgan Indians to the Falklands for instruction in English and agriculture. The Yahgan were astounded to hear a white man—Bridges—address them in their own language, and this made all the difference for the success of their venture.

Several Yahgans were taken to Keppel Island, and in 1866, Stirling even took four Yaghan boys to England, including one called Threeboy, who was a son of Jemmy Button. Lucas Bridges explains that when Jemmy was asked the name of this boy he had replied, "Three boy," thinking that the question related to the size of his family. The Indians who had spent time on Keppel Island were returned in 1867 to Laiwaia on Navarino Island, and a settlement for the missionaries was started in 1869 at Ushuaia. This was in fact a few months after Thomas Bridges had been summoned back to England by the South American Missionary Society for his ordination. (The Society changed its name from the Patagonian Missionary Society in 1864.) Ushuaia means "Inner Harbor to the Westward" in the Yahgan language and is in fact just outside modern Chile, in Argentina, on the north bank of the Beagle Channel. However, until an Argentinean boat arrived unannounced at Ushuaia in 1884 and the Argentinean flag was hoisted, the settlement had depended entirely on Punta Arenas in Chile for provisions and communications.

In October 1871, Thomas Bridges and his wife Mary Varder arrived in Ushuaia and were determined to stay. They were the first nonindigenous people to settle down permanently in Tierra del Fuego. A daughter, Mary, had been born in the Falklands, and then two boys followed soon after in Ushuaia—Thomas Despard Bridges and Lucas Bridges, the future author of *Uttermost Part of the Earth* (1951), building up to a family of five children. In 1886, Thomas Bridges became an Argentinean citizen and accepted a grant of land as a gift from a grateful nation. He settled on land on the Beagle Channel near Gable Island, which he had surveyed with Rev. Stirling. This became, and remains to this day, the Bridges' family farm, the Estancia Harberton.

Thomas Bridges spent more than thirty years producing a Yahgan–English dictionary of 32,000 words, which had a strange sequel. An American surgeon, Dr. Frederick Cook, turned up in Harberton in 1898 on the SS *Belgica* as a member of a Belgian scientific expedition to the Antarctic. Dr. Cook was interested in the dictionary and assured Thomas Bridges that there was a society in the United States that specialized in American indigenous languages and that could print the study. Bridges declined the offer, fearing that it might be lost in the Antarctic ice. However, he promised to give it to Dr. Cook when he returned from the survey.

Thomas Bridges died later that same year in Buenos Aires. Dr. Cook duly returned some months later, and the Bridges' family honored their father's promise. Sadly, although Dr. Cook did arrange the publication of the dictionary, in Brussels, he tried to pass it off as his own work. He made other fictional claims in his lifetime, including the discovery of the North Pole, and was described by *The New York Times* (May 21, 1910) as "one of the boldest fakers the world has ever known." This was the start of an odyssey for the dictionary; the original was lost in Brussels when the First World War started, only to turn up again in 1929 in Munster, and then it was published by Dr. Hestermann and Dr. Gusinde in a limited edition in Austria in 1933. The original was lost again when the Second World War broke out and then was found at the close of the war in the kitchen cupboard of a German farmhouse where Dr. Hestermann had left it for safe keeping. Parts of the original have never been recovered.

In 1946, the dictionary finally made its way to the British Museum in London, which in 1973 passed its collections of books and manuscripts to the British Library. The original works by Thomas Bridges surviving today in the British Library consist of seven volumes of his *Dictionary of the Yamana or Yahgan Language*, presented by his son Lucas Bridges (except for volumes 5 and 6). Volumes 2 and 3 were the manuscripts brought to Europe by Frederick Cook, and Volume 3 is lacking the final pages. Volume 4, the "new and last dictionary," was never completed and was brought to Europe by Alice Couty Bridges in 1929. In addition, the Library has a copy of *Yamana-English: A Dictionary of the speech of Tierra del Fuego* by Thomas Bridges (Ed. Ferdinand Hestermann and Martin Gusinde: 1933), along with Thomas Bridges' translations into Yahgan of the Gospel of Luke (1881), the Acts of the Apostles (1883), and the Gospel of John (1886).

Fuegian Indians survived into the late nineteenth and early twentieth centuries, but in dwindling numbers, and were usually seen by visitors begging and bartering from their canoes. One visitor, Annie Brassey, concluded in 1876 that "the Fuegians, as far as is known, have no religion of their own" (1878, 133). On leaving Punta Arenas her party was approached by a "frail craft" with Indians who

> came alongside, shouting "Tabáco, galléta" (biscuit), a supply of which we threw down to them, in exchange for the skins they had been waving; whereupon the two men stripped themselves of the skin mantles they were wearing, made of eight or ten sea-otter skins sewed together with finer sinews than those used for the boat, and handed them up, clamouring for more tobacco, which we gave them, together with some beads and knives. Finally, the woman, influenced by this example, parted with her sole garment, in return for a little more tobacco, some beads, and some looking-glasses I had thrown into the canoe. (*A Voyage in the Sunbeam* 1878, 135)

Another who witnessed this kind of spectacle was the British journalist William Russell in 1889. He describes how, after leaving Punta Arenas and passing Cape Froward, they met with canoes on their journey through the strait. He heard a Chilean on board his ship comment, "They are not Christians ... nor are they likely to become civilised, less so than ever now since the sheep-farmers shoot them. The latter say they must shoot Fuegians to prevent them stealing their sheep" (1890, 30–31). William Russell was sympathetic to the natives' plight, and concluded, "They have more to fear from civilisation as it is presented to them than from their cruel natural foes, cold and starvation" (1890, 31).

This view was echoed by the American anthropologist Samuel Kirkland Lothrop, who wrote, "The record of the white settlers in Tierra del Fuego, with of course certain splendid exceptions, is not one to be reviewed with pride; not the Indians but the Europeans have proved the greater savages. Missionary efforts, however well intended, have hastened the course of their neophytes to the grave" (1928, 23).

In 1888, the Chilean government gave permission for the Anglican mission, centered on Ushuaia, to establish outposts on Isla Grevy and at Cabo West on Isla Hermite, in the Wollaston group of islands just to the north of Cape Horn. In exchange, the Anglicans promised to maintain a lighthouse at Cabo West and set up lifeguard facilities. The Burleigh family volunteered to go to the station. It proved impossible to land at Isla Grevy, and the Burleighs decided to settle instead on Isla Bayly. After three years of sticking it out in the most appalling conditions, the Burleighs moved in 1892 to Tekenika, on Hoste Island. Rev. Stirling remarked that Tekenika was relatively better in terms of climate and soil, but this was not saying much, and in fact this station was later moved in 1906 to Bahía Douglas on Navarino Island, only to close finally in 1916 when it was estimated that only eighty Yahgan and 276 Ona Indians remained. There had been around four thousand Ona Indians before the settlers arrived. There is a national monument in Puerto Williams called "Casa Stirling," which is the portable house that was erected by the missionaries in Ushuaia and then carried to Isla Hoste and Bahía Douglas.

Lucas Bridges estimated that of the seven thousand to nine thousand natives who inhabited Tierra del Fuego when his father arrived nearly a century before, there were in 1947 fewer than 150 pure-blooded Indians who had survived, against a population of 9,560 white settlers.

The South American Missionary Society also attempted to work with another indigenous people in Chile—the Mapuche community of Araucanía in southern Chile. Allen Gardiner's son, Allen Gardiner Junior, was sent in 1860 to see what could be done. There were difficulties for Protestant Christianizing in that period in Catholic Chile, and the setting up of mission stations was out of the question, so after visiting Colcura, Lebu, and Tucapel, Gardiner became chaplain to the growing community of British residents in the coal mining region based on Lota, in a mission that started in 1861. Lota belonged then to Bishop Stirling's diocese with headquarters on the Falklands.

Zavala Cepada (2008) notes that a second mission was established in Lebu in 1867.

There were also British immigrants further south to be ministered to. They had arrived in a scheme of assisted immigration during the Presidency of José Manuel Balmaceda. The chaplain in Lota, Mr. Dodds, started the construction of the Anglican Church in Quino, although it was J. R. Tyerman who became the pastor in 1889, appointed by the South American Missionary Society. He celebrated the first service in Angol in that year, in the region settled by these immigrants.

Later in the century, in 1894, an effort was made to establish a mission among the Mapuches of Araucanía, centered on the town of Chol Chol, led by the Reverends Charles Sadleir and Philip Walker and a Scotsman named William Wilson. A church was built, as well as a school (1897) and dispensaries. Services were held in Spanish from 1894, starting in Quino, and then extending around to Traiguén, Victoria, Púa, Ercilla, Quilquilco, and Nueva Imperial. By 1905, two main centers had been established in Araucanía by the Missionary Society, in Chol Chol and in Quepe. The William Wilson School still exists today in Chol Chol. However, other religious denominations arrived on the scene, and slowly the influence of the Anglican faith waned along with the dwindling presence of British settlers until, by 1911, most of these immigrants around Quino had left for new lives abroad.

The largest British community in nineteenth century Chile was of course in Valparaíso. The Protestant faith in Valparaíso was initially celebrated by holding services on board British ships led by the ship's chaplain, but clearly this was sporadic and depended on a chaplain being available. From around 1825, there were also services held occasionally in the consulate, and later in the private homes of residents, presided over by Thomas Kendall and John Sewell. Thomas Kendall had arrived in Valparaíso as the private tutor to the children of the British vice consul, Henry William Rouse. Later, a warehouse was used on the Quebrada del Almendro, which is today Calle Urriola, until worshippers established St. Paul's Church in 1858, on Cerro Reina Victoria.

In 1837, the Chilean government authorized the consul general in Valparaíso to appoint an Anglican pastor who could maintain a school and hold religious services in his home. The first Anglican pastor was John Rowlandson, who had arrived as tutor to the children of Richard Price, a businessman. Joshua Waddington provided premises in the attic of his house for Rowlandson to set up a private school, and in December 1837, the first Anglican service was held. This was unofficial and not recognized by the British ecclesiastical authorities. Recognition came later, in 1841, when William Armstrong was appointed as the first consular chaplain officially recognized by the Church of England.

Observance of non-Catholic faith was difficult for many years, especially away from the more liberal-minded port of Valparaíso. Nevertheless, there were sporadic attempts. Charles Fletcher Hillman (1900) reports that in the 1860s Rev. Langridge was in Chañaral, and Rev. Stewart in Coquimbo, both appointed by the Anglican Church. Around the same time, also according to Hillman, Thomas Francis preached to his Welsh compatriots in Guayacán, and William Corrie, an Englishman, preached on Sundays in Talcahuano.

The difficulties arose, as Michelle Prain (2006) points out, from the fact that there was not yet in Chile the right to public religious worship in any form other than that of the Roman Catholic Church, set down in the constitution as the official religion, although freedom of conscience was guaranteed. This led to many conflicts, and clandestine worship, and was only resolved by the "interpretative law" of 1865, which modified Article Five of the 1833 Constitution. This now guaranteed freedom for religious worship, but only in private homes, and permitted non-Catholics to found schools for the education of their children in the principles of their religion. It was pressure from non-Catholic immigrants in Valparaíso that led to this change in the law.

Another source of discord for many years was the issue of marriage. In the early years of British immigration, when British non-Catholic couples wanted to get married, they did so in the consulate, or on board ships, and even on boats anchored temporarily in the bay of Valparaíso. This situation endured until January 1884, when, under the liberal government of Domingo Santa María, the Civil Matrimony Law was passed. This law removed the Catholic Church's monopoly on performing the legal registry of marriages, and this function passed henceforth to the state. The complementary Civil Registry Law of July 1884 provided for the orderly civil registry of these marriages, as well as births and deaths—a function formerly carried out by parish registers. While this resolved the issue of marriages taking place between couples of the same faith, it did not address the problem of mixed marriages. The Catholic Church simply prohibited such marriages, and the solution was either for the Protestant to renounce his or her faith and become a Catholic, agreeing to having the children raised in the Catholic faith, or for a special dispensation to be sought from the Vatican—a lengthy and generally unsuccessful process.

As the number of non-Catholic faiths and their congregations grew in Chile in importance and visibility, there was pressure to build churches. The first attempt to organize a place of worship for the

Protestant community in Valparaíso was made in 1835 by G. Hobson, the head of Alsop & Company. However, it was later, in 1856, that the Union Church was established in Valparaíso. This was the first Protestant church to be constructed in Chile (and in all of the west coast of Latin America), in Calle San Agustín, on land bought from the British merchant-trader Joshua Waddington. The decision to build the church was possibly motivated by the signing of the Treaty of Commerce and Friendship between Britain and Chile two years earlier. The church later moved in 1870 to another building, in Calle San Juan de Dios, which is now Calle Condell.

The church owes its existence to an initiative taken by a group of foreign residents in Valparaíso who were Protestant but not Anglican. In 1844, this group contacted the Foreign Evangelical Society in the United States, requesting that they send a missionary to work in their community. An American missionary named David Trumbull accepted the mission and was sent to Chile with the support of two missionary societies. He founded the congregation in 1847 that would later become the Union Church, which he led for more than forty years. The construction of the church was actually delayed until 1856 on account of the opposition of the Catholic Church in Chile, led by Archbishop Valdivieso, and even so, the church had to make concessions to comply with the law, including the absence of a bell tower, and a commitment that the choir would sing in a low voice! Trumbull was succeeded by vicars who mostly belonged to the United Free Church of Scotland, among them Revs. Dodge, Gray, Inglis, Aitkin, Collins, and McKnight. The church also set up the Union Church Young Men's Club aimed at providing entertainment to young people from abroad who might otherwise be drawn to vice.

Perhaps motivated by the setting up of the Union Church, St. Paul's Anglican Church was inaugurated in 1858 under the leadership of a vicar named Richard Dennett. The site on Cerro Reina Victoria was bought from José Guillermo Waddington Urrutia, the industrial engineer son of Joshua Waddington, with a loan provided by the Chilean businessman Agustín Edwards Ossandón. The church was constructed by William Lloyd, the railway engineer and architect who completed the Santiago–Valparaíso railway, and was declared in 1979 a historical monument in Chile.

Since St. Paul's Church was built seven years before the changes introduced by the 1865 interpretative law, its architecture, like that of the Union Church, had to disguise its real purpose, and this is why the construction is low, and there were no external elements that could identify it as a church. Later, in 1883, the church's interior was transformed, with stain glass windows and the purchase of its first organ. This organ was replaced in 1901 with another bought in England, following the death of Queen Victoria. The installation of the Queen Victoria Memorial Organ led to the church being enlarged, and this was finished in 1903. Considered the finest organ in South America in its time, it is still in use. Since electricity only came to Valparaíso in 1910, the organ was actually worked by a water-driven pneumatic mechanism. In 1894, the Anglican Institute, designed by John Livingston, was opened in the grounds of St. Paul's Church.

The first church in Santiago for the English-speaking Protestant community was the Union Church of Santiago, founded in 1885. In 1904, the British Protestant Church was established in Santiago under the chairmanship of the Anglican Bishop of South America and the Falkland Islands, and this became St. Andrew's Church in 1922. A new and larger St. Andrew's Church was subsequently built on Avenida Holanda and opened in 1947. In 1963, the Anglican diocese of South America was divided up, and Chile became a single diocese, with St. Andrew's Church assuming the role of cathedral church. The Union Church survived for many years, but in 1971, its building was sold and its congregation joined with that of St. Andrew's to form the Santiago Community Church, an interdenominational congregation. These premises are now shared with the Anglican Church of Providencia and the Anglican diocese. Another Anglican Church in Chile is St. Peter's Church in Viña del Mar.

Having asserted the right to worship and largely overcome the resistance to churches being built, Protestants still faced the problem of where to bury those who died in Chile who were non-Catholics. As in other matters, Valparaíso led the way when, in 1825, the first British cemetery in Chile was established on Cerro Panteón, intended for those of the Protestant faith—the "dissidents." It faces General Cemetery No. 1, which opened in the same year and was exclusive for the Catholics who died in that city. Later, in 1848, a second cemetery in the same area was opened for non-Catholics, Dissident Cemetery No. 2. Both these cemeteries are found on Calle Dinamarca and were declared national monuments in November 2005.

The founding of the first Protestant cemetery can be traced back to a petition made to Bernardo O'Higgins by forty-seven foreign residents and traders of Santiago and Valparaíso, mostly British, together with the Commander of the Royal Navy in the Pacific. They complained that in several cases when Protestants were close to death in Santiago they had been persuaded to abjure their religion in order to be given Christian burial and that others who had refused to convert to Catholicism had their bones disturbed after death and displayed in the port of Valparaíso. It seems certain that Protestants were sometimes buried on the beach in Valparaíso, and there are stories too of the bodies of non-Catholics being thrown into the sea after brief ceremonies.

In 1822, Maria Graham came across the "new burying ground" established just outside Valparaíso: "Separated from this only by a wall, is the place at length assigned by Roman Catholic superstition to the heretics as a burial ground; or rather, which the heretics have been permitted to purchase. Hitherto, such as had not permission to bury in the forts where they could be guarded, preferred being carried out to sea, and sunk; many instances having occurred of the exhumation of heretics, buried on shore, by the bigoted natives, and the exposure of their bodies to the birds and beasts of prey" (Graham May 31, 1822).

The appeal to O'Higgins was to stop such incidents "that shock the sentiments of humanity" and to give permission for the purchase of suitable land near Santiago and in the port of Valparaíso for the purposes of Protestant burial. Bernardo O'Higgins agreed to the request in December 1819 and authorized the sale of land for the founding of cemeteries for non-Catholics in the two cities.

In 1823, the *Cabildo* (municipal district) of Valparaíso agreed that land on the Cerro Panteón could be sold to the British consul (who had arrived that year) to serve as a cemetery for non-Catholics, and two years later this was effected when the municipality sold just under one hectare for this purpose. But Valparaíso was an exceptional case in the first half of the nineteenth century. The declaration in favor of free trade in 1811 had stimulated commercial activity in the port, and the arrival of British traders, as well as immigrants from other nations. This made for a cosmopolitan community with a degree of tolerance toward Protestantism that was unknown in the rest of Chile—a phenomenon that was frequently commented on by visitors to the port.

There is a monument in Dissidents' Cemetery No. 1 in Valparaíso to the memory of the American sailors who died on the US frigate *Essex* when this was engaged by a British force off the port in 1814. There is a Royal Navy vault in Dissidents' Cemetery No. 2 with names that span the period 1842 to the turn of the century. There are other links to the history of the British presence in Chile, such as the Mackay family mausoleum, including the founder of what became the Mackay School, Peter Mackay, and the tomb of Frederick Schwäger, closely linked to British and Chilean coal mining near Concepción, who died in Valparaíso in 1861.

In Santiago, however, for reasons that are not properly understood, no British cemetery was built as the result of O'Higgins' intercession, and for over thirty years dissidents who died in Santiago were brought to Valparaíso for burial or buried simply on one side of Santa Lucía hill. This may help explain why Britain took so long to recognize formally the independence of Chile. After the Treaty of Commerce and Friendship was signed in October 1854, during Manuel Montt's presidency, Minister Antonio Varas decreed in 1855 the opening of a section for dissidents in the Cementerio General in Santiago.

Later in the nineteenth century there were two legal watersheds in the history of cemeteries for non-Catholics that applied throughout Chile. Firstly, in 1871, a government decree provided for the burial of non-Catholics in spaces duly set aside for dissidents and for the creation of lay cemeteries funded and administered by the state or by municipalities. The second was the Ley de Cementerios Laicos (Lay Cemeteries Law), passed under President Santa María in August 1883, which permitted the burial of all people in cemeteries run by the state, regardless of their religion. This law also prohibited burials on private land, including church lands, and converted all existing burial places into lay cemeteries under the jurisdiction of the state. The Catholic Church hierarchy retaliated by forbidding Catholic burial rites at state cemeteries, and this led to bizarre and even macabre incidents throughout Chile. On occasion, bodies were secretly disinterred and buried again on church lands. There is also the apocryphal story of a lady of high society who announced that she would no longer pray with her rosary so as not to repeat the name of the president (Santa María).

Further north in Chile, many British immigrants came to work in the nitrates industry and faced similar problems over consecrated ground for their graveyards. There is a *cementerio inglés* that can be visited today in Coquimbo and a dissidents' cemetery in Caldera (a national monument) that was established in 1876. Duncan Campbell, administrator for the "British Presence in Southern Patagonia" Web site, has provided a list of the many British names that appear on graves in the Caldera Cemetery. This list includes the captain, officers, and passengers of the Glasgow-built steamship RMS *Atacama*, which foundered on the Chilean coast with the loss of many lives, and whose names are remembered in a memorial "erected by the fellow officers and friends on the West Coast."

However, the outstanding example of a cemetery that was successfully established in this region is the English Cemetery at Hacienda Tiliviche (sometimes spelled Tiviliche), which dates from 1876. This cemetery can be visited in the Quebrada de Tiliviche, inland of Pisagua in the Tarapacá Region, and it was declared a historical monument in June 1976. The cemetery was needed by the growing British-born population because of the distance from the port of Iquique and the absence in the nitrate fields of any organized cemetery, especially for non-Catholics. The cemetery was established on the Hacienda Tiliviche, and the owner's house has survived, with its typically English architecture. There are more than one hundred graves in the cemetery, mainly of British citizens, including James Humberstone, and the last burial took place in 1974.

According to G. W. Wright (1942) in his article "English Graves at Tiliviche," the cemetery was extended and consecrated by the Bishop of the Falklands in 1905.

Wright provides a list of the British names on the graves taken from the original plan of the graveyard, and was helped in this task by "the late James T. Humberstone, O.B.E." Six Humberstones appear with years of death between 1881 and 1897, and all appear to have "Died young." There are sixty names in all in this list, the earliest being George and Janet Steele, both buried in 1877. One poignant mention is "Keith, Adam; original proprietor of graveyard," whose descendants, according to Wright, still tended the cemetery in 1942.

Chapter 14

Sports

> *We travelled by special train with horse boxes attached, on the afternoon of July 25th 1889 [to Quilpué]. We were followed by a large contingent of the local populace and many huasos from the neighbouring farms, and what lent a little colour to the proceedings was that we were all dressed in good, old British style, that is to say, pink coat, white breeches, top hat, and hunting boots with tops.*
>
> —William Russell Young, 1933

A major presence in the history of British associations with sport in Chile, and the early development of sport in the country at large, is the Valparaíso Sporting Club founded in 1882. This was (and still is) mainly focused on horse racing, the history of which goes back to 1869, when the Valparaíso Spring Meeting was established. Initially, races were held on just one day each year—the second Friday of October—when all commerce enjoyed a day's holiday. In the early years, races were "for gentlemen riders only." Later, on June 1, 1882, the members of the Valparaíso Spring Meeting met to establish a club designed especially to promote horse racing, and the statutes for the Valparaíso Sporting Club were approved on September 5 that year. A key founder was John Stewart Jackson, who had settled in Chile in 1854 and set up Jackson & Company.

But before horse racing there came, naturally, the sport of cricket. There is a mention of a game of cricket in the memoirs of General William Miller—the British soldier who fought for independence in Chile and elsewhere in South America. He reports that cricket was played in 1818 between teams from two British warships in Valparaíso, HMS *Andromache* and HMS *Blossom*. Another game between Royal Navy teams from two warships in Valparaíso is recorded as taking place in

1829, and in 1863 a team made up of crewmen from HMS *Sutley*, *Clio*, and *Charybdis* was beaten by a local Valparaíso team.

Valparaíso Cricket Club was founded in 1860, and therefore it is the oldest British sports club in Chile and almost certainly the first sports institution to be established in Chile. The club started with a pitch on the Quebrada Verde hill, where the players arrived on horseback to play against sailors from British warships, and later transferred to the grounds of the Valparaíso Sporting Club in 1881. Michelle Prain (2007) mentions the names of cricket teams—Port, Hill, England, Rest of the World, and Navy. The first international game of cricket was played against Argentina in 1893, and the visiting players reportedly took three and a half days to reach Santiago, crossing the Andes by mule.

The weekly newspaper *El Lota*, published in Spanish on Sundays in the town of Lota, in the heart of the coal mining region, headlined a game of cricket on its front page in its edition of February 26, 1888. "El domingo último tuvo lugar en Coronel una partida de *cricket* jugada entre los clubs de Lota i Coronel [Last Sunday a game of cricket took place in Coronel, played between the clubs of Lota and Coronel]." The reporter praises two players in particular, Gualterio (Walter) Garner and Guillermo (William) Perry, especially the former who made more than eighty "corridas [runs]," "quedando ambos con sus bats al terminar el juego [both finishing the game not out]."

By 1960, cricket was no longer played at club level in Valparaíso, although, according to the Chilean Cricket Association, the cricket club continued to function, but as a ladies' hockey team! The game was kept alive throughout the 1960s by the Prince of Wales Country Club in Santiago.

Incredible as it may sound, there was also fox hunting. Russell Young records in his memoirs (1933) that he was a member of the Valparaíso Paperchase Club, founded by British residents in 1870, and the Reñaca Foxhunting Club. The "paperchase" consisted of galloping across the countryside with hounds following a scent laid down by pieces of paper. The Reñaca Hunt Club met in winter, on Sundays and holidays, and did involve hunting foxes, with the first pack of hounds specially brought out from England.

Fox hunting and cricket evidently did not catch on in Chile, but another British passion certainly did—that of football (soccer). In the early days, the game was played informally by crewmen from boats anchored in Valparaíso Bay, often against scratch teams from other boats or from among the resident British community, and the sport spread through other ports along the coast—Antofagasta, Iquique, Coquimbo, and Talcahuano.

Sources differ on the claim to be the first organized football club in Chile. One possibility is the Badmington Football Club in Valparaíso, which later became the Valparaíso Football Club, sometimes called the Old Valparaíso. The club was started by British immigrants, oddly enough, as part of the Valparaíso Cricket Club. An agreement was reached in the early years with the Cricket Club for the football team to use part of the cricket pitches in the Valparaíso Sporting Club to play football in the winter months. This football club was started by David Scott in 1889, but its formal organization had to wait until the Civil War had run its course, in 1892. The Valparaíso Football Club ceased to exist at the time of the First World War, when many players left to fight in Europe. Another possibility is that the first football club in Chile was the Mackay and Sutherland Football Club, established in 1882 in Cerro Alegre, where football was played in the grounds of the school.

The first intercity game was played in July 1893 in Parque Cousiño between Valparaíso Football Club and an improvised team from Santiago, the Santiago Club. The first international game was played in 1893 at the Valparaíso Sporting Club in Viña del Mar between a Chilean team from Valparaíso and an "Argentinean" side, which sources say was made up entirely of British citizens.

In 1894, representatives of Mackay and Sutherland, Valparaíso, Chilian, National, and Colegio San Luis football clubs met in the Casa de Botes (Boat House) in Valparaíso to set up a Committee of Sports with the aim of popularizing the game in the port. In the same year, a competition was organized in Valparaíso and was so successful that two new clubs were formed, Victoria Rangers and Valparaíso Wanderers. The committee met again in July 1895 to establish the first football association and was joined by representatives from Victoria Rangers, Athletic, and Valparaíso Wanderers (National Football Club may not have attended). The meeting was chaired by R. Bailey, who apparently imported the first football from England.

The first club to be organized in Santiago was the Santiago Club (1893), followed by Santiago City (1895) and Santiago Rangers (1896). Mr. Steel started up a football team in Coquimbo, and there was a team in Concepción called "el English." The earliest football competition was the MacClelland Cup, held in Valparaíso between 1898 and 1910, in which participated Santiago Wanderers, Badmington, Chilian, Mackay and Sutherland, Victoria Rangers, Gold Cross, Williamson, National, Union Edwards, George VI, Valparaíso Wanderers, and La Cruz football clubs.

Names of football clubs with unmistakably British names have come down to modern times in Chile. Santiago Wanderers was founded in

Valparaíso in 1892—the name was to differentiate the team from the Valparaíso Wanderers. Rangers de Talca was founded in Talca in 1902. John Greenstreet, one of the founders of the club, chose the name. The history of the Santiago Morning Football Club goes back to the Santiago Football Club (founded 1903) and the Morning Star Football Club (1909), which fused in 1936 to make the Santiago Morning. Everton de Viña del Mar was founded in 1909 as a football club in Cerro Alegre, Valparaíso, by a group mainly comprising descendants of British immigrants from Viña del Mar and Valparaíso led by David Foxley Newton. Other football teams today in Chile also have British connections through their names—Club de Deportes Lota Schwager, and Club Deportivo O'Higgins Rancagua.

Rugby may well have been played first in Iquique by the British nitrates workers and by sailors in the port of Valparaíso. The first organized club was the Badmington Football Club in Valparaíso, which changed its name in around 1920 to Badmington Sports Club on account of this diversification. The problem they faced with rugby, and with other sports that are so typically British, was opponents to play with, other than teams in Santiago and scratch teams from the boats in the harbor. Nevertheless, the game caught on, and in 1927, the Prince of Wales Country Club had a rugby team that played against Green Cross—the only other rugby team then in Santiago. The Chilean Rugby Federation was founded in 1953.

The history of golf in Chile starts with the Valparaíso Golf Club, founded in 1897, when nine holes were played in the Valparaíso Sporting Club. In 1910, land adjoining the Sporting Club was rented, providing an eighteen-hole course. When this land was sold in 1912, the Golf Club returned to the Sporting Club, and while eighteen holes were possible, given the demands of other sports such as cricket and tennis, the land available for golf began to be reduced, and it was decided in 1919 to look for another site. Eventually, a place called La Granadilla was found, and work started on a new course, which was inaugurated in August 1922.

Golf was played by expatriate British residents in Concepción near Laguna Redonda (the second club to be founded); in Valparaíso at the Playa Ancha Golf Club; and in Viña del Mar at the Granadilla Golf Club. This was followed over time by the Magallanes Country Club in Punta Arenas—which is the most southerly golf course in the world—and the Prince of Wales Country Club and Club Los Leones in Santiago. The latter started life as the Santiago Golf Club, with nine holes in the grounds of the Hipódromo Chile, before moving to Los Leones in 1921. The Iquique Golf Club (founded in 1916) was playing nine holes in 1919 in the Plaza del Colorado, and by 1923 the club had an eighteen-hole course. The national Golf Association of Chile was formed in 1934, bringing together the clubs that existed at that time—the Valparaíso Golf Club, the Concepción Golf Club, the Santiago Golf Club, and the Prince of Wales Country Club.

According to the Chilean Golf Federation, the first golf championship in Chile was played in 1905, for the Tarapacá Young Cup, between "recognized West Coast Clubs." At that time, the only two teams that existed were the Valparaíso Golf Club and the Concepción Golf Club, both composed mainly of British residents, and, initially, the host alternated every year. Since then the same cup has been contested every year, excepting four years when there was no competition. The name of the trophy is taken from Mr. Young, a manager of the Bank of London and Tarapacá, who donated the cup to be disputed between players on the Pacific coast in Valparaíso and Concepción, which led to the competition being called the West Coast Challenge. The first competition was won by Valparaíso, represented by Edgard Howe, Gerald Harvey, Harold Naylor, and Arthur Beecheno. The Concepción players were Edward Cooper (British vice consul in Coronel), George Guthrie, Charles McKay, and W. Keay. Such was the success of the competition that in 1916 the Junior West Coast Challenge Cup was started for "the second representative teams" of the clubs in Valparaíso, Santiago, and Concepción.

Tennis is today Chile's second most popular sport and was first played in Chile in 1882, when a British resident named Cox set up a rudimentary tennis court in Valparaíso. Some time later, three other British residents, named James, Hardy, and Sutherland, did the same in other parts of the port. The first tennis club to be established came later, in 1898, and was called the Viña del Mar Lawn Tennis Club, with one court at the Grand Hotel in Viña del Mar, until 1910, when courts were opened within the Valparaíso Sporting Club.

The game arrived later in Santiago, where a British resident named Denier founded a tennis court on Avenida Independencia. In 1904, the Royal Lawn Tennis Club was established in Santiago, followed by tennis being played from 1905 in the Prince of Wales Country Club and the founding of the International Tennis Club in 1916. The first national federation was founded in 1920 as the Asociación de Lawn Tennis de Chile, and in that year five courts opened in the Valparaíso Sporting Club. Tennis was played elsewhere in Chile; for example, there was the Iquique Lawn Tennis Club.

Other sports introduced into Chile were polo (the Valparaíso Polo Club), target-shooting (the British Rifle Club, 1910), fishing, and the hunting of partridges, dove, wild duck, and quail. The Viking Rowing Club was founded in 1899 in the Bay of Valparaíso and became later the Varuna Boating Club, the English Rowing Club, and in 1916, the British Rowing Club.

It is also possible that the British were instrumental in introducing skiing into Chile. When the idea of constructing a rail link across the Andes to Mendoza was being promoted by Juan and Mateo Clark, Chilean brothers of British descent, the Chilean government contracted a British engineering company in 1887 to undertake a survey of the route this railway might take. It seems that the British commissioned a group of Norwegians to examine the upper reaches of the mountain where snow is fairly constant and these men did so on skis. The novelty of skiing soon proved popular with the British railway engineers. The railway opened in 1910, and for many the train was a kind of ski lift, allowing a descent on skis through Portillo, which later became the internationally famous ski resort.

One last sport with British connections in Chile is that of mountain climbing. An expedition in January 1897 led by the British climber Edward Fitzgerald climbed the Anaconda Mountain and was the first to use the approach through the Horcones valley. Fitzgerald's guide and some members of his group reached the summit, although he himself did not. Two years later, William Martin Conway climbed to very close to the summit but stopped short out of deference to Fitzgerald—a very gentlemanly decision, but one he later regretted.

Chapter 15

The Battle of Coronel

> *Why, then, you will ask me, did he attack—deliberately, designedly, intentionally—a force which he could not have reasonably have hoped either to destroy or put to flight?*
>
> —First Lord Arthur Balfour at the York Minster unveiling of a memorial to Rear-Admiral Sir Christopher Cradock, 1916

The Battle of Coronel in 1914 was the first naval battle of importance in the First World War, and the first general engagement fought by the Royal Navy since the Battle of Trafalgar, 1805. The battle between two squadrons, German and British, took place off Chile on November 1, 1914, near the port of Coronel, so close to the coast that people were able to watch the explosions of the battle from the shoreline.

More books have been written about this battle and the subsequent British revenge at the Battle of the Falklands (on December 8, 1914) than any other naval engagement, with the exception of battles between entire fleets. Interest derives partly from the fact that the British commander, Rear Admiral Cradock, led a Royal Navy squadron against an enemy force for the first time since the days of sail—the Battle of Trafalgar, 109 years previously. In addition, the unthinkable happened—*Rule Britannia* was roundly defeated in this battle, and the pride and reputation of the Royal Navy, which had ruled the waves for two centuries, lay shattered in Chilean waters.

It was also a tragedy, given that of every ten officers and sailors who faced each other on that Day of All Saints, nine were to die in the war—the British on that very day. Another reason for continuing interest in the Battle of Coronel is that the defeat off the coast of Chile was so quickly and so decisively avenged at the Falklands/Malvinas—within only six weeks. These two battles at the outbreak of the First World War were also a watershed in the history of naval warfare; they were the last naval battles which any navy would wage along classical lines, since from this moment onward, mines, submarines, and aerial bombardment changed the nature and complexity of naval strategy.

The Battle of Coronel was very one-sided and, arguably, this fact accounts more than any other reason for the enduring interest shown in what happened, for why did Rear Admiral Cradock purposefully take on such an obviously superior German force?

The British squadron consisted of five ships. The flagship *Good Hope* was an armored cruiser built in 1902 with a maximum speed of twenty-three knots, a crew of nine hundred men made up almost entirely of reservists with no battle training, and armor considered so obsolete that she had been reduced to Third Fleet status before war was declared. The *Monmouth* was also an armored cruiser, built one year later than the *Good Hope*. Her crew of 675 men consisted mainly of Scottish fishermen and coast guards. Both ships, the *Monmouth* and the *Good Hope*, went down with all hands at the Battle of Coronel.

The third ship in the British squadron was HMS *Glasgow*, a light cruiser and significantly the only ship in the British squadron manned by long-service officers and seamen, and the only British ship to take part in both the Battles of Coronel and the Falklands. However, she was only a light cruiser with no significant armor, and her intended role was to scout in search of the enemy fleet, perhaps engaging other cruisers, but keeping away from battleships and larger armored cruisers. The fourth ship was the *Otranto*, an armed merchant cruiser. She was in fact a converted liner, capable of eighteen knots maximum speed, but she only managed fifteen or sixteen knots in the battle. The last member of the squadron, the *Canopus*, was a battleship with an armored hull, built in 1899 and destined for the scrap yard in 1915, had it not been for the war. She was crewed by reservists with no gunnery practice and so slow that when the battle started, she lagged 250 miles behind the action.

Ranged against this squadron was a crack German force of two armored cruisers and three light cruisers. This was the highly trained and modern East Asian Cruiser Squadron based, with the exception of the *Dresden*, on the German base of Tsingtau in the distant colony in China. The commander was Vice Admiral Maximilian Graf von Spee. His flagship was the *Scharnhorst*, built in 1908, and the second armored cruiser of the German squadron was the *Gneisenau*, both similar in speed and armor to the *Good Hope* but quite superior in every other respect. Together with the three light cruisers, the *Dresden*, the *Leipzig*, and the *Nürnberg*, this ensemble constituted a formidable adversary.

In order to understand why Cradock should have taken on such a superior force off Coronel, it is necessary to examine the orders he received and his understanding of the strategic objectives. On August 23, 1914, the British Admiralty decreed that the destruction of the *Scharnhorst* and the *Gneisenau* was of the first importance, but in fact they did not give the necessary priority to this objective. On September 14, Cradock received the following signal: "As soon as you have superior force, search the Magellan Straits with squadron, being ready to return and cover the River Plate or, according to information, search north as far as Valparaíso. Break up the German trade and destroy the German cruisers" (quoted in Bennett, 81). This "superior force" was supposed to include HMS *Defence* from the Mediterranean, a modern armored cruiser, but this order was later cancelled when danger seemed to recede. So much so that two days later, Cradock was instructed to attack German trade on the west coast of South America immediately, with the British Admiralty believing that "Cruisers need not be concentrated. Two cruisers and an armed liner would seem to be sufficient for Magellan Straits and west coast" (see Bennett, 82).

With this information, Cradock left the River Plate area on September 22, 1914, understanding that this was his main task. In addition, he set out to search for the *Dresden*—the only enemy warship he then thought he was likely to meet. Nevertheless, he was warned in a message dated October 5, which he received in the Falklands, that perhaps the *Scharnhorst* and the *Gneisenau* were working across the Pacific to South America and that they might have been joined by the *Dresden*. What the Admiralty had in mind at this stage was a concentration of British forces around the Falklands "to search and protect trade in combination" (quoted in Bennett, 91), with HMS *Glasgow* crossing into the Pacific to search as far north as Valparaíso.

Cradock disobeyed, or more likely misunderstood, Admiralty instructions. He replied on October 8 to say that he would concentrate around the Falklands and avoid dispersal of his forces, confining the *Glasgow*, the *Monmouth*, and the *Otranto* to a radius south of Valparaíso until the German cruisers were located. He added, on October 11, "Without alarming, respectfully suggest that in event of the enemy's heavy cruisers and others concentrating west coast of South America, it is necessary to have a British force on each coast strong enough to bring them into action" (see Bennett, 91–92). Winston Churchill sent a minute to the Admiralty in response to this signal: "It would be best for the British ships to keep within supporting distance of one another, whether in the Straits or near the Falklands, and to postpone the cruise along the west coast until the present uncertainty about *Scharnhorst-Gneisenau* is cleared up. They and not the trade are our quarry for the moment. Above all, we must not miss them" (see Bennett, 92).

This was all very sensible, but the actual signals sent by the Admiralty to Cradock were vague, saying that the Admiralty agreed to his concentrating his forces for "combined operations"—exactly where was not specified—and giving the news that other warships were on their way from Sierra Leone via Montevideo. At this point, the *Monmouth*, the *Glasgow*, and the *Otranto* were already on the Chilean coast, while the *Good Hope* was waiting for the *Canopus* at the Falklands.

The Admiralty then learned that Cradock was taking his squadron into the Pacific, contrary to their expectations and instructions, but they did not intervene because by late October a second squadron was concentrating near Montevideo under Rear Admiral Stoddart, and could be used if von Spee eluded Cradock's forces and entered the Atlantic intent on returning to Germany. There was also the Admiralty's understanding that even if the German warships were located, Cradock would not engage them but merely shadow them. At the same time, Cradock abandoned the *Canopus*, on account of her slow speed, and sailed on confident that he would be joined by the armored cruiser HMS *Defence*, which he assumed was now in Montevideo. Stoddart and the Admiralty had other ideas; that the *Defence* was to stay on the east coast in case the German squadron slipped through into the Atlantic, and Cradock was informed about this in a message he received at midday on the fateful day, November 1.

Winston Churchill wrote less than a decade later in *The World Crisis* (he was First Lord of the Admiralty in 1914), "I cannot accept for the Admiralty any share in the responsibility" for this defeat. Geoffrey Bennett quotes this opinion in his study *Coronel and the Falklands* (1962, 97), and finds it unacceptable, and so did many of Churchill's contemporaries.

Von Spee did not face such problems. On August 18, the German naval staff took the decision that he should have complete liberty of action, and they resolved to send him no further instructions. Nevertheless, von Spee would have been aware of general German strategy for his squadron, which was:

1. To engage British forces in foreign waters as much as possible in order to divert forces away from naval warfare in Europe.
2. To damage British trade. The victory at Coronel led to the temporary cessation of British trade on the west coast of South America. At that time, for example, access to Chilean nitrates was of special importance to both countries, given that it was still an ingredient

used in the manufacture of explosives. Germany developed synthetic substitutes later in the war.
3. To keep clear of Japanese forces in the north that might enter the war against Germany (Japan entered the war on October 23), and avoid Australian and New Zealand squadrons in the south.
4. To keep his cruiser squadron together and conceal aims and whereabouts as long as possible, so as to hold up a large number of enemy ships.

In addition, von Spee was aware that there existed a strong German and pro-German element along the Chilean coast, resulting from colonization and German investment in commerce. He had received a signal on August 1 describing Chile as friendly and neutral. Chile also had coal that he could purchase for his steam-driven squadron and agents from whom to glean intelligence.

Von Spee heard that the *Glasgow* was in Coronel and steamed south to find her. Under international law, the *Glasgow* had to depart within twenty-four hours, and she left on the morning of November 1 to rendezvous with Cradock fifty miles west of Coronel. Meanwhile, Cradock had intelligence that suggested that the *Leipzig* was in the area, and she was the only German ship he now expected to find. The two forces stumbled into each other off Coronel, to the north-west of Santa María Island, and spent the late afternoon maneuvering for advantage, with the British hoping to catch von Spee silhouetted by the sun behind him while they stood out to sea. Von Spee skillfully avoided falling into this trap and by 6:45 p.m. the tables had turned, and it was the German advantage to have the setting sun behind the British warships. Cradock ordered the auxiliary *Otranto* away, which left the *Monmouth*, the *Good Hope*, and the *Glasgow*, outclassed and outgunned, facing the more modern and better crewed *Scharnhorst*, *Gneisenau*, *Dresden*, *Nürnberg*, and *Leipzig*. Only the *Glasgow* survived, and both armored cruisers were sunk, with the entire crews of 1,440 killed on the *Good Hope* and the *Monmouth*. No Germans died in this engagement.

Two steamers, the *Valdivia* and the *Chiloé*, were chartered by the British government to search the area for possible survivors. The Chilean government sent the *Maipú*, for which the British Minister-Resident sent a note expressing his gratitude. A merchant ship, the *Rancagua*, also crisscrossed the sea near the coast, and the yacht *Gaviota* picked up a life vest, but that was all that was found.

The British revenge came quickly, on December 8, off the Falkland Islands, where both the *Scharnhorst* and the *Gneisenau* were sunk, and the German light cruisers forced back to the Magellan Strait. The *Nürnberg* and the *Leipzig* were caught and overcome, but the *Dresden* got away, and turned up at Punta Arenas to take on coal and water, as reported in *The Magellan Times* on December 18. This newspaper (published for the English speaking community in southern Chile) also editorialized about the victory in the Falklands: "The brilliant victory gained by the British Navy over the Germans off the Falklands has filled us with pride. We are glad to be able to record that all our countrymen behaved in that decorous way Britishers should, and quietly celebrated the good news among themselves with heartfelt joy" (*Magellan Times*, December 17, 1914).

The British hunting group arrived in Punta Arenas to find that the *Dresden* had just left. They posted guards at the entrances to the Magellan Strait and set off to comb the fiords of Tierra del Fuego. After hiding for three months, the *Dresden* entered the Pacific and was found by chance by HMS *Kent* on March 8, 1915. The *Dresden* made for the Juan Fernández Islands, but when the *Glasgow* also came on the scene and fired on her, she surrendered. The *Dresden*'s intelligence officer, Lieutenant Wilhelm Franz Canaris, came to the *Glasgow* with a flag of truce. The German crew then blew up the ship, after taking to the boats, and getting ashore, they requested internment for the rest of the war. The British followed and demanded the Chilean authorities give up the Germans, claiming that that they were prisoners of war, but to no avail. The German officers and crew were interned on the island of Quiriquina in the Bay of Concepción. Lieutenant Canaris managed to escape his internment and return to Germany, and by the time the Second World War started, he had become Admiral Canaris, in charge of the *Abwehr*, German Military Intelligence. Canaris was one of the leading military figures opposed to Hitler and was executed shortly before the end of the war on suspicion of plotting against the Nazi regime.

Testimony to the Battle of Coronel can be found in Chile. There is a plaque in memory of Cradock, his officers, and his men, in the Anglican Church in Concepción, and on November 8, 1989, a memorial was unveiled in the Plaza 21 de Mayo in Coronel by Admiral José Merino Castro and the Sociedad Anglo-Chilena. The only known tomb of a British seaman who took part and who died from his injuries, but in the Battle of the Falklands, can be found in Cemetery No. 1 in Talcahuano. His name is A. Munro, and he died on August 25, 1915. He was a reservist who served on HMS *Kent*, very probably one of the twelve sailors reported as wounded in the battle on this particular ship. There is a memorial in the cemetery in Punta Arenas erected by the German colony there in 1925 to the memory of the German officers and sailors who died in the Battle of the Falklands. Curiously, the text on the plaque, in both German and Spanish, gives the wrong date for the Battle of Coronel as November 2.

There remains the intriguing possibility, according to sources among the British community in Chile, that some bodies may have been washed up after the Battle of Coronel on the beach between Lebu and Punta Lavapie; perhaps they were buried in a small private Anglican cemetery belonging to a British family named Shand. This cemetery near the beach at Quidico still has the tombs of the Shands, but sadly it has proved impossible to verify this event through official documentation.

To return, by way of conclusion, to the initial question—why should Cradock have engaged such an obviously superior force?—Lord Arthur Balfour continued in his dedication at York Minster (quoted in Bennett 1962, 111):

> I think a satisfactory explanation can be given. [Von Spee] would be a great peril as long as his squadron remained efficient, and [if] Admiral Cradock judged that his squadron, that he himself and those under him, were well sacrificed if they destroyed the power of this hostile fleet, then I say there is no man, be he sailor or be he civilian, but would say that such a judgement showed not only the highest courage, but the greater courage of unselfishness; and that Admiral Cradock, by absolute neglect of personal interest and personal ambitions, had shown a wise judgement in the interests of his country. If I am right there never was a nobler act.

Chapter 16

The Decline of British Influence

Much of the enduring influence that the British enjoyed in Chile was mediated through commerce and industry, and, as we have seen, this presence was considerable in the late nineteenth and early twentieth centuries. At the outbreak of the First World War in 1914, although only 4.1 percent of the population in Chile were foreigners, 31.7 percent of commerce was in the hands of immigrants, principally from Europe, and many of them were British. More than 30 percent of Chile's imports at that time were from Britain, but from this year on, British business interests in Chile declined rapidly, and in Latin America in general.

Rory Miller (1991) has analyzed the generally held reasons for this decline, the first of which is the view that there was no strategic reaction to key events, and British investments were allowed to lie fallow. A second, and kinder, opinion is that Britain retreated from a region where the United States had a "manifest destiny" and concentrated sensibly on other parts of the world, especially in the British Empire. A third view is that external events proved too damaging, particularly the First and Second World Wars and the Great Depression.

Rory Miller's (1991) own conclusion is that 1914–1918 was a watershed since Britain emerged from the Great War as a debtor nation. She ceased from this time onwards to be an exporter of capital, exposing the fact that the strong pre–First World War commercial links had really been sustained by her capacity to lend. Miller adds that there is very little evidence to support the hypothesis that withdrawal from the region was deliberate, however sensible it might seem now for the country to have focused on the Empire after the Great War. Barton (2000, 262) makes the same point: "British traders struggled to remain competitive in the Chilean market place. They did not willingly vacate the market for imperial opportunities. They were frustrated by the lack of British government support, they failed to respond to market requirements, and they were forced out by more competitive, better supported export organizations."

The interwar years saw many criticisms within the region, of Britain's complacency, arrogance, conservatism, intransigence, lack of innovation, and even misjudgment, such as the Anglo-South American Bank's decision in the early 1930s to speculate heavily in nitrates. It also seemed in this period that the directors and top managers in Britain were increasingly out of touch with, and insensitive to, the realities on the ground in Latin America.

At the same time, the United States was coming on strong in Latin America following the First World War. This was a watershed for the commercial relations established in the nineteenth century, whereby the United States predominated in the nations of Central America, the Caribbean, and the northern countries of South America, while Britain dominated in the Southern Cone. This now changed, and in the interwar years, American businesses successfully challenged the British for supremacy in trade with Chile. In the 1920s, while Britain's nitrates interests declined, the United States was building up a portfolio in copper mining and industry that lasted throughout the first half of the twentieth century. While less important than the inroads made by American business in this period, it is interesting to note that despite her defeat in the Great War, Germany's exporters returned promptly and successfully to Latin America, although this renewed interest in the region was not sustained.

Then came the global slump, the Great Depression. Rory Miller (*Britain and Latin America in the Nineteenth and Twentieth Centuries*, 1993) provides figures that show that Britain exported just over £5 million of goods to Chile in the year before the Wall Street Crash in October 1929 and that this fell to just over £1.5 million by 1938. At the same time, imports from Chile also fell from around £7.5 million, through £3 million, to end the same period at £5.3 million, which created a considerable balance of trade in favor of Chile. This trend was reflected across Latin America and shows that by the mid-1930s Britain had become more important to the region as a market than as the traditional provider of manufactured goods. The Depression also meant that the prices paid for primary products from Latin America fell, and this stimulated a push for industrialization and diversification to reduce dependence on manufactured products from abroad.

The Depression had another negative effect on British commerce too, according to Rory Miller (1991), since it led to the complete rewriting of the rules of international trade and payments, cutting away at Britain's dominance in global financial affairs. At the same time, exports from Latin America fell away, and in Chile's case this was initially a nosedive—exports internationally after the Wall Street Crash were less than one-fifth of the pre-Depression period. This naturally produced problems with the balance of payments—a worldwide phenomenon—and countries abandoned traditional commercial treaties and instead sought new bilateral agreements. Countries belonging to the British Empire benefited from agreements reached in 1932 (the Ottawa agreements), but clearly this was not a help to Chile. Britain had to decide where its priorities lay in Latin America, and one response was to reach a mutually interesting agreement with Argentina in 1935.

Another factor relates to the British government's role in the interwar years. Barton (2000) points out that there was a marked absence of coordination between the key agencies of government and business to meet the new challenges in this period, and that as a result the hegemony of British commercial interests in Chile, held over more than a century since independence, was eclipsed and handed over to the United States.

Then came the Second World War.

Rory Miller (1991) makes the interesting point that, while the Second World War, unsurprisingly, contributed further to the decline of British interests in Chile, at the same time it proved to be the trigger for its salvation, in that host countries in the region began to nationalize British assets. These assets were generally run down because of the lack of investment, had become the targets of nationalism, and did not seem worth hanging on to for the longer term. For instance, in 1939 about 40 percent of British capital investment in the region was in railways alone, which were ripe for nationalization. Britain no longer held sway, it was soon weakened by the war effort, and British companies looked old-fashioned and vulnerable. The United States emerged from the war politically and economically dominant in the region and became increasingly important as a market for the region's exports and as a provider of manufactured goods. Between 1941 and 1950 the value of British investments in Latin America fell by more than 50 percent. Countries in Latin America benefited through the six years of the conflict from high prices for their produce, and Britain did not have the wherewithal to provide the machinery and tools needed in a region that was committed to industrializing.

This was the close of a golden era that had started with nineteenth-century investments by Britain in Chile, was renewed after World War I, then badly shaken by the Depression, and now heavily reduced as the result of the Second World War.

Chapter 17

The Imprint That Remains: Family Names and Geography

> *English names are borne by men high in the service of the State, and by politicians and landowners, the descendants of English, Irish and Scotch, who married Chilian ladies and settled in the country, and who for the most part, if not always, become intensely Chilian in feeling, and generally adopted the religion of the people.*
>
> —*William Howard Russell, 1890*

L. C. Derrick-Jehu is the author of a detailed study of British family names in Chile entitled *The Anglo-Chilean Community* (1965), and he warns the reader that no single researcher could account for the tens of thousands of British descendants in the country. Nevertheless, he was able to amass a database of around five thousand names.

Víctor Santa Cruz (1968) draws attention to another difficulty in following through on British names in Chile, and this derives from the order given by President Diego Portales in 1840 for foreigners living in the country to "Chileanize" their names. As a result, Harris became Arias, and Humphrey metamorphosed into Onofre. Santa Cruz wonders if Ibáñez is derived from Evans, a surname from Wales. Griffin (2006), however, refers to a John Evans from Ireland (possibly the first Irishman to settle down in Chile) who lived from 1737 in the region of Chillán and became prosperous. His great-great-grandson was Carlos Ibáñez, twice President of Chile in 1927–1931 and 1952–1958. More recently, the first president of Chile following the restoration of democracy certainly has a Welsh ancestry—President Patricio Aylwin—his great-grandfather came to Chile as a British consul. Other examples include James Humberstone, who became Santiago Humberstone, and John Williams, who turned into Juan Guillermos.

There are several interesting phenomena underpinning the history of British immigration into Chile. Unlike the general trend of immigration from other countries to Latin America in the nineteenth century and early twentieth century, none came to escape persecution or abject poverty. The possible exceptions are those who came from Catholic Ireland, where the chance of advancement for ambitious individuals was very limited in the eighteenth and nineteenth centuries. A surprising number came on doctors' orders for reasons of health. Many had contracts of work or at least the prospect of finding good employment on their arrival, and few came as part of assisted immigration programs. The early arrivals tended to see themselves as true immigrants and stay, marry, and have Chilean families, but from the mid-nineteenth century onward this changed. The following generations of arrivals usually regarded Chile as their temporary home, and the men typically intermarried with British wives, or left their wives at home, before retiring back to Britain.

However, a sizeable number did settle in Chile, and to give a flavor of the many British names that have imprinted themselves on Chile (in some cases becoming hispanicized), this is a short selection collated from Derrick-Jehu (1965), Mackenna (1884), and other sources.

Blest: Dr. William Cunningham Blest was a doctor and surgeon, born in County Sligo, Ireland. Dr. Blest is regarded as the "founder of Chilean medicine." He graduated from the Edinburgh Medical School in 1821, and arrived in Chile on account of his health in 1823, called over by his brother, who was head of a merchant house. In 1826, he presented to the Chilean government his *Observations over the Actual State of Medicine in Chile and a Plan to Improve It*, and in 1828 an *Essay over the Most Common Causes of Diseases Suffered in Santiago de Chile*. And well he might, since at that time public health was in a dreadful state, with unsanitary conditions prevailing, and there were only nine doctors in the city—most of them foreigners. He became a Chilean citizen, and in 1833, the director of the first school of Medicine created in Chile after independence. Later he became a deputy and a senator, and one of his sons, Alberto Blest Gana (1830–1920), is considered by many to be the most prominent Chilean novelist of the nineteenth century. Alberto is also remembered for leading the Chilean legation in Paris in the purchase of arms and munitions prior to the War of the Pacific. Another son was the poet Guillermo Blest Gana, born in Santiago in 1829.

Bunster: The story goes that Humphrey Bunster was sent on shore to get water in Chile in 1822, and was lassoed by a Chilean *huaso* (cowboy) and held prisoner! He evidently came to like Chile and was joined by his elder brother Grosvenor Bunster in 1827. According to Vicuña Mackenna (1884, 35), he became "the patriarch of the British in Valparaíso."

Cox: The family descends from Nathaniel Miers Cox. During the War of Independence he joined O'Higgins' army as first surgeon of the patriot army. He was at the battles of Cancha Rayada and Rancagua and endured the exile in Mendoza. He was given Chilean citizenship by O'Higgins in 1819 and later became a surgeon in the San Juan de Dios Hospital, dean of the school of medicine of the Universidad de Chile from 1843; military surgeon of Valparaíso from 1845; and the administrator of Santiago's Casa de Huérfanos (orphanage). He was apparently the first surgeon to undertake surgical operations in Chile.

Cooper: Edward Cooper was born in Reading and settled in Chile before 1869. He founded the milling firm of Cooper & Company in Concepción. Edward Cooper married Oriana Miller, and they had thirteen surviving children, producing thirty grandchildren, who mostly remained as residents in Chile. One of Edward's sons, also named Edward Cooper, was British consul in Coronel and Concepción for over fifty years.

Daroch: Rev. John Darroch-Campbell of the parish of Craignish in Scotland was born in 1670 and married Lady Ann Elizabeth Campbell of Glenorochy. Their second son, Joseph Archibald Darroch-Campbell, left to live in Panama and Peru, where he married María Teresa Modero y Ollo. Their second child, Juan José Darroch-Campbell y Moreno, was born in Lima, and this son arrived in Chile in 1750. Juan José served the Spanish crown very well, holding several key posts including that of *alcalde* (mayor) of Santiago. After he married in Chile, his first child was named Juan Antonio Daroch y Arlegui, born in Santiago in 1772, and from this time on, the second *r* and the additional surname of Campbell are dropped. The Daroch name has survived in Chile, with Vice Admiral Emilio Daroch Soto (Navy commander-in-chief 1947–1948), and Rear Admiral Arturo Troncoso Daroch (minister of education during the military government).

Edwards: According to the Chilean historian Diego Barros Arana (*Historia General*, vol. 7), George Edwards was a British doctor and surgeon on the first visit to Chile by the British frigate *Scorpion*, which was disguised as a whaler for contraband purposes. Another source names the whaler on which he arrived as the *Backhouse*, and others claim he landed from a British ship raiding Spanish possessions off the Pacific coast. What seems certain is that George Edwards fell in love with a Chilean woman named Isabel Ossandón e Iribárren, and that he jumped ship in Coquimbo in 1806.

His descendants have left their mark on Chile. His son Agustín Edwards Ossandón was the most financially successful of his eight children. He settled in Valparaíso in 1850 and founded the Bank of A. Edwards. Another son, Joaquín, was successful too, becoming a banker and mine owner and the provincial intendant of Coquimbo. George's grandson, Agustín Edwards Ross, was born in Valparaíso in 1852. He became senator for Valparaíso and *ministro de hacienda* (finance minister) in the administration of President Balmaceda. Agustín also acquired two newspapers, *El Mercurio* of Valparaíso, and *La Epoca* of Santiago, and established partnerships between his family's holdings in railways and nitrates and the major British companies.

Agustín Edwards MacClure, George's great-grandson, founded the Santiago edition of *El Mercurio*. He became a deputy in 1903, representing the Department of Quillota, foreign minister (1904 and 1905), minister of the interior (1910), and ambassador to Britain from late 1910 until after the First World War. On his retirement from the Chilean embassy in London, he became a director of the Anglo-South American Bank.

Faulkner: In 1804, the crew of a ship bound for Australia mutinied off the Chilean coast, and around one hundred of the passengers landed at Concepción, including Dr. Henry Faulkner, who later became governor of Quillita. The surname continues in Chile, probably in descent from this doctor.

King: There are descendants today in Chile of John King, who was born in Ayrshire in Scotland. He arrived in Chile in 1862, accompanying a group of railway workers from Glasgow to work on the Carrizal Railway. In 1866, King replaced the North American engineer George Stevenson and became the engineer-manager of the railway (see Couyoumdjian 2003). He married Margaret Webster Livingstone, and, although they returned to Britain in 1919, their fifteen children were born in Chile, with twenty-four grandchildren, ensuring a line of descendants in Chile with the surnames King, Barrett, Hardy, Martin, and Roper (see Derrick-Jehu 1965, 177).

Lyon: George Lyon founded one of the first merchant companies in Valparaíso soon after independence, in 1826. He was sent to Chile for reasons of health; it is possible that his family was influenced by Maria Graham's description in her *Journal* of Chile as "an earthly paradise and beneficial to the lungs." He had eleven children by his wife, Carmen Santa Maria, many of whom intermarried with traditional Chilean families.

MacIver: The MacIver family in Chile descends from a Scottish sailor named Henry MacIver, who was shipwrecked near Valparaíso in 1835. His son Enrique was born in Constitución in 1844, and his grandson was Enrique MacIver Rodríguez, who became minister of the interior and minister of finance in the presidency of Jorge Montt.

Perry: An Englishman named Thomas Perry arrived in Chile around 1852, with his wife Elisa Willis. He worked as an architect and designed and built a pier in Coqimbo. He moved to Valparaíso, and then to Lota, where he built piers in Coronel and Lota. He died in Lota and is buried in the cemetery there. One of his sons, Henry Perry (born 1855) administrated the Lota mines in two periods, 1889–1892 and 1900–1902, and also became mayor of Lota. Another son, William Perry, was a mining engineer and helped with the design of the gardens, artificial lakes, and bridges of Lota Park.

Tupper: the Tupper family is descended from William Vic-Tupper (born in Guernsey in 1800), who fought in the War of Independence. Francisco Puelma Tupper (born 1850) was one of the major promoters of public health in Chile and founder of the Sociedad Médica, and creator during the War of the Pacific of the health services for the armed forces.

Waddington: Vicuña Mackenna (1884, 34) refers to Joshua Waddington as "the true founder of modern Valparaíso." He was born 1792 in York, whence he went to Buenos Aires and then on to Valparaíso in 1818. Trading as Waddington, Templeman & Company, he financed copper mines at Copiapó and Coquimbo and invested in shipping, becoming very prosperous. There are two lasting testimonies to his name in Chile. The first is the sixty-kilometer Waddington Canal, which he had built to carry water to lands he had acquired in the Quillota Valley and which still exists today. The second is the present-day Plaza Waddington in Valparaíso. His son, Guillermo Waddington, was the first in the line of Chilean cabinet ministers with a British surname (in 1852).

Walker: Three Walker brothers—John, Robert, and Alexander—arrived in Chile around 1830 and worked in copper mining and export. Carlos Walker Martínez, who fought and died in the War of the Pacific, was Robert's son. Horacio Walker, who became minister for foreign relations, is also of this family.

White: Derrick-Jehu (1965, 174) believes that a man surnamed White settled in Chile before 1837. He adds that his descendants strongly believe that this ancestor was the illegitimate son of either King George IV or King William IV. The story is that when the immigrant was born, the father was Duke of York (which is actually not true of either of the kings), and hence the offspring was given the name of White (as in the White Rose of Yorkshire). Derrick-Jehu is impressed with how persistent the story is, and he wonders if perhaps there may be some truth in the family legend, but deriving from these kings' brother Frederick, who *was* Duke of York.

Williams: In 1843, the Chilean government sent an expedition under Welsh-born John Williams with the objective of establishing a permanent settlement on the shores of Magellan Strait. The Williams name lives on in the naming of Chile's most southerly settlement, Puerto Williams on the Beagle Channel, and the name of Isla Juan Guillermos (the rendering of his name in Spanish) in the Alacalufes National Park just north of the western exit of the Magellan Strait. Indeed, it is quite remarkable how many geographical places and features have over the centuries been named by, or after, British visitors to Chilean Patagonia and Tierra del Fuego.

Modern maps of the region provide evidence of these several enduring names, and here are some examples that resonate with the history of the British presence; we confine ourselves to the embroidery of archipelagos of southern Chile below the island of Chiloé down to the Magellan Strait and Tierra del Fuego.

Pirates, Buccaneers, Privateers, Corsairs, and Circumnavigators

Sir Francis Drake's circumnavigation (1577–1580):

- Elizabeth Island (Isla Isabel), in the Magellan Strait near Punta Arenas.
- Drake Passage.

Sir Thomas Cavendish's voyage (1586–1588):

- Port Famine (Puerto Hambre), Cavendish's renaming of the Spanish settlement of "Rey Felipe," where he found only corpses.

Sir John Narborough's expedition in the *Sweepstakes* and the *Batchelor* (1669–1671):

- Punta Arenas: "Sandy Point," named by John Narborough in 1670, whose description was "Good habitable land. Sandy Point. Lots of wild geese." The name was confirmed as Sandy Point by John Byron in 1764.
- Cape Froward, Narborough's name for the most southerly point of the continent.

- The Narborough group of islands.

Lord George Anson's expedition (1740–1744):

- The Wager and Byron Islands in the Guayaneco archipelago, referring to the wreck of HMS *Wager*, with a midshipman called Byron on board.
- Anna Pink Bay, named after the provisions boat *Anna*, which was abandoned at Juan Fernández Islands.

Explorers by Sea

Commodore John Byron's expedition (1764–1766), surveying the Magellan Strait:

- Byron Bay, Byron Island, Byron Shoal, and Byron Sound, names that today mark his progress through the strait. The ship *Dolphin* is remembered in Dolphin Cape and Dolphin Island, and the *Tamar* recorded in Tamar Island, Tamar Pass, Tamar Peninsula, and Port Tamar. The Mouat islands are named after the Captain of the *Tamar*, and King George Island (George III) and King George Bay date from this voyage.

Captains Samuel Wallis and Philip Carteret: expedition on the *Dolphin* and *Swallow* (1766–1768 [Wallis]/ 1769 [Carteret]):

- Punta Dúngeness, the last point of Chile in the east at the mouth of Magellan Strait, named by Samuel Wallis from its resemblance to the promontory in the English Channel.

Captain James Cook: first circumnavigation (1768–1771); second circumnavigation (1772–1775).

- Cape Gloucester, a headland named by Cook on his second voyage to Tierra del Fuego. York Minster, a promontory rising out of the sea that reminded him of a cathedral. This voyage charted and named Christmas Sound (he arrived there in December 1774) and Cook Bay to the north, which is in fact the western opening to the Beagle Channel, although of course he did not realize this. Cook also named Cape Desolation.
- Other features: Cook Bay, Puerto Cook, Isla Cook.

The *Beagle* surveys: Captains Philip Parker King and Pringle Stokes (1826–1829), Robert FitzRoy (1829–1830), and Robert FitzRoy (1831–1836):

- Otway Water, a reference to Admiral Otway, who headed the Royal Navy's South American Station from Brazil, to whom Parker King turned after the suicide of Pringle Stokes on board the *Beagle* on its first expedition.
- Stokes Island, Stokes Bay, Isla Pringle, Beagle Bay, Useless Bay (Bahía Inutil, named by Parker King), Parker King Bay, Isla Beagle, Isla King.
- Isla Skyring (named after Lieutenant Skyring, who took over the *Beagle* after Stokes' suicide before handing over to FitzRoy). Skyring Water (Seno de Skyring), which links to Otway Water by the FitzRoy Channel.
- FitzRoy named many landmarks and geographical features, despite clear Admiralty instructions to the contrary. Janet Browne (1995) lists several, including Admiral Otway, Queen Adelaide, Francis Beaufort, FitzRoy's sister Mrs. Rice Trevor, his uncles Grafton and Londonderry, and the names of Lyell, Buckland, Greenough, and Fitton, which were given to places around Clarence Island.
- Murray Narrows, named after the sailing master under FitzRoy on the *Beagle* on his first command, who had taken a whaleboat to find a more suitable anchorage during a storm, only to have it stolen by the Alacaluf Indians. Basket Island and Whaleboat Sound, also named after this incident—Murray and his companions wove a boat-shaped basket out of branches and leaves caulked with clay to paddle back to the *Beagle*. While chasing the culprits, FitzRoy named features of the landscape Isla Leadline, Cabo Long-chase, Isla Hide, Thieves Sound, Bahía Escape, and Thieves Cover. Cutfinger Cove recalls where one of FitzRoy's sailors almost cut off two fingers while chopping wood.
- Smythe Channel, named by Parker King and FitzRoy after a British Admiral they had served under in the Mediterranean.
- Beagle Channel. The island of Lennox at the eastern exit was named by FitzRoy and is perhaps called after the area north of Glasgow.
- Isla Herschel, just to the north of Cape Horn, named during the first *Beagle* voyage after the English astronomer John Herschel.

- Other features: Mount FitzRoy, FitzRoy Bay, Canal FitzRoy, Isla FitzRoy, Canal King, Boca Wickham (Lieutenant John Clements Wickham).

Henry Foster's scientific expedition on the *Chanticleer* to the South Atlantic (1828–1830):

- The Wallaston group of islands, named by Henry Foster to commemorate the British chemist and physicist William Hyde Wollaston. Isla Deceit in this group was also named by Foster.

Sir James Clark Ross's expedition in the *Erebus* and the *Terror* (1839–1843):

- Cape Ross, just north of Cape Horn.

British Naturalists in Chile

- Mount Darwin and the Darwin Cordillera, named by Robert FitzRoy.
- Darwin Sound (Seno Darwin), the Darwin Icefield, Darwin Bay, Canal Darwin, and Isla Darwin.

Chile's Wars

- Canal Bynon (who fought with Cochrane), Canal O'Higgins, Canal Simpson, Cochrane Strait, Puerto O'Brien, Isla O'Brien, Puerto Simpson, Isla Simpson, Isla Canning, Isla Patricio Lynch, and Canal Cochrane.

Visitors and Explorers on Land

Alexander Caldcleugh's stay in Chile (1821-ca.1836):

- Caldcleugh Canal, Caldcleugh Strait, Isla Caldcleugh.

British Communities in Chile

- Puerto Williams, Canal Williams, Isla Williams.

Religion

Allen Gardiner on Tierra del Fuego (1848 & 1850–1851):

- Banner Cove (Cabo Banner), on Picton Island at the eastern mouth of the Beagle Channel. Isla Gardiner, the small island in front of Banner Cove, which he called Garden Island due to the vegetables he planted there.
- Bahía Allen Gardiner, on Tierra del Fuego, near Cape Horn.
- Speedwell Bay, named after one of the ship's boats used by the missionary, landed from the *Ocean Queen*.

Finally, go to any town or village in Chile and there will be at least one street with a name that evokes names and exploits connected with the British presence in Chile. Taking Santiago as an example, there is the Avenida Libertador General Bernardo O'Higgins (the city's main avenue, known popularly as La Alameda), Parque O'Higgins, Calle General Mackenna, Avenida Vicuña Mackenna, Calle Lord Cochrane, Calle Jorge Canning, Calle O'Brien, and even a street called Drake.

All of this is rich testimony to the *mysterious sympathy* that has existed for centuries, and continues to exist, between Britain and Chile.

Appendix A

English Newspapers in Chile

> *The South Pacific Mail is found in every Nitrate Oficina, Mine, Ranch, Farm, and large industrial business in both Chile and Bolivia and affords the surest means of reaching members of all the English-speaking communities.*
>
> —*Advertisement published in 1925*

The Chilean historian Juan Ricardo Couyoumdjian provides an excellent history of the most famous, influential, and enduring of the newspapers published in English in Chile, *The South Pacific Mail*. Couyoumdjian's article "*Apuntes sobre un periódico inglés de Valparaíso* [Notes on an English newspaper in Valparaíso]" (1987), concentrates on the early history of the *Mail* from 1909 to 1925.

According to Couyoumdjian, there were two precursors for the *Mail*, both published in Valparaíso. Starting in 1876, there was the *Chilian Times*, which ceased to circulate in 1907, quite probably as a consequence of economic problems caused by the severe earthquake of 1906 that destroyed much of the city. This was followed in 1907 by the *Anglo-Chilean Times*, which circulated until the following year. This newspaper became the *South Pacific Mail*, whose first edition circulated on November 6, 1909. It was edited first in Valparaíso, until 1950, and then in Santiago, accompanying the shift in the economic center of gravity from the port to the capital. The *Mail* was a weekly newspaper published on Thursdays, entirely in English; it ceased to be published in 1965.

The first owner and editor of the *Mail* was Henry A. Hill. The launch was an immediate success with readers, and within three months it was being read in thirty different places in Chile and abroad, from Lima to Punta Arenas, a readership that increased to sixty towns a year later and included La Paz and Oruro in Bolivia. Couyoumdjian shows that the venture was apparently very successful commercially with advertisers: an edition of the *Mail* in 1913 comprises twenty-four pages, ten of which were entirely taken up by advertisements (including the first and last pages), and most of the rest had at least one paid announcement on each page.

By 1923, the newspaper was able to claim that it was "recognised as the OFFICIAL ORGAN of the English-speaking Communities in CHILE and BOLIVIA. Circulating throughout the West Coast of South America from CAPE HORN to PANAMA" (Escobar 1923, 228). The newspaper was renowned for its editorial stand, commenting on news of various kinds, but concentrating on business matters. The most famous writer for this newspaper was Oswald Hardy Evans, who became the main editorial writer in 1924. In essence, the *South Pacific Mail* represented the interests of the British community, and acted as a window for Chile on the world, but the owners always avoided any intervention in Chilean politics.

The second most important English newspaper in Chile was the *Magellan Times*, which started to circulate from January 1914 in Punta Arenas, and was published until 1932. This was also a weekly periodical, and the only English medium newspaper that proved able to compete with the *South Pacific Mail*. Founded by Arthur Riesco, the *Magellan Times* had a circulation of around a thousand copies by 1923, reaching all over Patagonia, both Chilean and Argentinean. During the First World War, the newspaper issued "A Call to Arms," with the text: "In the grave national emergency which now confronts the Empire, men are asked to come forward to serve their country. Those who are unable to pay their own passages to England will be assisted by the Magellan Times Patriotic Fund," (February 11, 1915). Money was raised by a campaign among its British readers for, among other ends, "Passages and allowances of 120 men sent to England to join H.M.'s Forces, £1479.34" and "Church Army Huts, £200." At the conclusion of the war, funds were also raised and sent to Buenos Aires to help soldiers returning there by paying their hotel bills for two weeks until they could find work.

These were not the only newspapers to circulate in English in Chile. The Biblioteca Nacional (National Library) in Santiago has an old document which lists all the dailies and periodicals published in Chile in the period 1812 to 1884 and registered in its archives—the *Cuadro Sinóptico Periodístico Completo de los diarios i periódicos en Chile publicados desde el año de 1812 hasta el de 1884 inclusive*. This list includes the following titles which appeared in English, all in Valparaíso:

The Marco Polo Observer: 1861 (one edition only; that is, in the Library archives).
The Neighbour: 1847 (sixty-four editions).
The Poetical Herald: 1861 (one edition only).
The Record (a monthly): 1871 onwards (187 editions—it probably continued past 1884).
The South American Magazine: 1868 (eleven editions).
The Valparaíso English Mercury: 1843–1844 (twelve editions).
The Weekly Mercantile Reporter: 1849–1850, a weekly, which became . . .
The Valparaíso Mercantile Reporter: 1850–1853.
The Valparaíso Herald: 1853–1854.
The Valparaíso and West Coast Mail: 1867–1875, a weekly.

Punta Arenas also boasted other periodicals in English. For example, Chamorro (1936) describes the *Times of Patagonia* as the "successor" to *The Magellan Times*. Martinic (2002) provides the names and years founded for the following periodicals in English:

The Punta Arenas Mail: 1900.
Gold Fields Gazette & Patagonian Advertiser: 1906.
Parish Notes St. James Church: 1906–1907.
The Punta Arenas English Magazine: 1907–1909.
The Standard: 1908.
The Observer & Patagonian Fortnightly: 1911.

Chile's national newspaper *El Mercurio* has British connections. It was founded in Valparaíso in 1827 and became a daily newspaper from 1829. Agustín Edwards Ross, grandson of the founder of the Edwards family in Chile, George Edwards, purchased the Valparaíso edition of the *El Mercurio* newspaper in 1880. His son, Agustín Edwards MacClure, was the founder of the Santiago edition of the *El Mercurio* newspaper.

Appendix B

British Diplomatic Representation in Chile

This following lists have been collated from several sources, including Escovar (1923), Chamorro (1936), Derrick-Jehu (1965), Couyoumdjian (2003), and www.patbrit.org.

Santiago

John James Barnard was designated Chairman of the English Committee of Santiago, effectively the first representative of Britain in Chile until the appointment of the first British consul in Valparaíso (in 1823), following the act in Chile that regulated the appointment of consuls. Lieutenant Colonel John Walpole was consul general from 1837 to 1841, and then also chargé d'affaires from 1841 to 1847. Stephen H. Sullivan was British chargé d'affaires during the time of the signing of the Treaty of Commerce and Friendship between Britain and Chile, in 1854. Admiral Sir William Taylour Thomson served as representative from 1858. He wrote a book describing the beauties of the south of Chile, especially south of the River Bío-Bío. From 1872, the British representative was designated minister-resident and consul-general.

Ministers-Resident and Consuls-General

Sir Horace Rumbold (1873–1876).
Sir F. J. Pakenham (1878–1885).
Hugh Fraser (1885).
Sir J. G. Kennedy (1888–1897, spanning the Civil War in Chile).
W. Henry Thomas, vice-consul in 1889.
Sir A. Gosling (1897–1901).
Sir G. Lowther Bart (1901–1905).

Arthur S. Raikes (1905–1907).
Sir Henry Bax-Ironside (1907–1909).
Sir Henry Lowther (1909–1913).
Sir Francis Stronge (from 1913, and during the First World War).
John Charles Tudor Vaughan.
Charles Bateman.
Sir Maurice de Bunsen (from 1918).
Arthur Grant Duff (from 1923).
Sir Thomas B. Hohler (from 1925).
Sir Henry Getty Chilton (from 1930). The British embassy (Chile) site quotes the diplomatic service list that gives Chilton as the first with the rank of British ambassador, with the British embassy established in 1932.
Sir Charles Bentinek (from 1937).

Valparaíso

In October 1823, George Canning appointed Christopher Richard Nugent as the first consul general to Chile. He arrived in Valparaíso in May 1824, accompanied by two vice consuls, Henry William Rouse and Matthew Carter. Carter was shortly afterwards British consul in Coquimbo. Other consuls in Valparaíso include John Walpole (1833) and Henry William Rouse (1837–1870, following his consul's post in Concepción). According to Derrick-Jehu, in his study of *The Anglo-Chilean Community* (1965, 164), it was rumored that Rouse was "a son of King George IV and an oriental lady."

Also Mentioned in Sources

Ernest George Berkeler (1866).
James de Vismes Drummond (1870).
John King, vice consul from 1873 to 1917 (see Couyoumdjian 2003).
William Henry Newman, consul in 1889.
Lewis Joel (1891), consul-general for more than three years, spanning the Civil War in Chile.
Joseph William Warburton (1894).
James Cox (1895; or Hayes Sadler, according to one source).
Thomas Berry (1897).
Sir Berry Cusack Smith (1903), consul general.
Frederick Peter Levy (1905).
Arthur Nightingale (1908–1909, a temporary appointment).
Alexander Finn (1909).

Allan Mac-Lean (1913–1917).
Ernest George Berkeler (1918).
James Mac-Iver Mac-Leod (1918–1923).
Constantine Graham (from 1923).

Punta Arenas

Consuls Resident in Punta Arenas

John Hamilton (1875, first representative and honorary vice consul).
James Henderson (or Henry?) Dunsmuir (1877).
Henry Reynard (1879).
Thomas Fenton (1881).
Rodolfo Stubenrauch (1895).
J. H. Meredith (1898).
Percy C. West (1899).
C. A. Milward (vice consul 1903–1910; consul 1910–1915), who was involved in the search for the *Dresden*.

All the above were honorary titles. The following were career diplomats:

J. Elliot Bell (1915).
Thomas B. Wildman (1919–1925).
(Honorary vice consuls T. C. Betteridge (1920); Douglas R. Lethaby (1924–1925)).
Kenneth J. M. White (1925–1927).
(J. Dickson, honorary vice consul from 1927).
J. Bowering (1928–1930).
Leslie Greer (1932).
M. E. (Roy?) Vibert (1932–1933).
H. W. Reid Brown (1933–1934).
Thomas Boyd (appointed 1936).

Concepción, Coronel and Talcahuano

Henry William Rouse was appointed vice consul in Concepción in 1827. Around 1838, he married Adela, daughter of Auguste Bardel, the French vice consul in Concepción.

When William Howard Russell visited Chile in 1889, he mentioned "our excellent Vice-Consul, Mr. Schwäger" in Coronel, adding that "he certainly could not very well exercise his hospitable disposition without adjuncts to the modest consular pay he receives from the Foreign Office, even though it be augmented by his fee of fifteen shillings for signing the papers of the British ships which visit the port" (1890, 34). Another source says that Frederick Schwäger (junior) remained as British consul in Coronel to 1900.

The book *Lota: Antecedentes Históricos* (1929, 48) names Mateo (Matthew) Wilson, who worked with Matías Cousiño in the early development of the coal mining region around Lota "and was later the British Consular Agent in Coronel."

Edward Cooper (senior) was born in Valparaíso in 1870 and became honorary vice consul in Coronel. He was active in consular posts from January 1900 until his retirement in 1952, which is apparently a record in the British Consular Service. Cooper followed Mr. Borowman as consul in Concepción in 1923, a post which also covered Coronel. His son, Edward Cooper Monk, later became the honorary consul in Concepción, from 1969 to 1976.

In Talcahuano, D. Robert Cunningham was British vice consul for many years. Fletcher Hillman (1900, 188) mentions William McKay and Fred Elton, "each of whom has had charge of Her Majesty's consulate at distinct periods in Talcahuano."

IQUIQUE

Britain appointed Maurice Jewell as the first consul in this port in June 1889. John Thomas North, the Nitrate King, was a partner with Jewell, importing machinery parts and tools for the nitrates industry, and they acted as local agents for steamship lines.

Select Bibliography

History of Chile, Major Studies

Barros Arana, Diego. *Historia jeneral de Chile*. Vols.1–16. Santiago de Chile: Imprenta Cervantes, 1884–1902.
Blakemore, Harold. "From the War of the Pacific to 1930." In *Chile Since Independence*, edited by Leslie Bethell, 33–86. Cambridge: Cambridge University Press, 1993.
Bulmer-Thomas, Victor, ed. *Britain and Latin America: A Changing Relationship*. The Royal Institute of International Affairs: Cambridge University Press, 1989.
Collier, Simon. "From Independence to the War of the Pacific." In *Chile Since Independence*, edited by Leslie Bethell, 1–31. Cambridge: Cambridge University Press, 1993.
Collier, Simon, and William F. Sater. *A History of Chile: 1808–1994*. New York & Cambridge: Cambridge University Press, 1996.
Encina, Francisco. *Historia de Chile desde la prehistoria hasta 1891*. Santiago de Chile: Editorial Ercilla, 1984.
Miller, Rory. *Britain and Latin America in the Nineteenth and Twentieth Centuries*. Harlow, UK: Longman Studies in Modern History, 1993.

The British Presence in Chile

Aldana, A, and A. E. Harris. *Chile and the Chilians 1810–1910*. London: James Adams, 1910.
Anglo-Chilean Society. *British Influence in Nineteenth–Century Chile*. London: Anglo-Chilean Society, 1982.
Edwards, Agustín. "Relaciones de Chile con Gran Bretaña." *El Mercurio*, Santiago de Chile, May 12, 1937, 5–8.
Edmundson, Eddie. "La presencia Británica." *Diario El Sur*, Concepción, Chile, June 16, 1989, 16.
———. "Calle Exeter and Rua Charles Darwin: British Studies on Your Doorstep." *British Studies Now*, 4 (August 1994): 5–6.

Escobar V., Aníbal. *Gran Bretaña en Chile.* Santiago de Chile: Imprenta La Ilustración, 1923.
Mayo, John. "Britain and Chile, 1851–1886: Anatomy of a Relationship." *Journal of Interamerican Studies and World Affairs* 23, no. 1 (1981): 95–120.
Nichols, Theodore E. "The Establishment of Political Relations between Chile and Great Britain." *The Hispanic American Historical Review* 28, no.1 (1948): 137–43.
Santa Cruz, Víctor. *Chile y Gran Bretaña.* Santiago: Casa Mackenzie, 1968.

INTRODUCTION

Vicuña Mackenna, Benjamin. *The First Britons in Valparaiso 1817–1827.* Valparaíso, Chile: W. Helfmann's Universo Printing Office, 1884.
Young, Henry Lyon. *Baroque Tales of Chile.* Ilfracombe, UK: A. H. Stockwell, 1963.

CHAPTER 1

Anson, George. *A Voyage Round the World in the Years 1740, 41, 42, 43, 44.* London: John and Paul Kapton, 1748.
Barros, José M. "La Expedición de Narborough a Chile: Nuevos Antecedentes." *Anales del Instituto de la Patagonia*, Punta Arenas, Chile: Universidad de Magallanes, 18 (1988): 35–60.
Bawlf, Samuel. *The Secret Voyage of Sir Francis Drake 1577–1580.* New York: Walker & Company, 2003.
Cummins, John. "'That Golden Knight': Drake and his reputation." *History Today* 46, no. 1 (1996): 14–21.
Drake, Sir Francis, and Francis Fletcher. *The World Encompassed by Sir Francis Drake: Being His Next Voyage to That to Nombre de Dios Formerly Imprinted, Carefully Collected Out of the Notes of Master Francis Fletcher.* London: Nicholas Bourne, 1628.
Hakluyt, Richard. *The Principal Navigations, Voyages, Traffiques & Discoveries of the English Nation Made by Sea or Overland to the Remote and Farthest Distant Quarters of the Earth at Any Time within the Compass of These 1600 Yeeres.* London: George Bishop & Ralph Newberie, 1589.
Isla, Federico Ignacio. *Los exploradores de la Patagonia, de Magallanes a Fitz-Roy.* Argentina: Universidad Nacional de Mar del Plata, 2002.
Kelly, James. "The Pirate, the Ambassador and the Map-Maker." *History Today* 48, no. 7 (1998): 49–55.
Lipschutz, A. "On the Reliability of Some Written Sources of the Seventeenth and Eighteenth Centuries." *American Anthropologist*, New Series, 52, no. 1 (1950): 123–26.

Ronald, Susan. *The Pirate Queen; Queen Elizabeth I, Her Pirates and Adventurers, and the Dawn of Empire*. New York: Harper Collins, 2007.
Riesenberg, Felix. *Cape Horn*. London: Readers Union, 1950. (Orig. pub. London: Robert Hale, 1941).
Rowse, Alfred Leslie. "Sir Richard Hawkins: Last of a Dynasty." *History Today* 30, no. 6 (1980): 24–27.
Sugden, John. *Sir Francis Drake*. London: Pimlico, 2006.
Thompson, William Judah. *Te Pito Te Henua, or Easter Island*. Washington: Government Printing Office, 1891.
Valderrama, Juan A. *Diccionario histórico-geográfico de la Araucanía*. Santiago: Imprenta Lagunas, 1928.
Vallar, Cindy. "Alexander Selkirk, the Real Robinson Crusoe." In *Pirates and Privateers: The History of Maritime Piracy* (2002), http://www.cindyvallar.com/selkirk.html (accessed May 11, 2009).
———. "A Buccaneer More Interested in Nature than Gold." In *Pirates and Privateers: The History of Maritime Piracy* (2004), http://www.cindyvallar.com/Dampier.html (accessed May 11, 2009).
Walter, Richard. *Anson's Voyage Round the World*. London: Rivingtons, 1901. Project Gutenberg, http://www.gutenberg.org/files/16611/16611-h/16611-h.htm (accessed May 11, 2009).

Chapter 2

Alexander, Caroline. *The Bounty: The true story of the mutiny on the Bounty*. London: Harper Perennial, 2003.
Collingridge, Vanessa. *Captain Cook: The Life, Death, and Legacy of History's Greatest Explorer*. London: Ebury Press, 2003.
Cook, James. *The Voyages of Captain James Cook*. Vol.4 (the second voyage). London: Longman, Hurst, Rees, Orme, and Brown, 1821.
———. *A Voyage Towards the South Pole, and Round the World in 1772, 1773, 1774, and 1775*. London: Longman, 1821.
FitzRoy, Robert. *Narrative of the surveying voyages of His Majesty's Ships Adventure and Beagle between the Years 1826 and 1836, describing their examination of the southern shores of South America, and the Beagle's circumnavigation of the globe*. Vol.2, *Proceedings of the second expedition, 1831–1836, Robert FitzRoy*. London: Henry Colburn, 1838.
Hawkesworth, John. *An Account of the Voyages Undertaken by the Order of His Present Majesty for Making Discoveries in the Southern Hemisphere*. Vols.1–3. London: Strahan, 1785.
Huntford, Roland. *Shackleton*. London: Abacus, 1996. (Orig. pub. London: Hodder & Stoughton, 1985).
King, Philip Parker. *Narrative of the Surveying Voyages of His Majesty's Ships Adventure and Beagle*, Vol. 1. *Proceedings of the first expedition, 1826–30*,

under the command of Captain P. Parker King, R.N., F.R.S. London: Henry Colburn, 1838.

Murphy, Dallas. *Rounding the Horn: Being the Story of Williwaws and Windjammers, Drake, Darwin, Murdered Missionaries and Naked Natives. A Deck's Eye of Cape Horn.* New York: Basic Books, 2005.

Ross, James Clark. *A Voyage of Discovery and Research in the Southern and Antarctic Regions, during the years 1839–43.* London: John Murray, 1847.

Shackleton, Ernest. "Lecture by Sir Ernest Shackleton." *The Magellan Times*, Punta Arenas, July 13, 1916, 3–7.

———. *South.* London: William Heinemann, 1919. Reprint, New York: Lyons, 1998.

Webster, W. H. B. *Narrative of a Voyage to the Southern Atlantic Ocean in the Years 1828, 29, 30, Performed in H.M. Sloop Chanticleer under the Command of the Late Captain Henry Foster, F.R.S. & by Order of the Lords Commissioners of the Admiralty.* London: Richard Bentley, 1834.

Weddell, James. *A Voyage towards the South Pole Performed in the Years 1822–24, Containing an Examination of the Antarctic Sea, to the Seventy-Fourth Parallel of Latitude, and a Visit to Tierra del Fuego, with a Particular Account of the Inhabitants.* London: Longman, Hurst, Rees, Orme, Brown & Green, 1825.

Wharton, W. J. L., ed. *Captain Cook's Journal during His First Voyage Round the World Made in H.M. Bark "Endeavour," 1768–71.* London: Elliot Stock, 1893.

Chapter 3

Ball, John. *Notes of a Naturalist in South America.* London: Paul, Trench, 1887.

Barlow, Nora. *Charles Darwin and the Voyage of the Beagle.* London: Pilot Press, 1945.

Browne, Janet. *Charles Darwin: Voyaging.* London: Pimlico, 1996.(Orig. pub. Jonathan Cape, 1995).

Chapman, Frank M. "Darwin's Chile." *The Geographical Journal* 68, no. 5 (1926): 369–85.

Darwin, Charles R. *Narrative of the Surveying Voyages of His Majesty's Ships Adventure and Beagle.* Vol.3, *Journal and Remarks. 1832–1836.* London: Henry Colburn, 1838. Republished as *Journal of Researches into the Geology and Natural History of the Various Countries Visited by H.M.S. Beagle.* London: Henry Colburn, 1839. Second edition with extensive revisions, London: John Murray, 1845.

———. *On the Origin of Species by Means of Natural Selection, or the Preservation of Favoured Races in the Struggle for Life.* London: John Murray, 1859.

———. Beagle *Diary (1831–1836).* Edited by R. D. Keynes. London: Cambridge University Press, 2001.

Darwin, Francis. *The Life and Letters of Charles Darwin.* Vols.1–2. London: John Murray, 1887.

Desmond, Adrian, and James Moore. *Darwin*. London: Penguin Books, 1992. First published by Michael Joseph, 1991.
Latcham, Ricardo. *La organización social y las creencias religiosas de los antiguos araucanos*. Colección "Biblioteca Nacional de Santiago," Chile. Santiago: Imprenta Cervantes, 1924.
Lothrop, S. K. "Richard E. Latcham 1869–1943." *American Anthropologist*, New Series 47, no. 4 (1945): 603–8.
Moorehead, Alan. *Darwin and the* Beagle. London: Penguin books, 1969.
Palmer, John Linton. "A Visit to Easter Island, or Rapa Nui, in 1868." *Journal of the Royal Geographical Society of London* 40 (1870): 167–81.
Routledge, Katherine. *The Mystery of Easter Island: The Story of an Expedition*. London: Sifton, Praed, 1919. Reprinted London: Adventures Unlimited Press, 1998.
Scott-Elliot, George Francis. *Chile: Its History and Development, Natural Features, Products, Commerce and Present Conditions*. New York: Charles Scribner's Sons, 1907. Reprinted by Barman Press, 2007.
Van Tilburg, Jo Anne. *Among Stone Giants: The Life of Katherine Routledge and Her Remarkable Expedition to Easter Island*. New York: Lisa Drew Books, Scribner's, 2003.

Chapter 4

Barros Arana, Diego. *La cuestión de límites entre Chile i la República Argentina: los tratados vigentes, las actas de los peritos, actas sobre el arbitraje, mapa de los dos límites limítrofes*. Santiago de Chile: Establecimiento Poligráfico Roma, 1895.
Cochrane, Thomas. *Narrative of Services in the Liberation of Chili, Peru and Brazil, from Spanish and Portuguese Dominion*. London: James Ridgway, 1859. Project Gutenberg: http://www.gutenberg.org/files/14914/14914-8.txt (accessed May 11, 2009).
Cordingly, David. *Cochrane: The Real Master and Commander*. New York: Bloombury USA, 2007.
"C. S. V." "Gran Bretaña y la Independencia de la América: 1812–1830." *El Mercurio*, Santiago, March 26, 1939.
———. "La Política de Canning y la Independencia Latinamericana." *El Mercurio*, Santiago, March 31, 1939.
Encina, Francisco A., and Leopoldo Castedo. "La Guerra del Pacífico." In *Historia de Chile*, vol. 8. Santiago: Editorial Santiago, 1999.
Foreign Office. *Award of H.M. Queen Elizabeth II for the Arbitration of a Controversy between the Argentine Republic and the Republic of Chile concerning Certain Parts of the Boundary between Their Territories*. London: HMSO, 1966.
Griffin, Arturo. "Conquistadores, Soldiers, and Entrepreneurs: Early Irish Presence in Chile," trans. Claire Healy. *Irish Migration Studies in Latin America*, 4, no. 4 (2006): 217–22.

Harvey, Robert. *Liberators: Latin America's Struggle for Independence, 1810–1830*. London: John Murray, 2000.
———. *Cochrane: The Life and Exploits of a Fighting Captain*. London: Constable and Robinson, 2002.
Kinsbruner, Jay. "Bernardo O'Higgins." *The Americas* 25, no. 3 (1969): 327–28.
Lambert, Andrew. *War at Sea in the Age of Sail*. London: Weidenfeld & Nicholson, 2000.
McFarlane, Anthony. "Independence and Revolution in the Americas." *History Today* 34, no. 3 (1984): 40–49.
Nichols, Theodore E. "The Establishment of Political Relations between Chile and Great Britain." *The Hispanic American Historical Review* 28, no. 1 (1948): 137–43.
Perry, Richard O. "Argentina and Chile: The Struggle for Patagonia 1843–1881." *The Americas* 36, no. 3 (1980): 347–63.
Rodriguez, Moises Enrique. *Southern South America*. Vol.2 of *Freedom's Mercenaries: British Volunteers in the Wars of Independence of Latin America*. Lanham, MD: Hamilton Books, 2006.
Proctor, Robert. *Narrative of a Journey across the Cordillera of the Andes, and of a Residence in Lima, and other parts of Peru in the years 1823 and 1824*. London: Hurst, Robinson, 1825.
Sater, William F. *Andean Tragedy: Fighting the War of the Pacific, 1879–1884*. "Studies in War, Society, and the Military," University of Nebraska Press, 2007.
———. *Chile and the War of the Pacific*. University of Nebraska Press, 1985.
Stevenson, William B. *A Historical and Descriptive Narrative of Twenty Years' Residence in South America*. London: Longman, Rees, Orme, Brown & Green, 1825.
Talbott, Robert D. "The Chilean Boundary in the Strait of Magellan." *The Hispanic American Historical Review* 47, no. 4 (1967): 519–31.
Thomas, Donald. *Cochrane: Britannia's Sea Wolf*. London: Cassell Military Paperbacks, 2001. First published by André Deutsch, 1978.
Tupper, Ferdinand B. *Memorias del Coronel Tupper*. Santiago: Editorial Francisco de Aguirre, 1972.
U.S. Bureau of Intelligence and Research, Office of the Geographer. *Argentina-Chile Boundary*. International Boundary Study 101. Washington, DC: GPO, 1970.

Chapter 5

Beerbohm, Julius. *Wanderings in Patagonia, or, Life among the Ostrich-Hunters*. London: Chatto and Windus, 1879.
Brassey, Annie. *A Voyage in the "Sunbeam."* London: H. Holt, 1878.

SELECT BIBLIOGRAPHY 257

Caldcleugh, Alexander. *Travels in South America during the Years 1819–20–21, Containing an Account of the Present State of Brazil, Buenos Ayres, and Chile.* London: John Murray, 1825.

———. "An Account of the Great Earthquake Experienced in Chile on the 20th February, 1835, with a Map." *Philosophical Transactions of the Royal Society of London* 126 (1836): 21–26.

Dixie, Florence. *Across Patagonia.* London: Bentley, 1880. Reprinted as *Riding across Patagonia.* Equestrian Travel Classics, Long Riders' Guild Press, 2001. Also available in Spanish, *A través de la Patagonia*, Punta Arenas, Chile: Ediciones Universidad de Magallanes, 1996.

Estrada Turra, Baldomero. "Los relatos de viajeros como fuente histórica: Visión de Chile y Argentina en cinco viajeros ingleses 1817–1835." *Revista de Indias*, Dept. de Historia de América, Centro de Estúdios Históricos, Consejo Superior de Investigaciones Científicos, Madrid, 47, no. 180, 1987.

Falkner, Thomas. *A Description of Patagonia, and the Adjoining Parts of South America.* London: Pugh, 1774.

Graham, Maria. *Journal of a Residence in Chile during the Year 1822, and a Voyage from Chile to Brazil in 1823.* London: Longman, Hurst, Rees, Orme, Brown, and Green, 1824. Reprinted by University of Virginia Press, 2003. Available in Spanish, *Diario de mi residencia en Chile.* Biblioteca Francisco de Aguirre, Colección Viajeros 1822–1823, no. 8. Santiago: Editorial Francisco de Aguirre, 1972.

———. "On the Reality of the Rise of the Coast in Chili." *Transactions of the Geological Society of London* 2, 1 (1824): 413–15.

Haigh, Samuel. *Sketches of Buenos Ayres and Chile.* London: James Carpenter & Son, 1829.

Hall, Basil. *Extracts from a Journal, Written on the Coasts of Chili, Peru, and Mexico.* Edinburgh: A. Constable, 1824.

Marchant, Andya. "The Captain's Widow: Maria Graham and the Independence of South America." *The Americas* 2 (1963): 127–42.

Mathison, Gilbert Farquhar. *Narrative of a Visit to Brazil, Chile, Peru and the Sandwich Islands during the Years 1821 and 1822. With Miscellaneous Remarks on the Past and Present State, and Political Prospects of Those Countries.* London: C. Knight, 1825.

Musters, George Chaworth. *At Home with the Patagonians: a Year's Wanderings over Untrodden Ground from the Straights of Magellan to the Rio Negro.* London: J. Murray, 1871. Reprinted London: Tempus Publishing, 2005.

Trifilo, S. Samuel. "Early Nineteenth-Century British Travellers in Chile: Impressions of Santiago and Valparaíso." *Journal of Inter-American Studies* 11, no. 3 (1969): 391–424.

Chapter 6

Alvarez Urquieta, Luis. *La pintura en Chile*. Santiago: Imprenta La Ilustración, 1928.
Bindis Fuller, Ricardo. *La pintura Chilena: desde Gil de Castro hasta nuestros dias*. Santiago: Philips Chilma, 1984.
Hurst, Alex A. *Thomas Somerscales, Marine Artist*. Brighton, UK: Teredo Books, 1988.
Pereira Salas, Eugenio. *Historia del arte en el Reino de Chile*. Santiago: Ediciones Universidad de Chile, 1965.
Raby, Peter. *Bright Paradise: Victorian Scientific Travellers*. London: Chatto & Windus, 1996.
Romera, A. R. *Historia de la pintura Chilena*. Santiago: Editorial Andrés Bello, 1976.
Valencia Avaria, Luis. *Símbolos pátrios*. Santiago: Editorial Nacional Gabriela Mistral, 1974.

Chapter 7

Abarca L., Jaime. *Presencia Británica em Valparaíso*. Viña del Mar, Chile: The British Council & Instituto Chileno-Británico de Viña del Mar, 1986.
Butland, Gilbert J. "The Human Geography of Southern Chile." *The Institute of British Geographers*, 24. London: George Philip & Son, 1957.
Campbell, Duncan, site administrator. *The British Presence in Southern Patagonia*. http://patbrit.org/eng/index.htm (accessed May 11, 2009).
Chamorro, Claudio. "Territorio de Magallanes y los elementos Británicos." In *Bajo el cielo austral*, 409–15. Santiago: Imprenta La Ilustracion, 1936.
Chatwin, Bruce. *In Patagonia*. London: Jonathan Cape, 1977.
Coo Lyon, José Luis. "Familias extranjeras en Valparaíso durante el siglo XIX." *Revista de Estudios Históricos* 15 (1968–1969): 37–84 and 19 (1974): 13–37.
Couyoumdjian B., Juan Ricardo. "Masonería de habla inglesa en Chile. Algunas noticias." *Boletín de la Academia Chilena de la Historia* 105 (1995): 185–208.
———. *Chile y Gran Bretaña durante la primera Guerra Mundial y la postguerra 1914–1921*. Ediciones Universidad Católica de Chile. Santiago: Editorial Andrés Bello, 1986.
Dooley, Elizabeth. *Streams in the Wasteland: A Portrait of the British in Patagonia*. Punta Arenas, Chile: Imprenta Rasmussen, 1993.
Estrada Turra, Baldomero, and R. Salinas Meza. "Inmigración Europea y movilidad social en los centros urbanos de América Latina (1880–1920)." *Estudios Migratorios Latinoamericanos* 2, no. 5 (1987): 3–27.
Estrada Turra, Baldomero. "La colectividad Británica de Valparaíso en el S. XIX a través de los testamentos." *Revista de Ciências Sociales* 31 (1987): 209–17.

———. "La colectividad Británica en Valparaíso durante la primera mitad del Siglo XX." *Historia (Santiago)* 39 no. 1 (2006): 65–91.
Fletcher Hillman, Charles. *Old Timers, British and American, in Chile*. Santiago: Imprenta Moderna, 1900.
Foreign Office. *Report on European Emigration to Chile*. Foreign Office Miscellaneous Series no. 158, "Reports on Subjects of General and Commercial Interest." London: HMSO, 1890.
Martinic B, Mateo. "La inmigración Europea en Magallanes 1891–1920." *Anales del Instituto de la Patagonia*, Serie "Ciencias Sociales," 18 (1988): 11–34.
———. *Punta Arenas en su primer medio siglo: 1848–1898*. Punta Arenas, Chile: Impresos Vabin, 1988.
———. "La participación de capitales británicos en el desarrollo económico del territorio de Magallanes: 1880–1920." *Historia (Santiago)* 35 (2002): 299–321.
———. *Los británicos en la región magallánica*. Valparaíso, Chile: Puntángeles de la Casa de Estudios de Valparaíso, 2007.
Narborough, John. *An Account of Several Late Voyages and Discoveries to the South and North*. London: Smith & Walford, 1694.
Nock, Laurie. "Los británicos en Magallanes." Punta Arenas: *Anales del Instituto de la Patagonia* 16 (1985–86): 23–43.
Ossa, F. V. *Concepción en el centenário nacional*. Concepción, Chile: Imprenta J. V. Soulodre, 1910.
Prain Brice, Michelle. "Presencia británica en el Valparaíso del Siglo XIX: Una aproximación al legado institucional y cultural de la colonia británica en Chile." *Bicentenário* 6, no. 2 (2007): 5–38.
Solberg, Carl. *Immigration and Nationalism, Argentina and Chile, 1890–1914*. Austin: University of Texas Press, 1970.
Young, William Russell. *Reminiscences of my Fifty-Five Years in Chile and Peru*. Santiago: Imprenta y Litografía Universo, 1933.

Chapter 8

Cavieres, Eduardo. *Comercio Chileno y comerciantes Ingleses 1820–1880: Un ciclo de história económica*. Monografías Históricas 2. Valparaíso: Universidad Católica de Valparaíso, 1988.
Centner, Charles W. "The 'Tacna' Case: An Episode in Anglo-Chilean Relations, 1874–75," *Pacific Historical Review* 11, no. 2 (1942): 161–67.
Chile. Santiago: Chilean Government publication, 1915.
Couyoumdjian B., Juan Ricardo. "El alto comercio de Valparaíso y las grandes casas extranjeras, 1880–1930. Una aproximación." *Historia (Santiago)* 33 (2000): 63–99.
Estrada Turra, Baldomero. *Valparaíso y el proceso de industrialización en Chile a fines del siglo XIX*. Monografías Históricas 1, Valparaíso: Instituto de Historia, Universidad Católica de Valparaíso, 1987.

Hardy Evans, Oswald. "Perilous Havens: Early Days on the Chilean Coast and South Pacific." *The South Pacific Mail*, April 20–July 27, 1951.
History UK. *The Darien Adventure*. http://www.historic-uk.com/HistoryUK/Scotland-History/DarienScheme.htm (accessed May 11, 2009).
Jones, Geoffrey. *Merchants to Multinationals: British Trading Companies in the Nineteenth and Twentieth Centuries*. Oxford: Oxford University Press, 2000.
Kinsbruner, Jay. "The Political Influence of the British Merchants in Chile during the O'Higgins Administration, 1817–1823." *The Americas* 27, no. 1 (1970): 26–39.
Lingwood, John E. *The Steam Conquistadores: A History of the Pacific Steam Navigation Company*. Widnes, UK: Swale Press, 1977.
Mayo, John. *British Merchants and Chilean Development: 1851–1886*. Boulder, CO: Westview Press, 1987.
———. "Before the Nitrate Era: British Commission Houses and the Chilean Economy, 1851–1880." *Journal of Latin American Studies* 11, 2 (1979), 263–303.
Malpas, D. and D. King. *Price Waterhouse in South America: The First 75 Years*. London: PriceWaterhouseCooper, 1989.
Miers, John. *Travels in Chile and La Plata*. New York: AMS Press, 1826.
Miller, Rory. "British Free-Standing Companies on the West Coast of South America." In *The Free-Standing Company in the World Economy, 1830–1996*, edited by Mira Wilkins and Harm Schröter, Chapter 8. Oxford: Oxford University Press, 1998.
Porteous, J. Douglas. "Easter Island: The Scottish Connection." *Geographical Review* 68, no. 2 (1978): 145–56.
Pregger-Roman, Charles G. "The Origin and Development of the Bourgeoisie in Nineteenth-Century Chile." *Latin American Perspectives* 10, no. 2–3 (1983): 39–59.
Rippy, J. Fred. "British Investments in Latin America, 1939." *The Journal of Political Economy* 56, no. 1 (1948): 63–68.
Vélez, Claudio. *Historia de la marina mercante de Chile*. Santiago: Ediciones de la Universidad de Chile, 1961.

Chapter 9

Astorquiza, Octavio, and Oscar Galleguillo V. *Cien años del carbón de Lota*. Lota, Chile: Compañia Carbonífera e Industrial de Lota, 1952.
Barclay, A. to James Douglas. "List of Labourers engaged for Vancouver's Island by Mr D. Landale," June 17, 1853. [HBC Archives, Winnipeg, A.6/30 fos. 118–18d].
Blakemore, Harold. "The Chilean Revolution of 1891: A Study in the Domestic and International History of Chile." *Historical Research* 31 (1958): 104–07.
———. *British Nitrates and Chilean Politics, 1886–1896: Balmaceda and North*. London: Athlone, 1974.

Select Bibliography

Bollaert, William. "Observations on the Coal Formation in Chile, S. America." *Journal of the Royal Geographical Society of London* 25 (1855): 172–75.

Bonilla, Ramiro, and Gregorio Corvalan. "Apuntes para la historia: Cronologia del carbón en la región del Bío Bío." *Revista Inculcar*, 2, no. 2 (1987): 35–39.

Brown, Joseph R. "The Chilean Nitrate Railways Controversy." *The Hispanic American Historical Review* 38, no. 4 (1958): 465–81.

Cameron, David to Archibald Barclay. San Francisco, March 10, 1854. [HBC Archives, Winnipeg, A.11/75 fo. 85d].

Centner, Charles W. "Great Britain and Chilean Mining 1830–1914." *The Economic History Review* 12, no. 1–2 (1942): 76–82.

Child, Theodore. "Coal-Mining in Chili." *Harper's Weekly*, February 14, 1891: 117–18.

Cowling Taylor, Richard. *Statistics of Coal: The Geographical and Geological Distribution of Mineral Combustibles or Fossil Fuel.* Philadelphia: J. W. Moore, 1848.

Edmundson, Eddie. "The Story of the Colinda." *Lipsan Usali*, no. 4 (1987): 20–23.

———. "Los británicos en la zona carbonífera." *Revista de la Sociedad de Historia de Concepción* 1 (1988): 23–24.

———. "Ayrshire to Arauco: The Voyage of the Colinda." *Geogscot* (1993): 8–9.

Hudson Beattie Valenzuela, Judith. *The Colinda* (forthcoming).

Lota: Antecedentes Históricos. Concepción, Chile: Compañia Minera e Industrial de Chile, 1929.

Mackay, Juan. *Recuerdos y apuntes 1820–1890.* Concepción, Chile: A. L. Murray, 1912.

Mazzei de Grazia, Leonardo. "Los británicos y el carbón en Chile." *Atenea*, no. 475 (1924): 137–67.

Monteón, Michael. "The British in the Atacama Desert: The Cultural Bases of Economic Imperialism." *The Journal of Economic History* 35, no. 1 (1975): 117–33.

———. "John T. North, The Nitrate King, and Chile's Lost Future." *Latin American Perspectives* Issue 133, vol. 30, no. 6 (2003): 69–90.

Rippy, J. Fred. "Economic Enterprises of the 'Nitrate King' and His Associates in Chile." *The Pacific Historical Review* 17, no. 4 (1948): 457–65.

Russell, William H. *A Visit to Chile and the Nitrate Fields of Tarapacá.* London: Virtue, 1890.

Soto Cárdenas, Alejandro. *Influencia británica en el salitre: origen, naturaleza y decadencia.* Santiago: Editorial Universidad de Santiago, 1998.

Stathers, Mary L. "The *Colinda* Voyage—An Emigration that Didn't Make It—Or Did It?" *The Scottish Genealogist* 34, no. 2 (1987): 325–27.

Veliz, Claudio. "Egaña, Lambert, and the Chilean Mining Associations of 1825." *Hispanic American Historical Review* 55, no. 4 (1975): 637–63.

Chapter 10

Banco de Chile. "Banco de A. Edwards: 1866–2001." www.fundinguniverse.com/company-histories/Banco-de-Chile-Company-History.html (accesssed May 11, 2009).

Joslin, David. *A Century of Banking in Latin America*. London: Bank of London and South America Ltd./Oxford University Press, 1963.

Chapter 11

Alliende Edwards, María Piedad. *Historia del ferrocarril en Chile*. Santiago: Goethe-Institut & Pehuén Editores, 1993.

Binns, Donald. *The Nitrate Railways Company Limited*. Skipton, UK: Trackside Publications, 2007.

———. *The Anglo-Chilean Nitrate & Railway Company (Ferrocarril de Tocopilla al Toco): A History of the Company and its Locomotives*. Skipton, UK: Trackside Publications, 1995.

———. "The Compañia de Salitres y Ferrocarril de Junín: A Brief Historical Outline." *Locomotives International* 14 (1992): 16–17.

Blakemore, Harold. *From the Pacific to La Paz. The Antofagasta (Chili) and Bolivia Railway Company (1888–1988)*. London: Antofagasta Holdings, 1990.

Couyoumdjian B., Juan Ricardo. "Dos ingenieros escoceses en Chile en el siglo XIX y comienzos del XX." *Boletín de la Academia de la Historia*, no. 112 (2003): 45–66.

Decombe E., Alberto. *Historia del Ferrocarril de Arica a La Paz*. Santiago: Ministerio de Industria i Obras Públicas, 1913.

Espech, Roman. *El Ferrocarril de Concepción a Los Rios de Curanilahue*. Instituto de Injenieros de Santiago: Imprenta Victoria, 1890.

Huidobro Díaz, Carlos. *Nuestros ferrocarriles*. Santiago: Ministerio de Fomento, 1939.

Long, W. Rodney. "Chile." In *Railways of South America*, part 3 of Trade Promotion Series #93. Washington, DC: U.S. Bureau of Foreign & Domestic Commerce, 1930.

Mair, Craig. *David Angus: The Life and Adventures of a Victorian Railway Engineer*. Stevenage, UK: The Strong Oak Press, 1989.

Marín Vicuña, Santiago. *Estudios de los ferrocarriles Chilenos*. Santiago: Imprenta Cervantes, 1900.

Morrison, Allen. *The Tramways of Chile, 1858–1978*. New York: Bonde Press, 1992.

Redman, Ronald N. "The Junín Story: To the North Pampa and Back." *Locomotives International* 14 (1992): 10–15.

"R. R. J." *Reseña histórica del ferrocarril entre Santiago i Valparaíso*. Santiago: Imprenta del Ferrocarril, 1863.

Thomson Newman, Ian, and D. Angerstein. *Historia del ferrocarril en Chile*. Santiago: Centro de Investigaciones Diego Barros Arana, Dirección de Bibliotecas, Archivos y Museos, 1997.

Thomson Newman, Ian. "La Nitrate Railways Co. Ltd.: La pérdida de sus derechos exclusivos en el mercado del transporte de salitre y su resposta a ella." *Historia (Santiago)* 38, no. 1 (2005): 85–112.

———. "Early Days on the Copiapó Railway." *Locomotives International* 47 (1999): 10–16.

———. "The Locomotives of the Railway between Santiago and Valparaíso." *Locomotives International* 41 (1998): 20–27.

———. *Red Norte: The Story of State-Owned Railways in the North of Chile*. Skipton, UK: Locomotives International, 1997.

Torres P., S. "El Ferrocarril de Concepción a Curanilahue." *Revista Inculcar* (1986): 17–22.

Turner J. M., and R. F. Ellis. *The Antofagasta (Chili) & Bolivia Railway: The Story of the FCAB and Its Locomotives*. Skipton, UK: Locomotives International, 1992.

Walker, Christopher, and Donald Binns. *Railways of Bolivia*. Skipton, UK: Trackside Publications, 2006.

Wheelwright, William. "Proposed Railway Route across the Andes, from Caldera in Chile to Rosario on the Parana, via Cordoba; With Report of Mr. E. A. Flint's Survey." *Journal of the Royal Geographical Society of London* 31(1861): 155–62.

Chapter 12

Zavala Cepeda, José M. "Los colonos y la escuela en la Araucanía: Los inmigrantes Europeos y el surgimiento de la educación privada laica y protestante en la región de la Araucanía (1887–1915)." *Revista Universum*, no. 23, 1 (2008).

Chapter 13

Bazley, Barbara. *Somos Anglicanos*. Santiago: Imprenta Interamericana, 1994.

Bridges, E. Lucas. *Uttermost Part of the Earth*. London: Hodder & Stoughton, 1951.

Every, Edward F. *The Anglican Church in South America*. London: Society for Promoting Christian Knowledge, 1915.

Guerra Rojas, Cristián. "La música en los inicios de los cultos cristianos no-católicos en Chile: El caso de la Union Church (Iglesia Unión) de Valparaíso, 1845–1890." *Revista Musical Chilena* 60, no. 206 (2006): 49–83.

Kirkland Lothrop, Samuel. *The Indians of Tierra del Fuego*. New York: Museum of the American Indian, 1928. Reprint Ushuaia, Argentina: Zagier & Urruty, 2002.

Levis, Cecil. "Colonos Anglicanos en la Araucanía." *Diario El Sur* (Concepción), January 3, 1988, "Actual" section.
Marsh, John W., and Waite Hocking Stirling. *The Story of Commander Allen Gardener RN.* London: James Nisbet, 1867.
Prain B., Michelle. "La Iglesia Saint Paul's de Valparaíso, patrimonio tangible e intangible de la era Victoriana." *Revista Archivum*, Año V. N° 6 (2006), 174–92.
Wright, G. W. "English Graves at Tiliviche." *Notes and Queries*. Oxford: Oxford University Press, 183 (1942): 216–17.

Chapter 14

Cricket: http://www.cricketchile.cl/en_news.php (accessed May 11, 2009).
Football: http://histofutbolchile.blogspot.com/2007/07/un-nuevo-deporte-llamado-football.html (accessed May 11, 2009).
Golf: http://www.golftours.cl/publico/article_7.shtml (accessed May 11, 2009).
Tennis: http://es.wikipedia.org/wiki/Tenis_en_Chile (accessed May 11, 2009).

Chapter 15

Bennett, Geoffrey. *Coronel and the Falklands*. London: Macmillan, 1962. Reprint, Pan, 1967.
Edmundson, Eddie. "La Batalla de Coronel." *El Mercurio* (Santiago), November 17, 1989, A2.
———. "La batalla de Coronel. 1 de noviembre, 1914." *Revista de la Sociedad de Historia de Concepción* 3 (1990): 21–22.
Hoyt, Edwin P. *Defeat at the Falklands: Germany's East Asia Squadron 1914.* London: Robert Hale, 1981.
Pitt, Barrie. *Coronel and Falkland.* London: Cassell, 1960.

Chapter 16

Barton, Jonathan R. "Struggling against Decline: British Business in Chile, 1919–33." *Journal of Latin American Studies* 32 (2000): 235–64.
Miller, Rory. "The Decline of British Interests in Latin America." *History Today* 41, no. 12 (1991): 42–48.

Chapter 17

Couyoumdjian B., Juan Ricardo. "Agustín Edwards y su primera misión en Londres 1911–1924." *Boletín de la Academia Chilena de la História* 117 (2008): 7–32.
Derrick-Jehu, L. C. "The Anglo-Chilean Community." *Family History* 3, no. 17–18 (1965): 157–84.

Appendix A

Couyoumdjian B., Juan Ricardo. "Apuntes sobre un periódico inglés de Valparaíso: 'The South Pacific Mail' entre 1909 y 1925." In *Valparaiso 1536–1986: Primera jornada de historia urbana*. Valparaíso: Instituto de Historia, Universidad Católica de Valparaiso, 1987, 185–94.

Cuadro sinoptico periodistico completo de los diarios i periódicos en Chile publicados desde el año de 1812 hasta el de 1884 inclusive, que la Biblioteca Nacional conserva empasados. Santiago: Biblioteca Nacional.

Index

Alacaluf Indians, 10, 28, 33, 197, 200, 240
Anglican faith
  Robert FitzRoy's cultural experiment with Fuegian Indians, 33–34, 41, 43
  See also cemeteries; churches; Gardiner, Allen; Lota; Matthews, Richards; Patagonian Missionary Society; South American Missionary Society; Valparaíso
Anglo-Chilean Society, London, 128
Anglo-Spanish War, 16–17, 132
Anson, George, Commodore (admiral; lord), 22, 23–24, 239
Antofagasta, 128, 129, 140, 143, 172, 173, 182, 183, 195, 196, 216
Araucanian Indians
  See Mapuche Indians
Arica
  Bartholomew Sharpe's attack, 18
  British presence, 128, 177, 180, 196
  Francis Drake's attack, 13
  John Watling's attack, 19
  Mackay's capture of the *Minerva*, 24
  Richard Hawkins' voyage, 16

Baden-Powell, Robert, 114
Balfour Lyon & Company, 145
Ball, John, 51

Balmaceda, José Manuel (president)
  colonization policy, 5, 208
  and John Thomas North, 163, 164–66, 172
banks
  Anglo-South American Bank, 114, 122, 138, 171, 173, 174, 180, 230
  Banco de A. Edwards, 171, 172, 173, 174, 236
  Bank of London and South America (BOLSA), 173–74
  Bank of Tarapacá and London, 121, 124, 163, 165–66, 170, 172–73, 174, 219
  London Bank of Mexico and South America, 161, 162, 170, 171, 174
  London and River Plate Bank, 170, 173
  London and South American Bank, 171
  Lloyds Bank, 173, 174
Banks, Joseph, 48–49
Barnard, John James, 134–35, 247
Basket, Fuegia, 33, 43, 198, 199, 200
Battle of Coronel, 53, 221–27
Beagle
  See Darwin, Sir Charles; FitzRoy, Robert; King, Philip Parker; Stokes, Pringle
Beerbohm, Julius, 90–91, 100, 116, 117–18
Blest, Dr. William Cunningham, 234

Bligh, William, 30
Bloody Mary, 1–2
boundary disputes
  Bolivia-Chile border disputes, 159, 160
  British arbitration in, 79–81
Brassey, Annie, 88, 89–90, 113, 117, 125–26, 157, 206
Bridges, Lucas, 33–34, 118, 123, 197, 202, 204, 205, 206, 207
Bridges, Thomas (explorer and plant collector), 50
Bridges, Thomas (missionary), 197, 200, 203, 204, 205–6
British Council, 128, 194, 195, 196
British Embassy, 128, 196, 248
buccaneers
  definition, 8
  See under individual names
Buchanan, Jones & Company, 143
Bunster, Humphrey, 234–35
Bunster, José, 3, 171
Button, Jemmy
  capture by Robert FitzRoy, 33
  in England, 198
  return to Tierra del Fuego, 43, 199–200, 202, 203–4
Bynon, James George (captain; vice admiral), 76–77, 241
Byron, John, 23, 27–28, 30, 84, 115, 239

Caldcleugh, Alexander
  botanist in Chile, 49
  on commercial opportunities, 49, 135–36
  experience of an earthquake, 85
  on the quality of coal, 148
  traveling in Chile, 7, 85, 109, 241
Callao
  commercial importance for Chile, 132–33, 136–37
  Francis Drake's attack, 13
  in War of Independence, 25, 64, 69, 72, 74, 76, 96
  in War of the Peruvian-Bolivian Confederation, 76–77

Canning, George, 4–5, 57–59, 135, 169, 241, 242, 248
Canning House, 59
Carrera, José Miguel, 61–62, 64
Carteret, Philip, 28, 30, 239
Castlereagh, Robert Stewart, Viscount Castlereagh, 4–5, 35, 57, 135, 169
Cavendish, Sir Thomas
  circumnavigation, 14–15, 238
  second voyage, 15
cemeteries for non-Catholics
  Caldera, 213
  Concepción, 127
  Coquimbo, 213
  Lota, 156, 237
  Punta Arenas, 33, 118, 226–27
  Santiago, 212–13
  Shand family cemetery, 227
  Talcahuano, 226
  Tiliviche, 213–14
  Valparaíso, 108, 211, 212
Chamber of Commerce, British (British-Chilean), 111, 115, 128
Chiloé Island, 23, 35, 44, 45, 47, 51, 63, 64, 65, 106, 115
churches, Anglican (Protestant), 111, 125, 208, 209, 210–11, 226, 245
Churchill, Winston, 223, 224
Clark, John (Juan) and Matthew (Mateo), 180, 186–87, 220
clippers, 40
Clipperton, John, 22
coal mining, 115, 147, 148–58, 162, 172, 179, 184, 185, 207, 212, 250
  See also railways, Arauco Coal and Railway Company
Cochrane, Thomas, Tenth Earl of Dundonald (admiral; lord)
  Casa de Lord Cochrane in Valparaíso, 113
  in Chilean War of Independence, 2, 63, 64, 65, 66, 67–74, 75, 76, 77, 135, 241, 242
  Cochrane and *Almirante Cochrane*, 79, 144

effigy on Arco Británico in
   Valparaíso, 55
 response to privateering in War of
   Independence, 25
 statue in Valparaíso, 114
Colinda, The, 154–56
Colonel North
   See North; John Thomas
colonization by British settlers
   in Araucanía, 5, 104–5
 Bernardo O'Higgins' plans, 103
 British official views on
   colonization, 5, 104–5
 on Chiloé Island, 105–6
 General Colonization Agency
   policy, 103–4, 105
 John Narborough's claim, 17
 of Punta Arenas and Magallanes,
   115–17, 124
 Welsh colonists, 4, 80–81
 See also immigration
Concepción, 35, 42, 45, 46–47,
   51–52, 60, 61, 62, 70, 100, 111,
   125–27, 138, 140, 141, 143,
   148, 149, 164, 172, 173, 184,
   185, 194, 196, 217, 218, 219,
   235, 249
Condell de la Haza, Carlos Arnaldo,
   78, 210
Consuls, British, in Chile, 45, 58,
   59, 105, 120, 128, 135, 150,
   151, 191, 208, 212, 219, 233,
   235, 247–50
Cook, James (lieutenant)
 cure for scurvy, 30
 first circumnavigation, 28–29,
   48–49, 198
 influence of William Dampier, 21
 naming of geography, 33, 239
 quoted by Annie Brassey, 89
 quoted by Charles Darwin, 42
 second circumnavigation, 29–30,
   31, 49, 84
 third voyage, 30, 31
 use of chronometers, 30
Cooper, Edward, 219, 235, 250
copper
 commerce, 114, 134, 135, 136,
   141, 158, 170, 171, 172,
   173, 230
 mining, 146, 147–48, 150, 151,
   160, 175, 237
Coronel
 consuls, 249–50
 Torre de los Ingleses, 153
 visitors' impressions: Annie
   Brassey, 125; William
   Howard Russell, 94
 See also Battle of Coronel
corsairs
 definition, 8
Cousiño, Matías, 150, 151–52, 154,
   155, 176, 250
Cowley, William Ambrosia
   (Ambrose), 20
Cox, Nathaniel Miers, 66, 235
Cradock, Sir Christopher, Rear
   Admiral, 221, 222, 223–24,
   225, 226, 227
cricket, 114, 125, 153, 215–16,
   217, 218
Crosbie, John and Joseph, 134
Cunningham, Robert Oliver, 51, 117
Cuming, Hugh, 49

Dampier, William
 first circumnavigation, 18, 19,
   20, 21
 quoted by Annie Brassey, 89
 second circumnavigation, 21–22
 third circumnavigation, 22
Darien Adventure, The, 131
Darroch (Daroch) family name, 235
Darwin, Charles
 in Chile, 41–48, 49, 85, 125, 199
 on Chilean views of the British,
   7, 20
 on a Cornish copper miner, 147–48
 experience of earthquake, 35,
   44–47, 87
 on Fuegian Indians, 32, 42, 89,
   90, 199, 200
 impressions of Valparaíso, 110, 112
 influence of William Dampier, 21

Darwin, Charles (*continued*)
joining the *Beagle* for the second survey, 34
and Joseph Hooker, 50
naming of geography, flora, fauna in Chile, 43–44, 48, 241
opinion of Robert FitzRoy, 36
On the Origin of Species, 36, 48, 50
on quality of Chilean coal, 149
saving the ship's boats in Tierra del Fuego, 43
on Tehuelche Indians, 42–43
Davis, Edward, 20–21
Davis (Davys), John, 15–16
Dawson, John, 161, 162, 172
Despard, Rev. George Pakenham, 202–3, 204
Dixie, Florence (lady), 83, 88, 91–94, 100, 118
Doterel, HMS, 118, 119
Drake, Sir Francis, 4, 8–14, 16, 91, 238, 242
Duncan Fox & Company, 107, 110, 114, 122, 127, 141, 142–43

Easter Island
Easter Island Exploitation Company, 142
Hugh Cuming's expedition, 49
James Cook's second voyage, 29
John Linton Palmer's visit, 53
Katherine Routledge's survey, 53
possible discovery by Edward Davis, 21
education, 98, 191–96, 209
See also schools
Edwards, George, 171, 235, 245
Edwards, Joaquín, 20, 150, 236
Edwards MacClure, Agustín, 236, 245
Edwards Ossandón, Agustín, 171, 182, 210, 236
Edwards Ross, Agustín, 19, 58, 106, 158, 171, 236, 245
Elizabeth I, Queen, 3, 4, 8, 9–10, 14, 16
Escobar, Aníbal, 113, 114, 122, 146, 192, 193, 244
Exeter, HMS, 127

Falkner, Thomas (father), 4, 83–84
Fenton, Dr. Thomas, 89, 118, 120, 122, 123, 249
firemen, associations of
British and Commonwealth Fire Rescue Company *J. A. S. Jackson*, 14th Fire Company, Santiago, 115
George Garland 11th Company of Firemen, Valparaíso, 112
FitzRoy, Robert (captain)
Charles Darwin's opinion of, 36
contact with Indians on Tierra del Fuego, 33–34, 198–200, 203
first command of the *Beagle* (1829–30), 33–34
with Fuegian Indians in England, 34
naming of geography, 43–44, 240–41
on prospects for coal mining in Chile, 149
return to England after second voyage, 36, 50
second voyage on the *Beagle* (1831–36), 34–35, 37, 41, 42, 43–47, 48, 50, 51, 79, 100, 115, 125, 201
Fletcher, Francis, 10, 11
football (soccer), 114, 125, 153, 216–18
Forster, John Reinhold, 29, 49
Forster, Robert, 74, 77
Foster, Henry, 36, 241
fox hunting, 216
freemasonry, 111–12
free-standing companies, categories of, 137–38
frontiers
See boundary disputes
Fuegian Indians, 18, 28, 29, 31, 32, 33, 34, 41, 42, 43, 44, 89, 90, 92, 198, 199, 201, 206–7
See also Alacaluf Indians; Basket, Fuegia; Button, Jemmy; Haush; Minster, York; Ona; Selk'nam; Yahgan (Yámana)

Index

Gardiner, Allen (captain), 118, 201–2, 203, 204, 207, 242
Garland, Thomas Bland, 151, 154, 155
Gibbs & Company, 107, 110, 114, 138–40, 141, 146, 158, 162, 164–65, 170, 178, 181
golf, 114, 128, 218–19
Graham, Maria [*or* Mary Dundas; Lady Callcott]
  on British merchants and commerce, 131, 134–35
  in Chile, 85–88, 236
  on coal mining in Chile, 148–49
  complaints among British naval officers in War of Independence, 25
  description of Bernardo O'Higgins, 60–61
  experience of an earthquake, 86–87
  impressions of Valparaíso, 103, 109, 110
  leaving Chile with Cochrane, 73
  on need for cemeteries for non-Catholics, 212
  risk of a French invasion of Chile, 57, 58
  sketching in Chile, 100
  on War of Independence, 62, 66, 71, 72, 73, 74
Graham Rowe & Company, 140
Greer, Leslie, 3, 124, 249
Grenfell, John Pascoe, 74, 76
Guise, Martin (captain), 69, 71, 72, 74

Haigh, Samuel, 9, 65, 84–85, 108, 109
Hakluyt, Richard, 10, 15
Hall, Basil, 47, 125, 136, 148
Hamilton, John, 120, 122, 249
Hardy Evans, Oswald, 244
Harvey, Robert, 161, 162, 163
Haush Indians, 198
Hawkins family
  John Hawkins, 9, 16
  Richard Hawkins, 16
  William Hawkins, 3
Helsby, Alfredo, 98, 101

Helsby, William Glaskell, 98, 100–101
Hooker, Joseph, 36, 50, 51, 201
Huáscar, 78–79
Hudson's Bay Company, 155–56
Humberstone, James, 167, 168, 214, 233
Huth & Company, 138

Illingsworth, John, 25
immigration from Britain
  to Arica, 128
  British concerns on immigration from Britain, 104–5
  characteristics of British immigrants, 107, 234
  to Concepción, 126
  General Colonization Agency (from 1882), 103
  Law of Selective Immigration (1845 decree), 103
  national censuses, 106–7, 118
  post-independence selective immigration (1824 law), 103
  President Balmaceda's policy, 104, 208
  to Punta Arenas and Magallanes, 118–20, 124
  Sociedad de Fomento Fabril (Industrial Promotion Agency; from 1893), 106
  Sociedad Nacional de Agriculture, General Office of Immigration (from 1872), 103
  to Valparaíso, 108, 112
  See also colonization; Scotland, immigrants from
independence, declaration of Chilean, 55–57, 62, 115
  See also War of Independence
Indians of Chile
  See Alacaluf; Fuegian Indians; Haush; Mapuche (Araucanian); Ona; Selk'nam; Tehuelches; Yahgan (Yámana)

Instituto Chileno-Británico de Cultura, 196
Iquique, 35, 38, 42, 47, 78, 99, 111, 128, 139, 141, 143, 153, 160, 161, 162, 163, 164, 165, 171, 172, 173, 176, 177, 178, 179, 182, 184, 195, 214, 216, 218, 219, 250

Jewell, Maurice, 161, 250
Juan Fernández Islands, 19, 20, 21, 22, 24, 31, 66, 73, 226, 239

King, John, 177, 236, 248

Latcham, Richard (Ricardo), 52–53
Lloyd, William, 176, 210
Lord Cochrane
See Cochrane, Thomas
Lota
   Anglican religion in Lota, 153, 207, 208
   coal mining, 151, 152, 153, 154, 156, 156, 162–63, 184, 237
   cricket in Lota, 216
   Edwyn Charles Reed in Lota, 52
   Lota Park (Parque Isidora Cousiño), 156–58
Lynch, Patricio, 78, 161, 241

MacIver, Henry, 236–37
Mackay (captain), 24
Mackay, John, 150–51
Mackay, Peter, 98, 192–93, 212
Mackenna, Benjamín Vicuña, 1, 5, 16, 64, 100, 108, 134, 137, 235, 237, 242
Mackenna, John (general), 63–64, 242
Magellan Times, The, 38, 39, 125, 226, 244, 245
Maine, Richard (captain), 37
Mapuche (Araucanian) Indians, 3, 5, 6, 12, 17, 52, 60, 61, 104, 148, 194, 201, 207, 208

Mary Tudor [*or* Mary I; Bloody Mary], 1–2
Mathison, Gilbert Farquhar, 66–67, 88, 109, 191
Matthews, Richard, 43, 199–200
Merrick, Andrew, 15
Miers, John
   as botanist in Chile, 49–50
   impressions of Valparaíso, 109
   opinion of commercial opportunities, 136, 147
Miller, William (major; general), 64–65, 69, 70, 75, 96, 215
Minster, York (Fuegian Indian), 33, 43, 198, 199, 200
Morrison & Company, 127, 144
Museo Nacional de Bellas Artes, Santiago, 2, 97, 98, 99
Musters, George Chaworth, 88–89

Narborough, Sir John, 4, 17–18, 115, 238–39
Nares, George (captain), 37
Nitrate King, the
   See North, John Thomas
nitrates, 2, 38, 114, 137, 139–40, 141, 143, 144, 147, 148, 158–68, 170, 171, 172, 173, 174, 177, 178, 179, 180, 184, 213, 218, 224, 230, 236, 250
   See also Gibbs & Company; North, John Thomas
North, John Thomas [*or* the Nitrate King; Colonel North]
   banking investments, 172
   and Chile's civil war, 165–66
   coal mining investments, 153–54
   nitrates investments, 2–3, 5, 138, 139, 160–61, 162–65, 166, 250
   railways, construction and investments, 177, 178, 181, 185
   with William Howard Russell, 94, 100, 126
North, Marianne, 95

O'Brien, George, 55, 74, 75
O'Brien, John Thomond, 65
O'Connor, Francis Burdett, 159
O'Higgins, Ambrose, 1, 4, 5, 31, 55, 59–61, 63, 126
O'Higgins, Bernardo
 design of Chilean coat of Arms, 96
 early years, 60–61
 Maria Graham's description, 60–61
 memorials in Chile, 55, 242
 petition for a cemetery for non-Catholics, 211–12
 as Supreme Director of Chile, 62–63, 68, 86, 103, 115, 135, 191
 in War of Independence, 61–62, 64, 65, 66, 72, 126, 235
 watercolor painter, 101
Ona Indians, 123, 198, 207

Pacific Steam Navigation Company (PSNC; Compañía Inglesa de Vapores), 94, 114, 116, 145–46, 149, 150, 164, 175
Palmerston (Henry John Temple), third Viscount Palmerston, 59, 169
Parker King, Philip (captain), 32, 33, 34, 37, 51, 79, 115, 240
Paroissien, James, 65, 96
Patagonian Missionary Society, 201, 202, 204
Perry family, 152, 157, 216, 237
Philip II, 1–2, 3, 9, 14
pirates
 definition, 8
 See under individual names
Prince of Wales Country Club, 114, 216, 218, 219
Prince of Wales' visit to Chile, 3, 59, 111, 113, 114
Prior, Melton, 100, 164
privateers
 definition, 8
 in War of Independence, 24–25
 See under individual names
Proctor, Robert, 63, 109–10, 112, 136

Puerto Williams, 39, 77, 207, 238, 241
Punta Arenas (Sandy Point)
 British presence, 33, 39, 88, 115–25, 172, 173, 195, 205, 218, 249
 voyagers and visitors: Beerbohm, Julius (1877, 1878–79), 90, 91, 117–18; Brassey, Annie (1876), 89, 117, 206; Byron, John (1764), 115; Cunningham, Robert Oliver (1866), 51; Dixie, Florence (1878–79), 94, 118; Narborough, Sir John (1670), 4, 17, 18, 115, 238; Nares, George (1876–78), 37; Shackleton, Ernest (1916), 38–39; Williams, John (1843), 115
 See also *Doterel*, HMS; *Magellan Times, The*; schools; sheep-farming

railways
 Anglo-Chilian Nitrate Railway Company, 140, 179, 184, 188
 Antofagasta (Chili) and Bolivia Railway Company (FCAB), 138, 179, 182–84, 195
 Antofagasta Nitrate & Railway Company, 159
 Arauco Coal and Railway Company, 153–54, 162–63, 179, 184, 185–86
 Arica and Tacna Railway Company, 177, 180
 Bío-Bío railway bridge, 185–86
 Caldera to Copiapó railway, 97
 Carrizal Railway Company, 160, 177, 236
 Junín Railway, 178–79, 189–90
 Nitrate Railways Company, 162, 163, 164, 165, 166, 177–78, 179, 180–82
 railway heritage in Chile, 188–90

railways (*continued*)
  Santiago and Valparaíso Railway, 175–76, 210
  Taltal Nitrate Railway Company, 179, 184, 188
Reed, Edwyn Charles, 51–52
Reynard, Henry, 120, 122, 124, 249
Robinson Crusoe, 19, 21, 22, 24
Rogers, Woodes, 22
Ross, Sir James Clark (captain), 36–37, 50, 201, 241
Rouse, Henry William, 45, 191, 208, 248, 249
Routledge, Katherine, 52, 53
rugby, 218
Russell, William Howard
  impressions of Concepción, 126
  impressions of Coronel, 94, 126, 249–50
  impressions of Valparaíso, 113
  with John Thomas North in Chile, 94, 100, 164, 177, 178, 185, 186, 233
  opinion of coastal shipping, 145
  opinion of Fuegian Indians, 206–7
  opinion of Lota Park, 157

St. Andrew's Society, 111, 113, 128
Salvation Army, 111, 113
San Martín, José de, 62, 63, 65, 66, 72–73, 84, 95–96, 191
Santiago
  Ambrose O'Higgins' improvements, 60
  British Chamber of Commerce, 111, 115, 128
  British presence in Santiago, 23, 31, 39, 50, 52, 53, 59, 60, 61, 62, 65, 66, 85, 86, 97, 98, 99, 100, 101, 104, 111, 114–15, 128, 135, 138, 139, 143, 144, 165, 172, 173, 175, 176, 184, 186, 187–88, 191, 193, 195, 196, 210, 211, 212–13, 216, 217, 218, 219, 234, 235, 242, 243, 247–48
  British schools in Santiago, 193–94
  Charles Darwin in Santiago, 42, 44, 47, 85
  Del Desagravio, 16
  Gilbert Farquhar Mathison's impressions, 88
  Prince of Wales' visit, 3, 59, 113
  Richard Latcham in Santiago, 52
  Samuel Haigh's impressions, 84
  See also cemeteries; railways
Sarmiento y Gamboa, Pedro de, 13–14
Saunders, Thomas, 120, 122
schools
  in Araucanía, 194–95
  Association of British Schools of Chile, 195–96
  British School of Punta Arenas (St. James School), 125, 195
  Grange School, 115, 193, 195
  Mackay School, 98, 192–93, 196, 212, 217
  St. John's English School, Concepción, 194, 195
  See also education
Schwäger, Frederick William, 153, 154, 156, 212, 218, 249–50
Scorpion, 133–34, 235
Scotland, immigrants from, 112, 124, 142, 150, 154, 155–56, 192, 210, 235, 236
Scott, Robert Falcon (captain), 37, 38
Scott-Elliot, George Francis, 51
scouting in Chile, 114
Searle, John, 97, 100
Selkirk, Alexander, 21–22
Selk'nam Indians, 28, 198
Shackleton, Ernest, 31, 37–40
Sharpe, Bartholomew, 18–20
sheep-farming
  British presence in sheep rearing, 120–24
  conflict with indigenous peoples, 92, 123–24
  on Easter Island, 142
  Estancia Fenton Station, 122, 123
  Gente Grande Farming Company, 122

Index

Patagonian Land & Estate Company, 122
Patagonian Sheep Farming Company, 122
Philip Bay Sheep Farming Company, 121
Porvenir sheep ranch, 121
Tierra del Fuego Exploitation Company (Sociedad Explotadora de Tierra del Fuego), 3, 121–22, 143
Tierra del Fuego Sheep Farming Company, 121
Shelvocke, George, 22
Simpson, Robert Winthrop (captain; rear admiral)
 remembered in Chile, 55, 241
 in War of Independence, 74, 75–76
 in War of the Peruvian-Bolivian Confederation, 76
skiing, 220
soccer
 See football (soccer)
Sociedad Anglo-Chilena, Santiago, 128, 226
Somerscales, Thomas Jacques, 97–99, 192
South American Missionary Society, British, 194, 204, 207–8
South Pacific Mail, The, 243–44
South Sea Company (South Sea Bubble), 131–33
Spry, John (captain), 69, 71–72
Stirling, Rev. Waite Hocking, 204, 205, 207
Stokes, Pringle (captain), 32–33, 34, 35, 51, 79, 240
streetcars
 See trams

Talcahuano, 35, 42, 45, 46, 52, 62, 64, 77, 79, 87, 104, 125, 127, 134, 140, 141, 149, 150, 209, 216, 226, 250
Tarapacá Waterworks Company, 144, 163

Tehuelche Indians, 28, 42, 80, 88–89, 90, 92–93
Temuco, 6, 52, 140, 179, 187, 189, 194–95
tennis, 114, 125, 128, 218, 219
Thomson, James, 191
Townsend, Frank, 122, 124
trams, 187–88
treaty
 of Friendship, Commerce and Navigation, 59, 210, 213
 of London, 16
 of Madrid, 16–17
 of Seville, 132
 of Utrecht, 22, 132

Ushuaia, 204–5, 207

Valdivia
 British presence, 111, 141, 154, 155, 189
 Charles Darwin's visit, 45
 Cochrane's naval campaign, 64, 68, 69–71, 76
 opening of port to commerce, 134
Valparaíso (and Viña del Mar)
 Arco Británico, 55, 113
 arrival of the *Colinda*, 155
 banking, 171–72, 173
 Beagle survey, 35, 42, 44, 46, 47
 British consuls, 58, 248–49
 British hospitals, 113
 British schools, Valparaíso and Viña del Mar, 191–93
 cemeteries for non-Catholics, 211, 212, 213
 clubs, 111–12
 Cochrane in Valparaíso, 68, 71, 73
 commerce and industry, 110–11, 134–37, 138, 139, 140, 141, 142, 143, 144, 145
 Edwyn Charles Reed at Natural History Museum, 51
 engagement with USS *Essex*, 62, 75, 108, 201
 Francis Drake's attack, 12–13

Valparaíso (*continued*)
  newspapers in English, 243, 245
  railway to Santiago, 175–76
  religion, non-Catholic, 208–11
  road to Santiago, 60, 176
  Seamen's Mission, 111
  sports in Valparaíso and Viña del Mar, 215–20
  Valparaíso Sporting Club, 114, 215, 216, 217, 218, 219
  visitors to Valparaíso: Alexander Caldcleugh's visit, 109; George Anson's voyage, 23, 24; George Vancouver's visit, 31; Gilbert Farquhar Mathison's visit, 88, 109; John Miers' impressions, 109; Maria Graham in Valparaíso, 85–87, 103, 109; Robert Poctor's visit, 109–10, 136; Samuel Haigh's visit, 84, 108; Thomas Bridges' collecting expedition, 50; Thomas Somerscales in Valparaíso, 98; William Howard Russell's impressions, 113; during War of Independence, 24, 64, 75
Vancouver, George (captain), 31
Vic-Tupper, William de, 65, 237

Waddington, Joshua, 114, 145, 147, 176, 191, 208, 210, 237
Wager, HMS, 23, 28, 239
Wallis, Samuel, 28, 30, 239
wars
  Anglo-Spanish War, 16–17, 132
  capture of USS *Essex* in War of 1812 (Britain–United States), 62, 75, 108, 201, 212
  Seven Years' War, 27
  War of the American Union, 77, 78, 159

War of Independence: Castlereagh's policy, 57; Charles Chatworthy Wood, 96; military affairs on land, 61–62, 235; naval engagements, 68–77
War of Jenkins' Ear, 23, 132
War of the Pacific, 77, 78, 80, 97, 98, 137, 140, 144, 158–62, 171, 172, 175, 177, 178, 180, 182, 184
War of the Peruvian-Bolivian Confederation, 76, 77
War of the Quadruple Alliance, 22
War of the Spanish Succession, 20, 21, 22, 132
Watt, Alexander Campbell, 156
Webb, Cornelius, 24
Weddell, James, 27, 31–32, 37, 198
Welsh colonists, 4, 80–81
Wheat King. *See* Bunster, José
Wheelwright, William, 145, 149, 150, 175, 176, 186
Whistler, James, 100
Whyte, Mark Beresford, 152
Williams, John
  Ancud expedition to Chilean Patagonia, 77, 79, 115–16, 117, 233, 238, 241
  in War of Independence, 77
  in War of the Peruvian-Bolivian Confederation, 77
Williamson Balfour & Company, 107, 110, 127, 138, 140, 141–42, 146, 170, 192
Wood, Charles Chatworthy, 95–97, 100, 175

Yahgan (Yámana) Indians, 28, 29, 31–32, 33, 48, 197, 198, 201, 202, 203, 204, 207
Yahgan language and dictionary, 200, 204, 205–6
Young, William Russell, 112, 171–72, 215, 216

Printed in Great Britain
by Amazon